*Count and Bishop in Medieval Germany*

University of Pennsylvania Press
MIDDLE AGES SERIES
Edited by Edward Peters
Henry Charles Lea Professor
of Medieval History
University of Pennsylvania

A complete listing of the books in this series
appears at the back of this volume

# Count and Bishop in Medieval Germany

## A Study of Regional Power, 1100–1350

*Benjamin Arnold*

upp

University of Pennsylvania Press

*Philadelphia*

Permission to use manuscript sources was kindly granted by the Bayerisches Haupstaatsarchiv München, Abteilung 1, and the Bayerisches Staatsarchiv Nürnberg.

Library of Congress Cataloging-in-Publication Data
Arnold, Benjamin.
    Count and bishop in medieval Germany : a study of regional power, 1100–1350 / Benjamin Arnold.
        p.   cm. — (Middle Ages series)
    Includes bibliographical references and index.
    ISBN 0-8122-3084-1
        1. Germany—Politics and government—To 1517.   2. Regionalism—Germany— History.   3. Nobility—Germany—History   I. Title.   II. Series.
JN3249.A76   1992
320.943—dc20                                                            91-24938
                                                                          CIP

*For*
*Elizabeth and J. Richardson Dilworth*

# Contents

# *Abbreviations*

| | |
|---|---|
| *AD* | *Archiv für Diplomatik* |
| AQ | Ausgewählte Quellen zur deutschen Geschichte des Mittelalters. Freiherr vom Stein-Gedächtnisausgabe |
| Bayr. Hsta. | Bayerisches Hauptstaatsarchiv München, Abteilung I |
| *BDLG* | *Blätter für deutsche Landesgeschichte* |
| *DA* | *Deutsches Archiv für Erforschung des Mittelalters* |
| EL | Eichstätt Lehenbücher, no. I |
| ES | Eichstätt Salbuch, Literalien, no. 165 |
| fasc. | fascicle |
| HBG, i–iii | M. Spindler (ed.), *Handbuch der bayerischen Geschichte*, vols. I to III |
| HRG, i–iv | A. Erler and E. Kaufmann (eds.), *Handwörterbuch zur deutschen Rechtsgeschichte*, vols. I to IV |
| Kl. | Kloster (abbey) |
| *JFLF* | *Jahrbuch für fränkische Landesforschung* |
| MB | Monumenta Boica |
| MDF | Mitteldeutsche Forschungen |
| MGH | Monumenta Germaniae Historica |
| MGH Consts. | MGH Constitutiones et acta publica |
| MGH Dipl. | MGH Diplomata regum et imperatorum Germaniae |
| *MIöG* | *Mitteilungen des Instituts für österreichische Geschichtsforschung* |
| *Reg. Eichst.* | F. Heidingsfelder, *Die Regesten der Bischöfe von Eichstätt* |
| *RVB* | *Rheinische Vierteljahrsblätter* |
| VF | Vorträge und Forschungen |
| *VSWG* | *Vierteljahrsschrift für Sozial- und Wirtschaftsgeschichte* |
| *ZBLG* | *Zeitschrift für bayerische Landesgeschichte* |
| *ZGOR* | *Zeitschrift für die Geschichte des Oberrheins* |
| *ZRGGA* | *Zeitschrift der Savigny-Stiftung für Rechtsgeschichte. Germanistische Abteilung* |

# Illustrations

## Maps

## Genealogical Tables

# Preface

For over a decade, English-speaking readers have been familiarized by Karl Leyser's *Rule and Conflict in an Early Medieval Society. Ottonian Saxony* with one of the most intriguing but at the same time most intractable questions in German history: the nature of the structures of command, and the problem of rendering them effective, in the strife-torn world of medieval Germany. Although this book is set in a different part of Germany and is based upon sources from another time scale, no work concerned with the medieval history of the German regions can fail to be indebted to Karl Leyser's example. The jurisdictions with which I am dealing here, and the careers of the counts and bishops who wielded them, gave rise to what has been characterized in twentieth-century German historiography as *Landesherrschaft*, "territorial lordship," although I hope to show how this useful phrase is not much more than a descriptive label without explanatory content. Nevertheless, a strong justification for writing this book has, I think, been summed up by John Freed, one of the most perceptive scholars of medieval German regional history as follows:

The formation of the German territorial lordship is a crucial topic, and it is extremely useful to inform English-speaking readers that it was not a case of usurpation of royal authority but a response to dynamic changes in German society, perhaps the most dynamic and creative period in German history until the nineteenth century. This issue has particular relevance again today when German reunification has suddenly and unexpectedly again become frontpage news.

Most of the book was written in 1989, a year punctuated by extraordinary bulletins of news from Germany. But as I shall outline in my introduction and in Chapter 2, the bulk of the source material I am using relies upon archival and other work initially undertaken for my doctoral dissertation.

I am extremely grateful to the Institute for Advanced Study at Princeton, New Jersey, which I had the privilege of visiting as one of the J. Richardson Dilworth fellows in the School of Historical Studies for the academic session of 1989–90, when I was provided with ideal conditions for completing this work and for undertaking related studies into the nature of ecclesiastical and aristocratic power in the medieval Western Empire.

# Introduction: Land and Lordship in the Medieval German Empire

During the rise of absolutism in the seventeenth century, of enlightened despotism in the eighteenth, and of the nation-state in the nineteenth, the German territorial structures inherited from the medieval past increasingly discomposed the minds of political theorists, philosophers, and historians. To Samuel von Pufendorf the Holy Roman Empire of the German Nation was a monstrosity; neither holy nor Roman nor an empire to Voltaire; an exasperating archaism to the perceptions of the Enlightenment and of Romanticism alike. The prevailing climate of disapproval began to find a political resolution when the might of revolutionary France redrew the German map under the Directory and Napoleon I. By means of Bismarck's wars from 1864 to 1871, the autonomy of Germany's territorial states guaranteed by several acts from the Golden Bull of 1356 and the Treaty of Westphalia of 1648 to the Congress of Vienna in 1815 was replaced by a German nation-state under the direction of Prussia. Nineteenth-century historical interpretation therefore tended to present the manifestation of provincial command structures in medieval Germany as a species of political malformation, which then stood in the way of emergent statehood and national identity, the latter linked by some schools to the aspirations of the Lutheran Reformation.

It can easily be seen that nineteenth-century tastes in historical interpretation inclined to portray a negative view of medieval and early modern German territories, apart from a few "success stories" such as the Austrian experiment, the rise of Brandenburg, and the Swiss Confederation. Nevertheless, nineteenth-century Germans admired obvious achievements dating from medieval times, notably the colonization of the eastern lands, the erection of cathedrals, and the rise of large towns, visible monuments of which existed all around them. So the failure of an early version of statehood or nationhood that the Capetians had supposedly engineered in France and the Plantagenets in England appeared to require an explanation. Normally it was sought at the summit of German medieval political life: in mistakes ascribed to the rulers of the Salian and Staufen dynasties (1024–1254); in the distractions offered by Italy as a dependent possession of the German crown since 961; and in the intensity and continuity of papal rivalry with the imperial office, suddenly setting in during the pontificate of Gregory VII (1073–1085). In one version of the story, the Staufen dynasty was held to have been diverted from its proper task of unifying the German kingdom under a coherent royal administration, and to have dissipated its resources in pursuit of an unattainable universal empire with its center of gravity located in the Mediterranean south.[1] One of the consequences was that the provinces of Germany were delivered into the hands of hungry ecclesiastical and secular princes during the thirteenth century. Historical pessimism tended to cast the crown as the failed force and the princes, lay and clerical, as the divisive force behind Germany's inept political evolution.

In the twentieth century several new approaches to the social, legal, economic, regional, and diplomatic study of medieval Germany dismantled the comprehensive but dejected explanations of the past, in itself a feat of academic detachment given that German military and nationalist power was twice overthrown within living memory. Historians of several schools in Austria, Switzerland, and Germany made intrepid efforts to reinterpret the medieval record material on its own terms, and tried to abandon the false question about subsequent national success and failure in German history. This detachment, coupled with some extraordinary talent and expertise especially in legal and diplomatic method, had fruitful results in the analysis of medieval Germany as a country made up of regional societies, and in the depiction of their inhabitants' varied contributions on the local horizon. Regional history became the most exacting task that the student could undertake just as overblown theories about medieval Germany's failed nationhood collapsed under the weight of their own improbability.

As I was assembling the materials for this book during 1989, I was aware of the year as the fiftieth anniversary of the publication of Otto Brunner's influential and controversial study from Vienna entitled *Land und Herrschaft*,[2] "Land and Lordship." As its subtitle announced, the book intended to present and to answer certain fundamental questions about the political and legal structure of the Austrian territories in the later Middle Ages. Brunner's work was based upon the study of political conflicts, juridical procedures, and legal language in use among the classes or orders in the potent upper reaches of society in the southeastern provinces of the medieval German Empire, as well as their effect upon the peasantry and townsfolk.[3] He drew conclusions about the land, its law, and princely rule over it working together as a type of social fusion,[4] in turn essential to creating the unified territorial principalities that formally passed under Habsburg rule after the conquest of 1276; Austria and Styria in 1282, then Carinthia and Carniola in 1335.[5] In persuasive and powerful language occasionally bordering upon invective, Brunner sought to destroy the basis for using modern, and indeed classical, definitions about law, politics, and statehood as normally irrelevant or meaningless for the medieval conception and practices of local rule over the varied lands and provinces of the German Empire.[6]

Brunner held that in the medieval Austro-Bavarian duchies and counties, *Land,* or "land," was not merely a neutral geographical analogue with some modern word such as area, region, province, or territory:

Hence it is a question of comprehending the structure of the land. Of the land it can be said that it features a community of justice and peace, which is united by ordained local law. Bearers of this union under justice and peace are the population of the land, the people constituting the political association of the land. This land may have, but need not have, a lord. Yet actually to function, the land stands in need of a director of its legal assemblies and a commander in war.[7]

The author did not by any means see this structure as a specifically late medieval outcome of the local political and legal history of the Austro-Bavarian regions. Such a conception of the "land" had had validity even in pre-Carolingian times: "It is an arrangement derived from a peculiar economic and political structure, which remains the common characteristic of a political union of persons cultivating and dominating the land, in spite of all variations in the course of historical evolution. It belongs to a world with a preponderant agrarian structure upon which the rise and expansion of towns altered nothing fundamentally."[8]

In emphasizing the antiquity of such notions—"The *civitas,* the people, the land are an association of men, either peasant or noble, who bear arms, a union knowing how to provide justice through conflict. For here every pursuit of justice is a combat, be it in the feud or in court"[9]— Brunner's work also showed in great detail what effect the reform of law after 1100 had for his organically conceived structure of a *Land:*

Under the general protection of the land's lord, "Land and people" stand as a totality. The lord's responsibility it is to defend peace and justice and to safeguard the *Landfrieden* [peace-keeping associations]. Protection of the peace, in itself an ancient duty of all rulers, possessed enhanced importance since the peace-movement of the high Middle Ages. Austrian regional law of the thirteenth century had already adopted the law of the *Landfrieden*. Thus the lord guaranteed the *salus publica*, the common good. . . . It is no coincidence that *Landfrieden* stood at the heart of the "law giving" of the Empire and of the territories.[10]

   In discerning the political roots of the integrative processes which eventuated in the late medieval version of the *Land* as early as the twelfth century,[11] Brunner was traveling with those German historians who were earnestly seeking to explain the origins of Germany's territorial multiplicity in medieval times not in simplistic and negative terms of the supposed collapse of imperial rule from above, but in terms of a much more creative and positive sociolegal scheme or process, "the rise of territorial lordship" in the multifarious regions and provinces of the old Empire, producing renovated political, economic, and jurisdictional structures from below. Although Brunner's book was undoubtedly the most interesting work actually to read among this quite wide genre, his statements about the species of creative integration set up between local law, the unity of the land, and princely rule did not find widespread favor as an interpretative or explanatory historiographical instrument.[12] Years later Hans Kurt Schulze, for example, summed up those critics of Brunner's who, having made their own regional exploration into the sources, found "the territorial unity of the land to have been not the point of departure but the end result of *Landesherrschaft*, lordship over the land."[13] Conceding that Austria and the other Habsburg lands must therefore have constituted an exception in German medieval regional history, another critic, Ferdinand Seibt, attempted to sum up as follows:[14] "What Brunner had accepted about a *Land* as a legal community of persons possessing the country in the sense of a constitutive, purported unity did not find countenance either in legal history or in regional history beyond Austria," while going on to praise Brunner's studies of the institutional interplay of prince, community, feud, peace keeping, local loyalties, and other features of regional political life in the Middle Ages.

   Nevertheless, Brunner's seminal insights about the nature of regionalized political society in medieval Germany remain suggestive and exciting rather than misleading or provably incorrect. He can show, for example, that princes and the powerful orders were so interested in constructions such as community, *Land,* and local law just because of the threat to them posed by the continued validity, under certain circumstances and restrictions, of aristocratic and other armed protest or feud right down to the imperial *Landfriede* of Worms issued in 1495:[15]

The feud inseparably belonged to the very life of the medieval state and to medieval politics like war to the sovereign state and national law of modern times. A realistic end to the feud, not just a prohibition which could not be enforced, would have altered fundamentally the total structure of the medieval state. Although we are thus forced to regard it as an intrinsic element of every medieval polity, this is not to say that the feud, however unavoidable, was not also a misfortune in the awareness of contemporaries. The entire religious and ecclesiastical mentality could not but regard it as a consequence of sin.

We shall be enabled to study decisive thirteenth- and fourteenth-century feuds over regional, ecclesiastical, and territorial issues in Chapters 3, 5, and 7.

As a meticulously researched survey of local political society and authority in their relation to larger medieval ideas of law and power, Brunner's *Land und Herrschaft* was matched by a number of disparate monographs concerned with "the rise of territorial lordship" in the German provinces. The best known of them was Walter Schlesinger's *Die Entstehung der Landesherrschaft,* first published in 1941.[16] Using sources from Thuringia and the Saxon marches, Schlesinger believed that he had uncovered the foundations for territorial lordship as exercised by the princes in slowly matured Carolingian and Ottonian local institutions. So the approach was quite different from Brunner's reliance upon political processes recoverable in much more detailed sources dating from the thirteenth, fourteenth, and fifteenth centuries.

In its legitimate pursuit of answers about "land" and "lordship" from regional sources, German historiography also sought for the origins and justification of aristocratic domination as a social phenomenon broader than the localities, provinces, and territories as such. In a short but influential study called *Adelsherrschaft im Mittelalter,* published in 1927, Otto von Dungern held that aristocratic powers of dominion and local rule had nothing to do with refashioned or usurped state powers but belonged to the nobility by inborn right of blood and descent, almost as though rights of local jurisdiction pertained to a celestially chosen and socially revered caste.[17] This kind of interpretation about innate aristocratic rights of authority cannot, of course, be confined to the German nobility. If it had validity, then it must apply to all entrenched western European nobilities who were passing on their lands, titles, offices, fortifications, manorial jurisdictions, and the mentality of a special God-given fitness for rule, by whatever exclusive scheme of descent. It does not at all derive from some dubious, idiosyncratic medieval version of "blood and soil" theory to be found only among the Germans, but would have had to be a phenomenon common to the entire Germanic and post-Frankish west, as well as to Britain, the Iberian peninsula, and the Italian south both before and after their reassimilation to the Latin world. It was perhaps chronologically unfortunate that some of the subsequent writers who wished to elaborate upon the possible origins of *Adelsherrschaft,* or "aristocratic domination," happened to publish between 1933 and 1945. This stimulated quite proper study of the pre-Carolingian Germanic past, but the subject was also, most lamentably, of interest for propaganda purposes to a certain uneducated type of misinformed National Socialist ideologue.[18]

There is nothing specifically political about Heinrich Dannenbauer's extremely original and wide ranging article "Adel, Burg und Herrschaft bei den Germanen" published in *Historisches Jahrbuch* in 1941,[19] the year of Hitler's invasion of the Soviet Union. Dannenbauer sought to establish a long pedigree for an independently authenticated type of aristocratic lord-ship valid throughout German medieval times. He daringly derived it from lordship over the households, military followings, and fortified residences of pre-Carolingian noblemen, quite autonomously of any state power or royal concession or usurpation of crown right. In this he was already anticipated by Otto Brunner[20] who had characterized with his usual terse verve "The house as the nucleus of all lordship."[21] The thrust of Dannen-bauer's argument was supported, in the main, by another important article published in democratic times by *Historische Zeitschrift* in 1953, Walter Schlesinger's "Herrschaft und Gefolgschaft in der germanisch-deutschen Verfassungsgeschichte."[22] Schlesinger convincingly reemphasized the im-portance of military retinues and the "personalized" rather than the institu-tional or political nature of aristocratic domination in early Germanic society; and he implied, like Dannenbauer, its continuing importance for later versions, including the "territorial," of the exercise of lordship by the princely orders in Germany.

These startling views did not find universal acceptance. Hans Kuhn, František Graus, and Karl Kroeschell were among a handful of historians and legal theorists who had serious doubts about the Germanic military following or retinue as a kind of crucible for aristocratic power; about the true significance and extent of lordship as exercised from the aristocratic "house," or fortification; and above all about the problems posed by pos-tulating some sort of continuity from an ill-documented Germanic past beginning with the works of Caesar and Tacitus and stretching through the Carolingian material to the archives of the twelfth- and thirteenth-century German churches.[23] There was, it must be admitted, a very long chronological gap between the pre-Carolingian arrangement of lord and retinue in Germanic society and the reign of aristocratic jurisdictional authority and autarky as *Landesherrschaft* in the centuries after 1100. Such well-founded doubts about the misty origins of an aristocratic style of domination independent of royal command or commission were, however, not necessarily destructive to the picture of autarkic princely authority as built up not only by Brunner and Schlesinger but also by the authors of many valuable local monographs based upon richer sociolegal documentation available for the period after about 1050 or 1100. After all, the Germanic *Gefolgschaft,* or retinue, in the barbarian past was one thing, incipient *Landesherrshaft* in the age of Otto of Freising, Anselm of Havelberg, Norbert of Magdeburg, and Otto of Bamberg, devoted and prolific writers, reformers, saints, statesmen, and territorial lords in an age of socioeconomic expansion was quite another. But the all-embracing explanatory optimism of the latter concept, *Landesherrschaft,* or "territorial lordship," has also been so mauled in recent historiography as to be virtually incapable of credible recovery.

Karl Kroeschell has argued with learned economy that "lordship" in the Middle Ages did not have a conceptual or institutional existence separately identifiable from the persons, titles, and offices under which it was exercised, thus incidentally strengthening Otto von Dungern's somewhat eccentric views about an "innate" *Adelsherrschaft,* although in a different guise. Kroeschell claims with great persuasiveness that "lordship" is basically a nineteenth-century sociological construct, which can at present be read only with a large measure of anachronism and questionable linguistic analogy back into the Middle Ages, to try to explain phenomena for which it is not at all apt. He considers that only upon the basis of more research can the question be answered whether lordship "existed as a homogeneous historical phenomenon or whether this concept simply has a polemical or ideological function in modern sociological and historical research."[24]

Nevertheless, the theory of "the rise of territorial lordship" even in a dismantled or fragmented state was crucial at a certain stage in German historiography[25] for showing how the local authority of the secular princes and the imperial Church, which was in all truth carried forward as the "territorial principality" assembled by the end of the Middle Ages, was not crown power usurped during the various internal disorders of the Empire experienced during the reign of Henry IV (1056–1106). Without doubt the work that has shown this most clearly, and has best stood up to the test of time partly because it was never attached to any version of "territorial lordship" theories, is Hans Hirsch's study of criminal jurisdiction in medieval Germany, *Die hohe Gerichtsbarkeit im deutschen Mittelalter,* first published as long ago as 1922. Hirsch was not really concerned about the problem of regions and territories at all, but with the taxing investigation of marked changes in the meaning and application of legal language that he discerned in the sources dealing with crime and punishment especially in the eleventh, twelfth, and thirteenth centuries. Arguably his book is the cleverest to have been written about medieval Germany in the twentieth century.[26] Hirsch realized that the criminal jurisdictions possessed in Germany in the thirteenth century by the secular princes, and by the greater churches as exercised through their appointed advocates, and therefore the very signature of princely authority which was to last for hundreds of years in Germany, had very little to do with crown right or ancient county jurisdiction usurped or otherwise taken over in the interests of consciously assembling and building up regional power.

Hirsch proclaimed that "high," or criminal, jurisdiction was, by the thirteenth century, virtually a new aristocratic jurisdiction devised under royal aegis itself since the imperial *Landfrieden* introduced by Henry IV in 1103,[27] and from the reforms to ecclesiastical advocacy made imperative by the general tone of religious improvement insisted upon by the reformed Papacy since the middle years of the eleventh century.[28] Another interesting implication of Hirsch's work was therefore further to remove aristocratic jurisdiction and dominion of the post-1100 princely type from possible roots in Germanic *Hausherrschaft,* or "lordship exercised from residences," long before Dannenbauer and Schlesinger had presented their modernized version of theories discovering them there. Hirsch's insights and interpretations about the comparative jurisdictional modernity of the twelfth and thirteenth centuries therefore tended to short circuit later controversies about law, its derivation, and application, simply because his understanding of extremely difficult and meager sources about legal procedures showed how it was possible to galvanize a new jurisdictional reform into action in medieval German society once its expansive needs were making themselves felt at all levels by about 1100. This is why the German twelfth and thirteenth centuries constituted an era of extraordinary legal experiment and innovation[29] in terms of *Landrecht,* or regional law;[30] of "feudal" law, or *Lehnrecht;*[31] of town law;[32] and even of Roman law, although its recovery was of more moment in the Italian lands of the Empire.[33]

Although so much of great significance was happening to German legal enterprise in that era, for example, in the interaction of *Landrecht* and *Lehnrecht*,[34] I believe it is still valid to speak of "the rise of territorial lordship" in a descriptive or symptomatic sense, but not as a legal explanation for the increasing complexity of aristocratic local domination in Germany after 1100. And the imaginative originality of Brunner's approach in *Land und Herrschaft* is still apparent fifty years later, one reason being his robust address to a large question in medieval European history: How did the lords maintain control over the land, its people, and their resources, and what jurisdiction justified their exploitation in lords' favor? A credible answer to this was provided in a scholarly fashion by the regional monographs on territorial lordship; that the changing social structures of the regions, not the crisis-ridden constitutional history of the Empire, contained the materials for promoting the German secular and ecclesiastical aristocracy into princes[35] with an extremely varied and uncommonly successful local autarky,[36] lasting in many cases until modern times.

This book is certainly about land and lordship, without directly subscribing to Brunner's exacting but limited definitions of those words' validity for medieval German political and social history. In edging away from a formal concept of lordship for medieval Germany, except in the legally construed constitutional and "official" cases of *dominium* and *dicio*, *potestas* and *ius*, "power and right," exercised by properly elected bishops and abbots, ecclesiastical advocates, and kings, it has been necessary to adopt another form of discourse much more reliant upon the politically favored persons born into the aristocratic order and upon their careers; in the case of this regional study, representative ones for all of twelfth-, thirteenth-, and fourteenth-century Germany. Although there undoubtedly were *Länder,* or regions, dominated by princes and lesser lords to be found everywhere in Europe,[37] the processes in Germany point away from conscious ideas about institutions to be reformed into *Landesherrschaft,* and rather toward a politically creative order of title-bearing princes, secular and clerical,[38] who used their inherited traditions of rule to remodel regional authority during the twelfth and thirteenth centuries toward what was actually identified in the royal chancery by the 1230s as a *terra,* or "land," with a *dominus,* or "lord."[39] I think that an instructive example of aristocratic personalities and careers at work in this sense is provided by the counts and bishops of the Franconian-Bavarian border diocese of Eichstätt, for whom telling though circumscribed sources have survived from the crucial formative period in territorial history stretching from the papal-imperial compromise of 1122, the Concordat of Worms, to the collapse of Bavarian hegemony in 1346, which transferred the imperial mantle to a new international dynasty, the Luxemburgs of Prague.[40]

Years ago at Oxford University I wrote a thesis under the supervision of Professor Karl Leyser, the leading scholar on medieval German history in the English-speaking world, on the bishops of Eichstätt and their knights entitled *"Ministeriales and the Development of Territorial Lordship in the Eichstätt Region, 1100–1350."* For a long time I have thought that the Eichstätt region, almost unknown in historical scholarship generally except as the mission ground and final home of St. Willibald,[41] was well worth revisiting in print because the sources for the theme "count and bishop" were so revealing.[42] However, I no longer believe in *ministeriales* as a category of knightly persons and families particularly to be distinguished, except in their servile legal status, from any other social grouping of medieval European knights, and wrote a book called *German Knighthood 1050–1300* (Oxford, 1985) to sustain the point.[43] I no longer believe in "the development of territorial lordship" either, except as one of several possible modern descriptions for the concretion of aristocratic authority, jurisdiction, and autonomy in medieval Germany. I hope I have rendered the rise of princely political power and independence, which did indeed happen, somewhat more intelligible in another book, *Princes and Territories in Medieval Germany,* to be published by Cambridge University Press in 1991. I also think that a geographical description such as "the Eichstätt region" could be attacked as a contemporary misnomer, simply because the border between the medieval duchies of Franconia and Bavaria sliced the Eichstätt diocese down the middle. The region is not the same as the diocese, but was the geographical and political dimension within which succeeding bishops, with great tenacity and inventiveness, survived the threat of their secular neighbors, the counts, and came out with a durable territorial structure of their own, which they were able to recast between 1280 and 1320 as a credible and long-lasting principality.[44]

\*   \*   \*

In preparing this "study of regional power," I found that even the most sympathetic rereadings of Schlesinger's *Die Entstehung der Landesherrschaft* and Brunner's *Land und Herrschaft* had less to relate that was relevant to the structures of authority in the other regions of Germany than I had hoped. Since this effect could hardly be attributed to failings in their versatile and painstaking scholarship, I concluded that the problem was one of chronology. German regional history is so diverse that analyses of Thuringia and the Saxon marches in the Carolingian and Ottonian eras, and of Austria and its neighbors in the Empire from the later thirteenth through to the early sixteenth centuries—the hard cores, in short, of Schlesinger's and Brunner's research—cannot be tortured into providing schemes and models for other regions. In the Eichstätt region, the essential surviving sources on the evolution of territorial command stretch through quite a different time scale: from the reign of Henry V, the last Salian, in the twelfth century to that of Louis IV, the Bavarian, in the fourteenth.

In abandoning models and theories in favor of the personalities who now come to life only from meager legal and chronicle sources selected by chance, time, and archival malpractice, it would be a mistake not to recognize the advantages that episcopal office, in the sense of a continuous governing authority with temporal as well as ecclesiastical powers, gave to the incumbents of Eichstätt in common with most of the other German bishops. Ever since late Carolingian times the bishops of Germany had, however unwillingly, been entrusted with secular tasks matched by gifts of material resources protected by juridical immunities to enable them to carry them out.[45] Although the Reformed Papacy had hesitated about the wisdom of permitting this tradition to continue, especially in 1111 when Paschal II had contemplated abandoning episcopal regalia in Germany back into the hands of the crown,[46] the imperial bishops of the twelfth and thirteenth centuries took for granted their dual role as ecclesiastical reformers and as landowning princes with temporal responsibilities.[47] Although the bishops may have been shorn by their feoffees, plundered by their advocates, and restrained by their cathedral chapters,[48] it is nevertheless remarkable how similar the temporal rights and methods wielded by both secular and ecclesiastical princes turned out to be.[49] For bishops the main disadvantage was that the prestigious and powerful criminal jurisdictions, the principal outward sign of the rise of all princely authority in Germany and evolving further in the twelfth and thirteenth centuries under the aegis of the royal *Landfrieden*,[50] could in theory be exercised only through delegated advocates as secular magistrates because, according to canon law, churchmen should not be responsible for shedding blood. Although it was continually flouted, this principle had done much since late Carolingian and Ottonian times to rein in ecclesiastical rule under the power of advocates as legal representatives appointed from among the local secular aristocrats, who were permitted by custom to inflict capital sentences.

As we shall see, much of the Eichstätt region's history was dominated by the question of the advocate's power. In this case, the authority of the cathedral church and that of the advocatial dynasty, the counts of Grögling and Dollnstein, later called Hirschberg, were mismatched in that the latter, in order to enjoy the benefit of resources belonging to the church, over-stepped their commission. However, Eichstätt was not to become one of that handful of German sees reduced to complete subservience by unscru-pulous secular neighbors. Yet there were times when it appeared that the counts of Hirschberg's advocatial domination of episcopal assets would destroy the bishopric's credibility as a temporal power, in the sense of the traditions handed on since the Ottonian era. This did not happen. The thirteenth-century bishops were not frightened by their chapter's capitula-tions; they struck back at the feoffees who robbed them; and as an elected or provided line that could not, like secular dynasties, die out, they stood to gain when the Hirschberg house was itself extinguished in 1305, the most significant date in the temporal history of the see until the suppression of the principality in 1802. The point was not only that in 1305 the bishopric inherited the extensive Hirschberg lands, but also that the advocacy over the cathedral church, the source of so much recrimination and discontent, was not renewed.

Why was this so? Although the sources do not say so directly, the main reason was that the only candidates for the advocacy, Dukes Rudolf I and Louis IV of Upper Bavaria, had in any case received by the same testament the superior or criminal jurisdiction, the *Landgericht,* over the Hirschberg lands just bequeathed to the church of Eichstätt. These events followed hard upon the pontificate of Boniface VIII (1294–1303), when the curia had decided to recognize episcopal possession of purely secular jurisdictions, a fait accompli already several centuries old, and embodied its findings in the *Liber sextus*.[51] The unspoken implication was that bishops who had not so far been politically powerful enough to do so might now emancipate themselves from the domination of advocates, and this is one thing that the demise of the Hirschbergs achieved for Eichstätt in 1305.[52]

Another reason why the bishops of Germany could in most cases hold their own against secular rivals, advocates, and feoffees was that their prestige and authority as churchmen advanced again under the aegis of the papal reform movement. Once the problem of their investiture had in principle been solved by the Concordat of Worms in 1122,[53] the German bishops, like all others, benefited from explicit papal measures to enhance their spiritual arm.[54] Pope Innocent III (1198–1216) did much for the episcopal office in this respect[55] so that in a see such as Eichstätt the threat or reality of appeals to the metropolitan at Mainz or to the Roman curia still carried weight. In the diocese there was, in other words, a sacral dimension of power beyond the politics of landowning and advocatial jurisdiction: the pontifical authority of a consecrated bishop protected in normal circumstances by juridical immunity, with an apparatus of ecclesiastical command conferred upon him in canon law. The German bishops were, in addition, *principes imperii,* or "princes of the Empire," as direct vassals of the crown for their temporalities.[56] In Eichstätt's case the advocate was not a *princeps imperii,* and potentially the prestige of *princeps* and bishop outclassed the status of count and advocate, the latter being technically an appointed official of the cathedral church. The consequences of the rivalry between these offices, of bishop and of advocate, especially in the period from 1225 to 1305, were crucial for the political future of the Eichstätt region, and will be elucidated in Chapters 3, 4, and 5. But before introducing the Eichstätt diocese and region in detail in Chapter 2, we need to move on from the models and theories of *Landesherrschaft,* land and lordship, and the significance of episcopal office to improvise an account of Germany's political regionalism in the Middle Ages.

*Notes*

1. See the discussion in W. Smidt, *Deutsches Königtum und deutscher Staat des Hochmittelalters während und unter dem Einfluss der italienischen Heerfahrten. Ein zweihundertjähriger Gelehrtenstreit im Lichte der historischen Methode zur Erneuerung der abendländischen Kaiserwürde durch Otto I.* (Wiesbaden, 1964).

2. *Land und Herrschaft. Grundfragen der territorialen Verfassungsgeschichte Österreichs im Mittelalter* (Vienna, 1939). I have used the new and slightly revised edition published at Darmstadt in 1973.

3. Ibid., pp. 1–110, 165–239.

4. Ibid., esp. pp. 357–440.

5. MGH Consts. iii, nos. 339–45, pp. 325–31 (1282), and J. Leuschner, *Deutschland im späten Mittelalter,* Deutsche Geschichte, vol. III, 2d ed. (Göttingen, 1983), pp. 119–24, trans. by S. MacCormack as *Germany in the Late Middle Ages,* Europe in the Middle Ages. Selected Studies, vol. XVII (Amsterdam, New York, and Oxford, 1980), pp. 93–98.

6. Brunner, *Land und Herrschaft,* esp. pp. 111–64.

7. Ibid., pp. 234f.: "Es gilt daher, die Struktur des Landes zu erfassen. Vom Lande ist zu sagen: Es stellt eine Rechts- und Friedensgemeinschaft dar, die durch ein bestimmtes Landrecht geeint ist. Träger dieser Rechts- und Friedensgemeinschaft ist das Landvolk, sind die Landleute, die den politischen Verband des Landes

bilden. Dieses Land kann, muss aber nicht einen Landesherrn haben. Wohl aber bedarf das Land, um tatsächlich zu funktionieren, eines Leiters seiner Gerichtsversammlungen und eines Führers im Krieg."

8. Ibid., p. 187: "Es ist eine bestimmte Ordnung von einer eigentümlichen wirtschaftlichen und politischen Struktur, der bei aller Verschiedenheit im Laufe der geschichtlichen Entwicklung doch das gemeinsame Merkmal eben eines politischen Verbandes landbebauender und landbeherrschender Leute bleibt. Es gehört einer Welt von überwiegender Agrarstruktur an, woran auch Aufstieg und Ausbreitung der Städte grundsätzlich nichts ändern."

9. Ibid., p. 31: "Die civitas, der Stamm, das Land sind ein Verband wehrhafter Männer bäuerlicher oder adeliger Art, die sich selbst im Kampfe Recht zu schaffen Wissen. Denn Kampf ist hier jede Verfolgung des Rechts, sei es in der Fehde, sei es im Gericht."

10. Ibid., pp. 363–65: "Unter dem allgemeinen Schutz des Landesherrn stehen 'Land und Leute' als Ganzes. Aufgabe des Landesherrn ist es, Friede und Recht zu schützen, den Landfrieden zu wahren. Der Friedensschutz, an sich eine alte Pflicht jedes Herrschers, hat seit der Landfriedensbewegung des hohen Mittelalters gesteigerte Bedeutung. Das Österreichische Landrecht des 13. Jahrhunderts hat das Landfriedensrecht bereits rezipiert. Damit wahrt er die salus publica, das gemeine Wohl. . . . Es ist kein Zufall, dass die Landfrieden im Mittelpunkt der 'Gesetzgebung' des Reichs und der Territorien stehen."

11. Ibid., pp. 199–205. For more recent considerations of this theme in Austrian history, see E. Schrader, "Zur Gerichtsbestimmung des Privilegium minus," *ZRGGA* 69 (1952): 371–85; H. Appelt, "Die Erhebung Österreichs zum Herzogtum," *BDLG* 95 (1959): 25–66; H. Fichtenau, *Von der Mark zum Herzogtum. Grundlagen und Sinn des "Privilegium Minus" für Österreich*, Österreich Archiv. Schriftenreihe des Arbeitskreises für österreichische Geschichte, 2d ed. (Munich, 1965); M. Mitterauer, "Zur räumlichen Ordnung Österreichs in der frühen Babenbergerzeit," *MIöG* 78 (1970): 94–120; F. Reichert, *Landesherrschaft, Adel und Vogtei. Zur Vorgeschichte des spätmittelalterlichen Ständestaates im Herzogtum Österreich*, Beihefte zum Archiv für Kulturgeschichte, vol. XXIII (Cologne and Vienna, 1985); K. Lechner, *Die Babenberger. Markgrafen und Herzoge von Österreich 976–1246*, Veröffentlichungen des Instituts für österreichische Geschichtsforschung, vol. XXIII, 3d ed. (Vienna, Cologne, and Graz, 1985), pp. 118–251.

12. The most important review was by Heinrich Mitteis, "Land und Herrschaft. Bemerkungen zu dem gleichnamigen Buch Otto Brunners," *Historische Zeitschrift* 163 (1941): 255–81 and 471–89, reprinted in H. Kämpf (ed.), *Herrschaft und Staat im Mittelalter*, Wege der Forschung, vol. II, 2 eds. (Darmstadt, 1956 and 1972), pp. 20–65.

13. Schulze, *Adelsherrschaft und Landesherrschaft. Studien zur Verfassungs- und Besitzgeschichte der Altmark, des ostsächsischen Raumes und des hannoverschen Wendlandes im hohen Mittelalter*, MDF, vol. XXIX (Cologne and Graz, 1963), p. 207: "Auch in den deutschen Ostmarken ist die territoriale Einheit des Landes nicht der Ausgangspunkt, sondern das Ergebnis der Entwicklung der Landesherrschaft gewesen." For the term *Landesherrschaft* and the controversies, see now F. Merzbacher, "Landesherr, Landesherrschaft," in HRG ii, cols. 1383–88.

14. Seibt, "Land und Herrschaft in Böhmen," *Historische Zeitschrift* 200 (1965): 292: "was Brunner vom 'Land' als Rechtsgemeinschaft landesbeherrschender Leute im Sinne einer konstitutiven, nämlich vorgegebenen Einheit angenommen hatte, fand weder in der Rechts- noch in der ausserösterreichischen Landesgeschichte Anerkennung."

15. Brunner, *Land und Herrschaft*, p. 106: "Die Fehde gehört untrennbar zum mittelalterlichen Politik wie der Krieg zum souveränen Staat und zum Völkerrecht der neueren Zeit. Ein wirkliches Aufhören der Fehde, nicht bloss ein Verbot, das nicht durchgeführt wurde, musste die Gesamtstruktur des mittelalterlichen Staates von Grund auf ändern. Sind wir so gezwungen, die Fehde als wesentliches Element jeder mittelalterlichen Verfassung zu betrachten, so ist damit doch nicht gesagt, dass die Fehde, so unumgänglich sie war, doch eben und auch im Bewusstsein der Zeitgenossen nicht ein Unglück gewesen sei. Das ganze religiös-kirchliche Denken konnte sie nur als Folge der Sünde betrachten." On these problems see also H. Patze, "Grundherrschaft und Fehde," in Patze (ed.), *Die Grundherrschaften im späten Mittelalter*, VF, vol. XXVII, part 1 (Sigmaringen, 1983), pp. 263–92, and E. Kaufmann, "Fehde," "Friede," in HRG i, cols. 1083–93, 1275–92, and "Notwehr" in HRG iii, cols. 1096–1101.

16. I have used the new edition published at Darmstadt in 1973.

17. I have used the second edition, published at Darmstadt in 1972 as vol. 197 of *Libelli*. For short guides to the concepts surrounding noble domination, see R. Scheyhing, "Adel," in HRG i, cols. 41–51; H. K. Schulze and W. Ogris, "Dominium," ibid., cols. 754–57; W. Ogris, "Gewere," ibid., cols. 1658–67 and "Munt, Muntwalt," in HRG iii, cols. 750–61; E. Kaufmann, "Potentes," in ibid., cols. 1846–48. It is not possible to cite much of the vast scholarly literature on the German aristocracy, but taken together, the following provide an incisive chronological conspectus of ideas and debates: F. Irsigler, *Untersuchungen zur Geschichte des frühfränkischen Adels*, Rheinisches Archiv, vol. LXX (Bonn, 1969), his chap. 3 being in translation in T. Reuter (ed.), *The Medieval Nobility. Studies on the Ruling Classes of France and Germany from the Sixth to the Twelfth Century*, Europe in the Middle Ages, Selected Studies, vol. XIV (Amsterdam, New York, and Oxford, 1978), pp. 105–36; R. Wenskus, *Sächsischer Stammesadel und fränkischer Reichsadel*, Abhandlungen der Akademie der Wissenschaften in Göttingen, phil.-hist. Klasse, 3d ser., vol. XCIII (Göttingen, 1976); G. Tellenbach, "Vom karolingischen Reichsadel zum deutschen Reichsfürstenstand," in T. Mayer (ed.), *Adel und Bauern im deutschen Staat des Mittelalters*, new ed. (Darmstadt, 1976), pp. 22–73, and in Kämpf (ed.), *Herrschaft und Staat*, pp. 191–242, also in translation in Reuter (ed.), *Medieval Nobility*, pp. 203–42; K. J. Leyser, "The German Aristocracy from the Ninth to the Early Twelfth Century: A Historical and Cultural Sketch," *Past and Present* 41 (1968): 25–53, and in his *Medieval Germany and Its Neighbours 900–1250* (London, 1982), pp. 161–89; H. Fichtenau, *Lebensordnungen des 10. Jahrhunderts. Studien über Denkart und Existenz im einstigen Karolingerreich*, Monographien zur Geschichte des Mittelalters, vol. XXX (Stuttgart, 1984), pp. 185–323; K. Schmid, *Gebetsgedenken und adeliges Selbstverständnis im Mittelalter. Ausgewählte Beiträge* (Sigmaringen, 1983), pp. 183–267; A. Schulte, *Der Adel und die deutsche Kirche im Mittelalter*, Kirchenrechtliche Abhandlungen, vol. LXIII–IV (Stuttgart, 1910); H. Kallfelz, *Das*

*Standesethos des Adels im 10. und 11. Jahrhundert* (Würzburg, 1960); O. von Dungern, "Comes, liber, nobilis in Urkunden des 11. bis 13. Jahrhunderts," *Archiv für Urkundenforschung* 12 (1932): 181–205.

18. For the most convenient introduction to Nazi ideology in relation to historiography, see now M. Burleigh, *Germany Turns Eastwards. A Study of Ostforschung in the Third Reich* (Cambridge, 1988).

19. Vol. 61, pp. 1–50; subtitled "Grundlagen der deutschen Verfassungsentwicklung," it was subsequently revised for republication in Kämpf (ed.), *Herrschaft und Staat,* pp. 66–134. The original version began: "Die Welt des Mittelalters ist eine aristokratische Welt. Staat und Kirche und Gesellschaft werden vom Adel beherrscht. Eine Anzahl grosser Familien, angezeichnet durch vornehme Geburt und weitausgedehnten Besitz, untereinander vielfach versippt, gebietet über Land und Leute . . . Sie stellen in ihre Gesamtheit neben dem König 'das Reich' oder 'das Volk' dar. Die Taten und Untaten dieser weltlich-geistlichen Aristokratie machen die Geschichte jener Jahrhunderte aus, mit ihnen füllen die Chronisten der Zeit die Blätter ihre Bücher. Von anderen Leuten ist nichts zu vermelden . . . Das Volk auf dem Land ist zum grössten Teil abhängig, unfrei in mannigfaltigen Abstufungen. Es hat zu gehorchen, zu arbeiten und Abgaben zu entrichten. Zu sagen hat es nichts. Es hat im Grunde keine Geschichte." This accurate view of "Das Volk" would have enraged party ideologues had they bothered to read it. The German aristocracy was despised by National Socialism, a German Workers' Party that would have found the idea of princes representing "Volk" and "Reich" absurd.

20. *Land und Herrschaft,* pp. 240–356.

21. Ibid., p. 254.

22. Vol. 176, pp. 225–75. Reprinted in Kämpf (ed.), *Herrschaft und Staat,* pp. 135–90, it is partially translated in F. L. Cheyette (ed.), *Lordship and Community in Medieval Europe. Selected Readings* (New York, Chicago, Toronto, and London, 1968), pp. 64–99.

23. H. Kuhn, "Die Grenzen der germanischen Gefolgschaft," *ZRGGA* 73 (1956): 1–83; F. Graus, "Über die sogenannte germanische Treue," *Historica* 1 (1959): 71–121, and "Herrschaft und Treue. Betrachtungen zur Lehre von der germanischen Kontinuität," ibid. 12 (1966): 1–44; K. Kroeschell, *Haus und Herrschaft im frühen deutschen Recht. Ein methodischer Versuch,* Göttinger rechtswissenschaftliche Studien, vol. LXX (Göttingen, 1968), and the discussion in R. Wenskus, *Stammesbildung und Verfassung. Das Werden der frühmittelalterlichen gentes* (Cologne and Graz, 1961), pp. 346–74. See Schlesinger's later statements in "Randbemerkungen zu drei Aufsätzen über Sippe, Gefolgschaft und Treue" and "Verfassungsgeschichte und Landesgeschichte," in his *Beiträge zur deutschen Verfassungsgeschichte des Mittelalters,* 2 vols. (Göttingen, 1963), pp. 286–334 (in vol. I) and 9–41 (in vol. II). See also H. K. Schulze, "Hausherrschaft" in HRG i, cols. 2030–33, and K. Kroeschell, "Gefolgschaft," ibid., cols. 1433–37.

24. "Herrschaft" in HRG i, col. 107, and see his "Verfassungsgeschichte," in H. Quaritsch (ed.), *Gegenstand und Begriffe der Verfassungsgeschichtsschreibung,* Beihefte zu "Der Staat." Zeitschrift für Staatslehre, öffentliches Recht und Verfassungsgeschichte, vol. VI (Berlin, 1983), pp. 47–77. Kroeschell's critical stance is shared by R. Koselleck, "Begriffsgeschichtliche Probleme der Verfassungsgeschichtsschrei-

bung," ibid., pp. 7–21; H. K. Schulze, "Mediävistik und Begriffsgeschichte," in K.-U. Jäschke and R. Wenskus (eds.), *Festschrift für Helmut Beumann zum 65. Geburtstag* (Sigmaringen, 1977), pp. 388–405, and "Reichsaristokratie, Stammesadel und fränkische Freiheit. Neuer Forschungen zur frühmittelalterlichen Sozialgeschichte," *Historische Zeitschrift* 227 (1978): 353–73; F. Graus, "Verfassungsgeschichte des Mittelalters," ibid. 243 (1986): 529–89; and M. Mitterauer, "Formen adeliger Herrschaftsbildung im hochmittelalterlichen Österreich. Zur Frage der 'autogenen Hoheitsrechte,'" *MIöG* 80 (1972): 265–338. W. Schneider's *Wider die These von der "Adelsherrschaft,"* Arbeiten zur alamannischen Frühgeschichte, vol. IX (Tübingen, 1980) overstates the case.

25. Other important authors concerning themselves with the interrelated themes of lordship, community, aristocratic power, and territorial structures included K. S. Bader, "Herrschaft und Staat im deutschen Mittelalter," *Historisches Jahrbuch* 62–69 (1949): 618–46; K. Bosl, "Herrscher und Beherrschte im deutschen Reich des 10.–12. Jahrhunderts," in his *Frühformen der Gesellschaft im mittelalterlichen Europa. Ausgewählte Beiträge zu einer Strukturanalyse der mittelalterlichen Welt* (Munich and Vienna, 1964), pp. 135–55, in translation in Cheyette (ed.), *Lordship and Community,* pp. 357–75; K. Jordan, "Herrschaft und Genossenschaft im deutschen Mittelalter," in his *Ausgewählte Aufsätze zur Geschichte des Mittelalters,* Kieler historische Studien, vol. XXIX (Stuttgart, 1980), pp. 173–84; W. Kienast, "Germanische Treue und Königsheil," *Historische Zeitschrift* 227 (1978): 265–324; T. Mayer, "Analekten zum Problem der Entstehung der Landeshoheit, vornehmlich in Süddeutschland," *BDLG* 89 (1952): 87–111; H. Mitteis, "Formen der Adelsherrschaft im Mittelalter," in his *Die Rechtsidee in der Geschichte* (Weimar, 1957), pp. 636–68; H. Quirin, "Herrschaftsbildung und Kolonisation im mitteldeutschen Osten," *Nachrichten von der Akademie in Göttingen,* phil.-hist. (Klasse, 1949), pp. 69–108; H. Schmidinger, *Patriarch und Landesherr. Die weltliche Herrschaft der Patriarchen von Aquileia bis zum Ende der Staufer,* Publikationen des österreichischen Kulturinstituts in Rom, Abhandlungen, vol. I (Graz and Cologne, 1954).

26. I have used the second edition, published at Graz and Cologne in 1958. As Theodor Mayer pointed out in his "Nachwort" (pp. 241–67) to that edition at p. 267: "Der Versuch, das Reich von oben her in einen Staat umzubilden, ist nicht geglückt, die Staatlichkeit musste von unten her aufgebaut werden. Dass wir diese Grundlagen der deutschen Verfassung zu erkennen vermögen, verdanken wir in hohem Ausmasse Hans Hirsch und seiner 'Hohen Gerichtsbarkeit'; Hirsch hat die Eigenart und Bedeutung der treibenden Kräfte, aber auch die Grenzen für ihre Wirksamkeit gezeigt. Deshalb besitzt sein Werk auch heute noch epochemachende Bedeutung."

27. On this vital manifestation in German legal history, see E. Wadle, "Heinrich IV. und die deutsche Friedensbewegung," in J. Fleckenstein (ed.), *Investiturstreit und Reichsverfassung,* VF, vol. XVII (Sigmaringen, 1973), pp. 141–73, and "Der Nürnberger Friedebrief Kaiser Friedrich Barbarossas und das gelehrte Recht," in G. Köbler (ed.), *Wege europäische Rechtsgeschichte. Karl Kroeschell zum 60. Geburtstag,* Rechtshistorische Reihe, vol. LX (Frankfurt am Main, etc., 1987), pp. 548–72; O. Engels, "Vorstufen der Staatwerdung im Hochmittelalter. Zum Kontext der Gottesfriedensbewegung," *Historisches Jahrbuch* 97–98 (1978): 71–86;

J. Gernhuber, *Die Landfriedensbewegung in Deutschland bis zum Mainzer Reichsland-friede von 1235,* Bonner rechtswissenschaftliche Abhandlungen, vol. XLIV (Bonn, 1952), and "Staat und Landfrieden im deutschen Reich des Mittelalters," in *La Paix,* Recueils de la Société Jean Bodin pour l'histoire comparative des institutions, vol. XV, part 2 (Brussels, 1961), pp. 27–77; H. Angermeier, "Landfriedenspolitik und Landfriedensgesetzgebung unter den Staufern," in J. Fleckenstein (ed.), *Probleme um Friedrich II.,* VF, vol. XVI (Sigmaringen, 1974), pp. 167–86; E. Kaufmann and H. Holzhauer, "Landfriede," in HRG ii, cols. 1451–85. The earliest text of a royal *Landfriede* to survive is from 1152; MGH Dipl. Frederick I, no. 25, pp. 39–44. Some of the content of Henry IV's *Landfriede* is known from report; MGH Consts. i, no. 74, pp. 125f. Those of Henry V, Lothar III, and Conrad III have unfortunately perished.

28. It is not possible to cite much of the huge literature, but for the impact of ecclesiastical reform and polemic in Germany, see H. Jakobs, *Kirchenreform und Hochmittelalter 1046–1215,* Oldenbourg—Grundrisse der Geschichte, vol. VII (Munich and Vienna, 1984), pp. 15–36, 208–12; U.-R. Blumenthal, *The Investiture Controversy. Church and Monarchy from the Ninth to the Twelfth Century,* Middle Ages Series (Philadelphia, 1988), pp. 64–181; C. Morris, *The Papal Monarchy. The Western Church from 1050 to 1250,* Oxford History of the Christian Church (Oxford, 1989), pp. 109–33, 154–73, 182–204; M. Herberger, "Investiturstreit," in HRG ii, cols. 407–12; H. Kämpf (ed.), *Canossa als Wende,* Wege der Forschung, vol. XII (Darmstadt, 1963); Fleckenstein (ed.), *Investiturstreit und Reichsverfassung;* H. Hirsch, "The Constitutional History of the Reformed Monasteries During the Investiture Contest," in G. Barraclough (ed.), *Mediaeval Germany 911–1250,* part 2, *Essays by German Historians,* Studies in Mediaeval History, vol. II, new ed. (Oxford, 1961), pp. 131–73; W. Ullmann, "Von Canossa nach Pavia. Zum Strukturwandel der Herrschaftsgrundlagen im salischen und staufischen Zeitalter," *Historisches Jahrbuch* 93 (1973): 265–300; S. Weinfurter, "Reformkanoniker und Reichsepiskopat im Hochmittelalter," ibid., 97–98 (1978): 158–93; P. Classen, *Gerhoch von Reichersberg. Eine Biographie* (Wiesbaden, 1960); and the texts of the Concordat of Worms in MGH Consts. i, nos. 107f., pp. 159–61 (1122).

29. See H. Krause, "Gesetzgebung," in HRG i, cols. 1611–13; W. Ebel, *Geschichte der Gesetzgebung in Deutschland,* Göttinger rechtswissenschaftliche Studien, vol. XXIV (Göttingen, 1958), pp. 42–56; K. Kroeschell, *Deutsche Rechtsgeschichte,* vol. I, *Bis 1250* (Reinbek bei Hamburg, 1972), pp. 152–240, and "Recht und Rechtsbegriff im 12. Jahrhundert," in *Probleme des 12. Jahrhunderts. Reichenau—Vorträge,* VF, vol. XII (Constance and Stuttgart, 1968), pp. 309–35; E. Kaufmann, *Deutsches Recht. Die Grundlagen,* Grundlagen der Germanistik, vol. XXVII (Berlin, 1984), pp. 20–27; P. Classen (ed.), *Recht und Schrift im Mittelalter,* VF, vol. XXIII (Sigmaringen, 1977).

30. See A. Laufs and K.-P. Schroeder, "Landrecht," in HRG ii, cols. 1527–35; G. Köbler, "Land und Landrecht im Frühmittelalter," *ZRGGA* 86 (1969): 1–40; K.-H. Ganahl, "Versuch einer Geschichte des österreichischen Landrechtes im 13. Jahrhundert," *MIöG,* Ergänzungsband 13 (1935): 229–384; M. Weltin, "Das österreichische Landrecht des 13. Jahrhunderts im Spiegel der Verfassungsentwicklung," in Classen (ed.), *Recht und Schrift,* pp. 381–424; W. Barkhausen, "Die Gesetzgebung Wichmanns von Magdeburg," *DA* 4 (1940–1941): 495–503.

31. The word is no neologism; see O. Schade, *Altdeutsches Wörterbuch*, vol. I, 2d ed. (Halle, 1882), p. 541 for *lêhenrëht*. From the large literature see K.-H. Spiess, "Lehnsgericht," "Lehnsgesetze," and "Lehn(s)recht, Lehnswesen," in HRG ii, cols. 1714–21, 1725–41; K.-F. Krieger, "Die königliche Lehnsgerichtsbarkeit im Zeitalter der Staufer," *DA* 26 (1970): 400–33; H. Mitteis, *Lehnrecht und Staatsgewalt. Untersuchungen zur mittelalterlichen Verfassungsgeschichte*, new ed. (Weimar, 1958), pp. 415–63; W. Goez, *Der Leihezwang. Eine Untersuchung zur Geschichte des deutschen Lehnrechtes* (Tübingen, 1962); H.-G. Krause, "Der Sachsenspiegel und das Problem des sogenannten Leihezwangs. Zugleich ein Beitrag zur Entstehung des Sachsenspiegels," *ZRGGA* 93 (1976): 21–99; M. Herberger, "Leihezwang," in HRG ii, cols. 1826–29; K. Bosl, "Das ius ministerialium. Dienstrecht und Lehnrecht im deutschen Mittelalter," in his *Frühformen der Gesellschaft*, pp. 277–326.

32. See, for example, H. Patze, "Stadtgründung und Stadtrecht," in Classen (ed.), *Recht und Schrift*, pp. 163–96; W. Ebel, "Über die rechtsschöpferische Leistung des mittelalterlichen deutschen Bürgertums," in T. Mayer (ed.), *Untersuchungen zur gesellschaftlichen Struktur der mittelalterlichen Städte in Europa*, VF, vol. XI (Constance and Stuttgart, 1966), pp. 241–58, and "Lübisches Recht," in HRG iii, cols. 77–84; G. Buchda, "Magdeburger Recht," ibid., cols. 134–38; W. Schlesinger, "Forum, villa fori, ius fori. Einige Bemerkungen zu Marktgründungsurkunden des 12. Jahrhunderts aus Mitteldeutschland," in *Aus Geschichte und Landeskunde* (Bonn, 1960), pp. 408–40, and "Das älteste Freiburger Stadtrecht. Überlieferung und Inhalt," *ZRGGA* 83 (1966): 63–116; B. Diestelkamp, "Welfische Stadtgründungen und Stadtrechte des 12. Jahrhunderts," ibid. 81 (1964): 164–224. See also G. Köbler, "Civis und ius civile. Untersuchungen zur Geschichte zweier Rechtswörter im frühen deutschen Mittelalter," ibid. 83 (1966): 35–62, and H. Drüppel, *Iudex civitatis. Zur Stellung des Richters in der hoch- und spätmittelalterlichen Stadt deutschen Rechts*, Forschungen zur deutschen Rechtsgeschichte, vol. XII (Cologne and Vienna, 1981).

33. On this huge subject see, for example, H. Appelt, "Friedrich Barbarossa und das römische Recht," in G. Wolf (ed.), *Friedrich Barbarossa*, Wege der Forschung, vol. CCCXC (Darmstadt, 1975), pp. 58–82; W. Stelzer, "Zum Scholarenprivileg Friedrich Barbarossas (Authentica 'Habita')," *DA* 34 (1978): 123–65, and *Gelehrtes Recht in Österreich von den Anfängen bis zum frühen 14. Jahrhundert*, MIöG Ergänzungsband 26 (Vienna, Cologne, and Graz, 1982); C. M. Radding, *The Origins of Medieval Jurisprudence. Pavia and Bologna 850–1150* (New Haven and London, 1988).

34. Eike von Repgow's private compilation, the *Sachsenspiegel*, is about both; see K. A. Eckhardt, *Sachsenspiegel Landrecht* and *Sachsenspiegel Lehnrecht*, MGH Fontes iuris, new ser., vol. I, 2 parts, 2d ed. (Göttingen, Berlin, and Frankfurt am Main, 1955–1956). In Eckhardt, *Lehnrecht*, p. 19, between paragraphs 180 and 181, we find, "Hir is gesproken van dem lantrechte, dit is dat lenrecht." See E. Molitor, "Der Gedankengang des Sachsenspiegels. Beiträge zu seiner Entstehung," *ZRGGA* 65 (1947): 15–69; K. Kroeschell, "Rechtsaufzeichnung und Rechtswirklichkeit. Das Beispiel des Sachsenspiegels," in Classen (ed.), *Recht und Schrift*, pp. 349–80; R. Lieberwirth, *Eike von Repchow und der Sachsenspiegel*, Sitzungsberichte der sächsischen Akademie der Wissenschaften zu Leipzig, phil.-hist. Klasse, vol. CXXII, part 4 (Berlin, 1982); H. Schlosser, "Eike von Repgow," in HRG i, cols. 896–99,

and F. Ebel, "Sachsenspiegel," in HRG iv, cols. 1228–37. See both concepts of law in practice in E. E. Stengel, "Land- und lehnrechtliche Grundlagen des Reichsfürsten-standes," *ZRGGA* 66 (1948): 294–342; G. Theuerkauf, "Der Prozess gegen Hein-rich den Löwen. Über Landrecht und Lehnrecht im hohen Mittelalter," in W.-D. Mohrmann (ed.), *Heinrich der Löwe*, Veröffentlichungen der Niedersächsischen Archivverwaltung, vol. XXXIX (Göttingen, 1980), pp. 217–48; K. Heinemeyer, "Der Prozess Heinrichs des Löwen," *BDLG* 117 (1981): 1–60.

35. On the usage, see G. Theuerkauf, "Fürst," in HRG i, cols. 1337–51; H. Koller, "Die Bedeutung des Titels 'princeps' in der Reichskanzlei unter den Saliern und Staufern," *MIöG* 68 (1960): 63–80; E. Schröder, "Herzog und Fürst. Über Aufkommen und Bedeutung zweier Rechtswörter," *ZRGGA* 44 (1924): 1–29; G. Köbler, "Amtsbezeichnungen in den frühmittelalterlichen Übersetzungsgleich-ungen," *Historisches Jahrbuch* 92 (1972): 334–57.

36. I have analyzed those materials in my forthcoming *Princes and Territories in Medieval Germany* (Cambridge, 1991), chaps. 8–12.

37. I derived much benefit through comparing German regions with studies on conditions elsewhere in Europe, notably R. H. Hilton, *A Medieval Society. The West Midlands at the End of the Thirteenth Century* (London, 1966); K. B. McFarlane, *The Nobility of Later Medieval England. The Ford Lectures for 1953 and Related Studies* (Oxford, 1973); J. C. Holt, "Politics and property in early medieval England," *Past and Present* 57 (1972): 3–52, and the subsequent debate in 65 (1974): 110–35; J. Larner, *The Lords of Romagna. Romagnol Society and the Origins of the Signorie* (London, 1965); P. Toubert, *Les Structures du Latium médiéval. Le Latium méridional et la Sabine du IXe siècle à la fin du XIIe siècle,* Bibliothèque des Écoles françaises d'Athènes et de Rome, vol. CCLI, 2 parts (Rome, 1973); T. Dean, *Land and Power in Late Medieval Ferrara. The Rule of the Este, 1350–1450,* Cambridge Studies in Medieval Life and Thought, 4th Series, vol. VII (Cambridge, 1988); R. Fossier, *La Terre et les hommes en Picardie jusqu'à la fin du XIIIe siècle,* Publications de la Faculté des Lettres et Sciences humaines de Paris-Sorbonne, series "Re-cherches," vols. XLVIII–IX (Paris and Louvain, 1968); G. Duby, *La Société aux XIe et XIIe siècles dans la region mâconnaise,* Bibliothèque générale de l'École Pratique des Hautes Études, 2 eds. (Paris, 1953 and 1971); E. Perroy, *Les Familles nobles du Forez au XIIIe siècle. Essais de filiation,* Centre d'études foréziennes. Thèses et mémoires, vols. VIII and IX (Saint-Etienne and Montbrison, 1976–1977), and G. Devailly, *Le Berry du Xe siècle au milieu du XIIIe. Étude politique, religieuse, sociale et économique,* École pratique des Hautes Études. Sorbonne VIe section, Civilisations et sociétés, vol. XIX (Paris, 1973), taking their varied approaches with, for example, G. Heinrich, *Die Grafen von Arnstein,* MDF, vol. XXI (Cologne and Graz, 1961); B. Herrmann, *Die Herrschaft des Hochstifts Naumburg an der mittleren Elbe,* MDF, vol. LIX (Cologne and Vienna, 1970); W.-A. Kropat, *Reich, Adel und Kirche in der Wetterau von der Karolinger- bis zur Stauferzeit,* Schriften des Hessischen Landesamts für geschichtliche Landeskunde, vol. XXVIII (Marburg, 1965); T. Mayer, *Mit-telalterliche Studien. Gesammelte Aufsätze* (Lindau and Constance, 1959 [for Swabia]); J. Prinz, *Das Territorium des Bistums Osnabrück,* Studien und Vorarbeiten zum Historischen Atlas Niedersachsens, vol. XV, new ed. (Göttingen, 1973); W. Ribbe (ed.), *Das Havelland im Mittelalter. Untersuchungen zur Strukturgeschichte*

*einer ostelbischen Landschaft,* Berliner Historische Studien, vol. XIII and Germania Slavica, vol. V (Berlin, 1987); R. Sablonier, *Adel im Wandel. Eine Untersuchung zur sozialen Situation des ostschweizerischen Adels um 1300,* Veröffentlichungen des Max-Planck-Instituts für Geschichte, vol. LXVI (Göttingen, 1979), and E. Zickgraf, *Die gefürstete Grafschaft Henneberg-Schleusingen,* Schriften des Instituts für geschichtliche Landeskunde von Hessen und Nassau, vol. XXII (Marburg, 1944).

38. Their titles and offices are discussed in my *Princes and Territories,* chaps. 4–7.

39. MGH Consts. ii, no. 285, pp. 401f. (1224); nos. 304f., pp. 418–20 (1231); no. 171, pp. 211–13 (1232).

40. See F. R. H. Du Boulay, *Germany in the Later Middle Ages* (London, 1983), pp. 19–63; P. Moraw, *Von offener Verfassung zu gestalteter Verdichtung. Das Reich im späten Mittelalter 1250 bis 1490,* Propyläen Geschichte Deutschlands, vol. III (Berlin, 1985), pp. 235–59, and "Kaiser Karl IV. im deutschen Spätmittelalter," *Historische Zeitschrift* 229 (1979): 1–24. On the changing conditions, see also K.-F. Krieger, *Die Lehnshoheit der deutschen Könige im Spätmittelalter (ca. 1200–1437),* Untersuchungen zur deutschen Staats- und Rechtsgeschichte, new ser., vol. XXIII (Aalen, 1979), and E. Schubert, *König und Reich. Studien zur spätmittelalterlichen deutschen Verfassungsgeschichte,* Veröffentlichungen des Max-Planck-Instituts für Geschichte, vol. LXIII (Göttingen, 1979).

41. Stefan Weinfurter's valuable recent edition of *Die Geschichte der Eichstätter Bischöfe des Anonymus Haserensis. Edition—Übersetzung—Kommentar,* Eichstätter Studien, new ser., vol. XXIV (Regensburg, 1987) may make it better known. So may B. Appel, E. Braun, and S. Hofmann (eds.), *Heilige Willibald 787–1987. Künder des Glaubens. Pilger, Mönch, Bischof,* Katalog der Ausstellung der Diözese Eichstätt (Eichstätt, 1987).

42. For the diversity in scholarly approach to the history of the adjacent regions in the Middle Ages, see, for example, H. Schwarzmaier, *Königtum, Adel und Klöster im Gebiet zwischen Oberer Iller und Lech,* Veröffentlichungen der Schwäbischen Forschungsgemeinschaft bei der Kommission für bayerische Landesgeschichte, 1st ser., Studien zur Geschichte des bayerischen Schwabens, vol. VII (Augsburg, 1961); K. Bosl, *Oberpfalz und Oberpfälzer. Geschichte einer Region. Gesammelte Aufsätze,* ed. K. Ackermann and E. Lassleben (Kallmünz/Opf., 1978); J. Jahn, *Augsburg Land,* Historischer Atlas von Bayern, Teil Schwaben, vol. XI (Munich, 1984), pp. 1–207.

43. One reviewer (*American Historical Review* 91 [1986]: 646) thought that the book might more profitably have been entitled *The German Ministerialage.* Ministerialage is a suggestive neologism and must be a rendering of the German "Ministerialität" (as in H. Rössler and G. Franz, *Sachwörterbuch zur deutschen Geschichte,* vol. II [Munich, 1958], "Ministerialität," pp. 738–40), itself an invention of nineteenth century *Fachsprache,* which won acceptance over the less euphonious "Dienstmannschaft" as used, for example, in P. Heck, "Der Ursprung der sächsischen Dienstmannschaft," *VSWG* 5 (1907): 116–72, and K. Bosl, "Vorstufen der deutschen Königsdienstmannschaft" (1952) in his *Frühformen der Gesellschaft,* pp. 228–76. In *Mediae latinitatis lexicon minus* (Leyden, 1976), J. F. Niermeyer discerned eleven different uses or senses for the word *ministerialis* in medieval Latin

(pp. 684–87), but an equivalent for "Ministerialität" did not exist. The nearest words were *familia* as used in M. Heuwieser, *Die Traditionen des Hochstifts Passau, Quellen und Erörterungen zur bayerischen Geschichte*, vol. VI (Munich, 1930), no. 628, p. 231 (1149–1164), or F. Schumi, *Urkunden- und Regestenbuch des Herzogtums Krain*, vol. II (Laibach/Ljubljana, 1887), no. 282, pp. 219f. (1261), and *militia* as used in C. Erdmann and N. Fickermann, *Briefsammlungen der Zeit Heinrichs IV.*, MGH Die Briefe der deutschen Kaiserzeit, vol. V (Weimar, 1950), no. 18, pp. 211–13 and no. 35, pp. 233f. (1063), or H. A. Erhard, *Codex diplomaticus historiae Westphaliae*, vol. II (Münster, 1851), no. 252, p. 41 (1146), the latter example also cited by Niermeyer. On the pitfalls of equating modern *Fachsprache* and historiographical devices with medieval words and meanings, see W. Stach, "Wort und Bedeutung im mittelalterlichen Latein," *DA* 9 (1952): 332–52; G. Köbler, "burg und stat—Burg und Stadt?" *Historisches Jahrbuch* 87 (1967): 305–25; Schulze, "Mediävistik und Begriffsgeschichte."

44. See Chapters 5 to 7.

45. See Chapter 2, n. 20.

46. MGH Consts. i, no. 90, pp. 140–42, and S. Chodorow, "Paschal II, Henry V, and the Origins of the Crisis of 1111," in J. R. Sweeney and S. Chodorow (eds.), *Popes, Teachers, and Canon Law in the Middle Ages* (Ithaca and London, 1989), pp. 3–25. See also C. Servatius, *Paschalis II. (1099–1118). Studien zu seiner Person und seiner Politik*, Päpste und Papsttum, vol. XIV (Stuttgart, 1979), esp. pp. 223–27, 238–41, 252f., 264–72.

47. H. Hürten, "Die Verbindung von geistlicher und weltlicher Gewalt als Problem in der Amtsführung des mittelalterlichen deutschen Bischofs," *Zeitschrift für Kirchengeschichte* 82 (1971): 16–28, and E.-D. Hehl, *Kirche und Krieg im 12. Jahrhundert. Studien zu kanonischem Recht und politischer Wirklichkeit*, Monographien zur Geschichte des Mittelalters, vol. XIX (Stuttgart, 1980).

48. K. Ganzer, "Zur Beschränkung der Bischofswahl auf die Domkapitel in Theorie und Praxis des 12. und 13. Jahrhunderts," *Zeitschrift der Savigny-Stiftung für Rechtsgeschichte. Kanonistische Abteilung* 88 (1971): 22–82, and 89 (1972): 166–97, and Morris, *Papal Monarchy*, pp. 545–49.

49. This point is forcibly made by H. Thieme in "Reich, Reichsverfassung," HRG iv, col. 513. See, for example, Bishop Conrad I (1153–1171) of Eichstätt's neighbor Herold of Würzburg as *episcopus et dux*, "Bishop and Duke," in MGH Dipl. Frederick I, no. 546, pp. 3–7 (1168).

50. See my forthcoming *Princes and Territories*, pp. 186–210.

51. See F. Merzbacher, "Bischof," HRG i, col. 444 and "Hochgerichtsbarkeit," HRG ii, col. 174.

52. For the details, see Chapter 6.

53. See P. Classen, "Das Wormser Konkordat in der deutschen Verfassungs-geschichte," in Fleckenstein (ed.), *Investiturstreit und Reichsverfassung*, pp. 411–60.

54. Morris, *Papal Monarchy*, pp. 219–26, 387–409; Merzbacher, "Bischof," HRG i, cols. 439–46. In English the best account of episcopal office in the age of reform is by R. L. Benson, *The Bishop-Elect. A Study in Medieval Ecclesiastical Office* (Princeton, 1968). For an important German example, see S. Weinfurter, *Salzburger Bistumsreform und Bischofspolitik im 12. Jahrhundert. Der Erzbischof Konrad I. von*

*Salzburg (1106–1147) und die Regularkanoniker,* Kölner Historische Abhandlungen, vol. XXIV (Cologne and Vienna, 1975), and K. Zeillinger, *Erzbischof Konrad I. von Salzburg 1106–1147,* Wiener Dissertationen aus dem Gebiete der Geschichte, vol. X (Vienna, 1968).

    55. See W. Imkamp, *"Pastor et sponsus.* Elemente einer Theologie des bischöflichen Amtes bei Innocenz III," in H. Mordek (ed.), *Aus Kirche und Reich. Studien zu Theologie, Politik und Recht im Mittelalter. Festschrift für Friedrich Kempf* (Sigmaringen, 1983), pp. 285–94; P. B. Pixton, "Watchmen on the Tower: The German Episcopacy and the Implementation of the Decrees of the Fourth Lateran Council, 1216–1274," in S. Kuttner and K. Pennington (eds.), *Proceedings of the Sixth International Congress of Medieval Canon Law 1980,* Monumenta Iuris Canonici, series C, Subsidia, vol. VII (Vatican City, 1985), pp. 579–93; R. P. Stenger, "The Episcopacy as an Ordo According to the Medieval Canonists," *Medieval Studies* 29 (1967): 67–112; Morris, *Papal Monarchy,* pp. 527–35.

    56. G. Theuerkauf, "Fürst," HRG i, cols. 1340–49.

# 1. Regions and Political Power in Medieval Germany

The medieval kingdom of the Germans, the *Teutonicum regnum* as it was described by the twelfth-century imperial chancery,[1] was the largest component of the Roman Empire reestablished in the west by Otto the Great in 962.[2] But in their political structure, neither the kingdom nor the Empire exhibited many of the distinguishing marks of the sovereign state. In theory the western emperor possessed the autocratic powers of a Roman *princeps,* and for this reason some of the legislative acts of the Staufen rulers were actually inserted into the *Corpus Iuris civilis.*[3] In practice the German kingdom was an agglomeration of autonomous regional jurisdictions exercised by dynastic magnates, powerful cities, and the princes of the Church.

At the summit of this congeries stood the royal court, the crown enjoying great influence in the realm more by virtue of homage, fealty, and service rendered by the above mentioned authorities than through effective administrative organs of its own.[4] By tradition the crown was in any case involved primarily with international diplomacy, with the religious affairs of Christendom as a whole, and with recruiting armies for the expeditions to Italy, and for campaigns seen as necessary in Germany itself, in Burgundy, or in eastern Europe. So the tacit division of realistic governing authority between the court and the regional powers did not of itself inspire or predict conflicts and jealousies about who should be exercising rule in Germany. Besides, German rulers possessed rights that enhanced their power and prestige above malcontent combinations of their rivals. The king was the guardian of justice and of the *Landfriede;* he was lord of the German Church as a visible hierarchy owing the crown valuable services in return for its temporalities; and the king was owner of a widespread fisc, which, despite aristocratic depredations especially in the north of Germany, was again increasing in value and extent due largely to economic expansion and to inheritances in the twelfth century.[5]

Few of the German cities held extensive territory. Most of them derived their significance from commerce, defensive diplomacy, and military preparedness behind their fortifications. The secular princes, the bishops, and the imperial abbots also owned towns, markets, mints, and tolls. Their power was based primarily upon the economic, demographic, and military resources of the countryside where they owned numerous castles, manors, forests, and monasteries, each with its appropriate jurisdiction. From the tenth century until the end of the old Empire over eight hundred years later, the crown was never quite outfaced by these formidable local powers who were technically its subjects and vassals. The Empire was, however, too large for one government or a single imperial administration ever to be an effective controlling force. So the successive imperial dynasties were obliged to accept a set of circumstances that could not be reversed until the nineteenth century: that autonomous regions under the hereditary rule of the bishops, abbots, and secular princes, interspersed with independent city-states and lands of imperial knights, constituted the German political structure.[6] In 1648 this was formalized by the Treaty of Westphalia as the *ius territorii et superioritatis*.[7] It was, in other words, local sovereignty under imperial suzerainty, untidy in legal thought but a reasonable reflection of political reality in Germany.

The causes for the relatively fragmented nature of the German medieval polity are to be found not in the misfortunes, weakness, or mistakes of imperial dynasties, but in the huge geographical extent of the Empire and in the vigor of aristocratic and ecclesiastical rule in its localities. Established in the eighth and ninth centuries during the Carolingian occupation of the provinces east of the Rhine, ecclesiastical and aristocratic domination received phenomenal new impetus from demographic and economic expansion between the later eleventh and the early fourteenth centuries.[8] The ambition of the secular princes, the needs of the cities, and the temporal powers of the Church may frequently have provided causes for conflict with the crown. But there was no conscious policy on the part of regional authorities favoring the erosion of the crown's powers either. On the other hand, the royal court had necessarily to settle for the regional autarky of the Church and lay magnates, if not the towns, even before the confrontations of Henry IV's reign (1056–1106) added the savor of ecclesiastical controversy to German politics.[9]

The history of the German *regnum,* or realm, shows that there was, within the vast geographical construction that itself decisively expanded toward the east in the twelfth and thirteenth centuries, space for an exalted concept of kingship, a powerful Church, ambitious princes, and rising cities. The narrative sources often bemoan the violence and double-dealing with which they tended to conduct their mutual affairs. By 1146 the most distinguished historian of them all, Bishop Otto of Freising, thought that events in Germany had reached such a pass that the "evil city," the *civitas perversa,* would be on the point of imminent collapse were it not for the prayers of the saints, ushering in the end of the world as forecast in Scripture. Quoting St. Paul on the overshadowing sentence of death, "we consider that on account of our many sins and the immoderate impurity of this turbulent age, the world can hardly persist for very long."[10] However, none of the sinful powers in Germany was mighty enough to overthrow the established rights of the others, or pretended, except in times of indignation, to be able to do so. Such times were perhaps 1076 to 1088, 1198 to 1208, and 1245 to 1254 when the princes of Germany, with considerable backing from the papacy, endeavored to remove the established imperial dynasties; 1110 to 1111 when Henry V appears to have planned the abolition of the temporal authority of the German Church; and 1232 to 1235 when the crown issued unsuccessful legislation depriving the cities of their autonomy.

Time and again German medieval history compels us to look to the regions for an understanding of the ways in which authority was exercised. The regions were complex. They reflected not only the pre-Carolingian histories of settlement, the territorial acquisitions of East Francia in the ninth and tenth centuries, and the internal and external colonizations of the twelfth and thirteenth, but also the shifting property rights and jurisdictions of the crown, the Church, and the aristocracy through the generations.[11] The regions are also confusing because they exhibited few hard and fast political boundaries until early modern times. Land ownership, rights over persons, and the variety of jurisdiction did not fall into unified geographical portions but were physically quite interspersed, reflecting the history of inheritance and partition, gift, exchange and purchase, feud and expropriation, all affecting large expanses of territory. The see of Mainz, for example, whose cathedral town and diocesan center were in the Rhineland, did not actually own very extensive lands there compared with its possessions farther afield, in the Main valley and in Thuringia.[12] The individually formulated jurisdictions in Germany, be they over manors, counties, ecclesiastical foundations with their lands, towns, or forests, had differing origins and purposes; they overlapped considerably in their geographical outlines; and they grew or atrophied according to the effective authority of their princely owners. Regional complexities increased with the immense multiplication of villages, monasteries, communications, markets, and fortifications from the later eleventh century. Furthermore, much German territory and jurisdiction was held as hereditary fief, so that the realities of possession in a given region hinged upon long-standing struggles between two parties, lord and vassal, to vindicate their ultimate control.[13]

As a result of all this, the regions of medieval Germany offer few convincing generalizations about their political structure and historical direction.[14] For centuries the vast provinces of the Carolingian conquest and settlement preserved their names; in the center, Franconia, in the south, Bavaria and Swabia, in the north, Saxony and Thuringia, in the west, Lotharingia and Frisia. These large areas did not in themselves provide a social basis for emergent regional unity. On the contrary, they tended toward subdivision, and their very names changed meaning. Lotharingia shriveled into a hereditary dominion, albeit an extensive one, around the castle of Nancy.[15] Thuringia was recreated as a landgravate under a new dynasty after 1130.[16] The name of Saxony shifted east of the River Elbe onto new colonial ground as its ducal and electoral titles changed hands between 1180 and 1423.[17] Swabia disintegrated quite rapidly at the end of the eleventh century and its ducal title, effective only over a portion of the old duchy, was completely subordinated by the end of the twelfth century as part of the Staufen imperial fisc.[18] Bavaria shed its southeastern marches of Austria, Styria, and Carinthia between the tenth and the twelfth centuries, and was entirely reconstructed after 1180 as a new dynastic duchy made out of about forty comital inheritances and fifty monastic advocacies as well as the hereditary lands of the palatine house of Scheyern and Wittelsbach.[19] So the old military duchies of the late Carolingian and Ottonian world finally gave way, by the beginning of the twelfth century, to a body of ecclesiastical and secular landowners several hundred strong. It was this all-powerful and interrelated group, the effective rulers of the regions, who began to construct territorial principalities held together by reformed criminal jurisdictions, new or enlarged stone castles garrisoned by *ministeriales,* and economic expansion in town and country, during the twelfth and thirteenth centuries.[20]

To the ambitious magnate, the German countryside did not present any internally coherent or socially integrated regional unities that could then be subverted and occupied. In practice the regions were newly carved out by the princes themselves: through inheritance and feud, the assart of very extensive woodlands, the settlement of lands newly available in the colonial east, and the foundation everywhere of towns, monasteries, manors, and castles after about 1050. These processes are reflected in the regional nomenclature of Germany. Although the old provincial and ducal names survived, there emerged a new and much longer set of regional names, which were the dynastic names of the secular princes and the cathedral and abbey names of the prelates. The great majority of the dynastic names were themselves derived from major castles erected as residences in the later eleventh and twelfth centuries, indicating the integration, or at least the interdependence of the princely family, its strongholds, and its political domination of the region in question.[21]

It is easy to see how the marked regionalism of medieval times, merging into the "particularism," or *Sonderweg,* of the early modern era, affected German history to the end of the Holy Roman Empire in 1806 and beyond. But German regionalism was more than a medieval compromise that it is necessary to examine as a precondition of the Imperial Reform movement, the Lutheran Reformation, and the Thirty Years War. It was one of the driving forces in German political life in the Middle Ages. It was not a negation, the supposed failure of kingship, that created this state of affairs, but the strength of an entrenched elite of princes based upon hereditary landowning, sharing power admittedly with much disorderly rivalry and intrigue, with the crown, ecclesiastical institutions, and the more prominent towns. The positive and vital nature of German regionalism, and its durability until its virtual collapse in the face of new nationalistic forces in the nineteenth century, makes it difficult to write coherent German history except in regional terms. Each province is distinctive,[22] every region exhibits different forms of political power, of social structure, and of economic modes. The historiography of the regions is also affected by modern administrative arrangements, which cut across the medieval and early modern divisions, compounded by the subsequent distribution of institutions of higher learning as well as the archive material itself. During the secularization of ecclesiastical Germany in 1802 and 1803 when the bishops and abbots were deprived of their territorial administrations and their lands were sequestrated by the lay princes,[23] the latter usually carried off episcopal and monastic archives to their capitals, not only out of antiquarian zeal but to hinder any subsequent restoration of ecclesiastical government.

So the writing of German regional history is inevitably affected by later events, and this poses many hazards. In the process of time Bavaria, for example, has retreated from its tenth-century Alpine marches, most of which now constitute the Austrian republic, but it has acquired as if in compensation the eastern reaches of Swabia, principally the city and bishopric of Augsburg, and about half of medieval Franconia, including the rich and extensive sees of Würzburg and Bamberg. Bavaria underwent several incarnations: the Agilofing duchy eventually suppressed by Charlemagne in 788; its vast successor in the Ottonian and Salian Empire; its truncated sequel under the Welf dynasty (1070–1180); the duchy reconstituted under the Wittelsbachs, frequently partitioned from 1255 and finally reunited in 1503; the expanded electorate under the Munich line in the seventeenth century; and then the new kingdom established in the Napoleonic era, which survives as the modern *Land Bayern*. These remarkable metamorphoses raise many problems for the consistent presentation of its history. The most notable recent undertaking in the field, the collectively written *Handbuch der bayerischen Geschichte* (1967–1975) edited by Max Spindler in four volumes and nearly five thousand pages, cuts the knot by treating of medieval Bavaria in the first two volumes, and the medieval history of its modern extensions into Swabia and Franconia in the third. This may be satisfactory from the Bavarian standpoint, but it appears completely artificial to the student of medieval Franconia and Swabia, which find themselves partitioned in a manner at variance with the medieval realities. Nevertheless, it is hard to see how this splendid work, to which a large team of scholars made contributions of high quality, could fulfill every requirement.

In 1980, when the time came to celebrate the eight hundredth anniversary of the installation of Count-Palatine Otto of Wittelsbach as duke, the magnificent historical exhibitions and their catalogues, packed with scholarly articles summarizing the most recent research, circumvented such problems by alighting upon three eras thought to be representative of Bavaria's greatness under the Wittelsbachs: their earliest ducal regime (1180–1347) culminating in the reign of Emperor Louis IV the Bavarian; the reign of Elector Maximilian I (1597–1651), when the culture of the Catholic Reformation triumphed in Bavaria; and the conversion of Bavaria into a kingdom under Maximilian IV Joseph (1799–1825), embellished by its own distinctive version of the Empire style.[24]

✳   ✳   ✳

In proposing to examine the political and social structures of any German region under its medieval forms of command, it is useful to recall the injunction of Marc Bloch:

Whatever particular aspect of European social life is being studied, and at whatever period, the student must find his own geographical framework, fixed not from outside but from within, if he wishes to escape from a world of artificiality.[25]

In German medieval history it is actually possible to impose several such "geographical frameworks" over the same landscape. The north of Germany, for example, consisted of a large-scale economic fabric containing the Hansa towns, but cut again in agrarian terms by the "north-south" Elbe and Saale river line, crossed in the twelfth century by the colonization of the Slav lands.[26] The Rhineland with its navigation from Basel down to the terminal port at Cologne, for a long time the richest and largest town in northern Europe, formed another economic construction, yet the riverain regions were beset by intense political subdivision.[27] The leagues of Rhineland cities headed by Mainz[28] were usually at loggerheads with the several bishops, themselves under pressure from hostile counts who got the better of them in the expansion of their territories.[29]

To pursue the example of Cologne. It belonged to the Rhineland and was its principal river port; to the northern economic sphere as a great Hansa city; and to the low countries as the terminal of its land routes leading in from Bruges, Ghent, and Brussels, Rotterdam, Dordrecht, and Amsterdam.[30] Its archbishops attempted and failed to impose quite a different kind of regional identity in the twelfth and thirteenth centuries, based upon their substantial diocese on both sides of the Rhine, which included Saxon as well as Lotharingian territory. For the purpose they had possessed themselves, by the end of the twelfth century, of *ducatus,* or ducal title and authority, not only in Westphalia but between the Rhine and the Meuse as well.[31] As imperial princes the archbishops were powerful,[32] yet they turned out to be no match for the townsmen of Cologne or for the combinations of their secular neighbors based in their hereditary counties. After Archbishop Siegfried's decisive defeat by them at the Battle of Worringen in 1288, the see's ducal authority was evacuated of all realistic content, and the archbishops' ambition to rule the counts and margraves of the Netherlands, the Rhineland, and Westphalia, let alone the city of Cologne itself, came to nothing. So the diocese, or *terra Coloniensis et termini episcopatus,* as it was described when arranging for its military defense in the 1160s,[33] failed to break the counterforce of city, princes, and rival churches such as Liège and Münster, or to create a realistic "political region" out of Cologne's diocese.

Cologne was a mighty city and the archbishops were powerful princes, yet the definition of its region is a complex question. The Alpine county of Tirol provided a simpler answer. Essentially it was a new dynastic creation, based upon the possession of fortifications and forests, the exploitation of ecclesiastical advocacies, and the domination of long-distance communications rather than landowning as such. The prosperous valleys of the Inn and Adige rivers, where they flow through the mountains, were linked by the well-trodden Reschen and Brenner passes, the approaches strategically secured by the counts' exercise of their advocacies over the extensive lands of the bishops of Chur and Brixen in the neighborhood of the passes. The way out to the Lombard plain involved the virtual occupation of the see of Trent, so here the counts, by means of their advocacy, endeavored to suppress the independence of the bishopric. In 1282 it was recognized that this new Tirol county, the *terra in montanis,* or "land in the mountains," belonged neither to the duchy of Bavaria nor to Swabia.[34] In the past these mountains and valleys had certainly belonged to Bavaria and the failure, by 1282, of any legal or archival memories to this effect showed how Tirol had vindicated its practical independence as a new region. In the Netherlands, to take another example, the duchy of Brabant combined an ancient regional name with the dynastic inheritances of the counts of Louvain, ornamented since the early twelfth century with the vestigial ducal title to lower Lotharingia.[35]

Although the Franconian name survived for its people, in its legal customs, and in the shadowy *ducatus,* or dukedom, of the bishops of Würzburg, the actual identity of Franconia was disintegrating after 1100.[36] Again it was the establishment of realistic territorial dominions that brought this about. After extensive feuds in which their claims had to be vindicated against the burgraves of Nuremberg and the counts of Henneberg respectively, the bishops of Bamberg and Würzburg were left with substantial principalities, chiefly assarted from woodland, by the end of the thirteenth century.[37] Cut off from these bishoprics by the forest territory of Fulda Abbey,[38] the Hessian portion of the ancient duchy took a different path from about 1130 under its principal lords, the newly promoted landgraves of Thuringia. Some members of this dynasty used the title "count of Hesse," the ancient regional name going back in all probability to Germanic times.[39] Its new identity as a county in the twelfth century, and as an independent landgravate in the latter part of the thirteenth, was underlined by the ambition of the new Brabantine house of Hesse, which seized possession in 1247, the title finally being recognized in 1292.[40]

In Saxony and its eastern marches the same tendency, the rise of dynastic authority, established new regions in the twelfth and thirteenth centuries. Notable examples were the marches of Brandenburg, reestablished by the new Ascanian margrave Albert the Bear between 1134 and 1170,[41] and Meissen, expanded after 1123 by the Wettin margrave Conrad the

Great and his descendants.[42] The Welf dominion of Duke Henry the Lion in Saxony proper was not entirely thrown down in 1180. The huge alodial inheritances stretching from the River Werra right across Saxony to the lower Elbe remained in possession of his descendants, and were reconstituted as the duchy of Brunswick-Lüneburg in 1235.[43] There are many other instructive examples of the increasing identification of region and dynastic authority: Holstein under the Saxon comital dynasty of Schauenburg or Schaumburg in the twelfth century; the palatine county of the Rhine refounded by Conrad of Staufen and his successors after 1156;[44] Austria and Styria united in 1192 under the Babenberg ducal dynasty, which failed in 1246;[45] upper Swabia under the Habsburgs in the later thirteenth century, and the county of Württemberg in the fourteenth.[46]

From an examination of the sources for and the history of jurisdictions in the twelfth and thirteenth centuries, it becomes clearer that the dynamism of princely command, overtly expressed as autonomous criminal jurisdiction possessed by ecclesiastical and secular princes and exercised by their commissioners,[47] was reorganizing Germany's political geography into a new complex of regions. In this process the great churches appear to have lost by the usurpations and depredations of their aristocratic vassals as extensive fiefs changed hands over the generations. But as an undying corporation, the Church also gained from alodial legacies, sometimes whole dynastic counties, and from the resumption of fiefs when princely families died out. The result was that by the time the Staufen royal fisc had virtually disappeared into the hands of the princes, the cities, the imperial knights, and the Church toward the end of the thirteenth century,[48] the lay aristocracy owned perhaps two thirds of Germany and the Church one third, apart from the interstices occupied by independent cities. So the crown now had to rely principally upon its own comital and ducal inheritances as a series of new men and dynasties, chiefly from the houses of Habsburg, Wittelsbach, and Luxemburg, were elected to the throne between 1246 and 1440.

From the foregoing account it can clearly be seen that the provincial structures in their social, legal, and economic content were consciously manipulated by titled noblemen, ecclesiastical office holders, city councils, and kings themselves, to maintain, defend, and expand their regional control in medieval Germany. That the crown could accept aristocratic and ecclesiastical competition and autonomy was a tradition. The lapidary comment of a recent historian of Lothar III's time (1125–1137) can stand for the entire German Middle Ages: "On the basis of its actual ascendancy, the aristocracy had since Frankish times made good its pretensions to joint rule."[49] The emperor was head but the princes in reality constituted the *regnum*.[50] What they knew they were entitled to do with this realm by virtue of their inherited right was to administer it as an immense complex of regional jurisdictions. Their efforts, their successes, and even their rivalries over the generations point to an elitist political method applicable in terms of local dominion. And in turning now to one such region of the medieval Empire, that inner borderland where the duchies of Bavaria, Franconia, and Swabia and the dioceses of Eichstätt, Würzburg, Regensburg, and Augsburg marched with each other,[51] we can attempt a closer analysis of the historical and social realities, and the successive ruling personalities, upon which regional political authority were based.

*Notes*

1. E.g., MGH Dipl. Lothar III, no. 101, pp. 162f. (1136); ibid., Conrad III, no. 81, pp. 143f. (1142); ibid., Frederick I, no. 658, pp. 161–65 (1176). See also F. Hausmann, *Reichskanzlei und Hofkapelle unter Heinrich V. und Konrad III.*, MGH Schriften, vol. XIV (Stuttgart, 1956); R. M. Herkenrath, *Regnum und Imperium. Das Reich in der frühstaufischen Kanzlei (1138–1155)*, Sitzungsberichte der österreichischen Akademie der Wissenschaften, phil.-hist. Klasse, vol. CCLXIV, part 5 (Vienna, Cologne, and Graz, 1969); W. Koch, "Die Reichskanzlei unter Kaiser Friedrich I.," *AD* 31 (1985): 327–50; H. Appelt's "Vorrede" to MGH Dipl. Frederick I, vol. I, pp. VII–XIV, and the further literature cited there.

2. H. Zimmermann (ed.), *Otto der Grosse*, Wege der Forschung, vol. CCCCL (Darmstadt, 1976); *Das Königtum. Seine geistigen und rechtlichen Grundlagen*, VF, vol. III (Lindau and Constance, 1956); H. Keller, "Das Kaisertum Ottos des Grossen im Verständnis seiner Zeit," *DA* 20 (1964): 325–88, and "Grundlagen ottonischer Königsherrschaft," in K. Schmid (ed.), *Reich und Kirche vor dem Investiturstreit. Gerd Tellenbach zum 80. Geburtstag* (Sigmaringen, 1985), pp. 17–34. See also C. Erdmann, "Das ottonische Reich als Imperium Romanum," *DA* 6 (1943): 412–41, and in his *Ottonische Studien*, ed. H. Beumann (Darmstadt, 1968), pp. 174–203.

3. H. Dilcher, "Authenticae," in HRG i, cols. 276f.

4. For recent views in English of the powers of the crown in the Staufen era, see H. Fuhrmann, *Germany in the High Middle Ages, c. 1050–1200*, trans. T. Reuter, Cambridge medieval textbooks (Cambridge, 1986), pp. 135–86; K. J. Leyser, "Frederick Barbarossa and the Hohenstaufen polity," *Viator* 19 (1988): 153–76; A. Haverkamp, *Medieval Germany 1056–1273*, trans. H. Braun and R. Mortimer (Oxford, 1988), pp. 221–59; D. Abulafia, *Frederick II. A Medieval Emperor* (London, 1988), pp. 63–86, 226–48; and my forthcoming *Princes and Territories*, chaps. 1–2.

5. Good summaries of royal and imperial rights and powers can be found in

HRG ii: A. Erler, "Kaiser, Kaisertum," cols. 518–30; E. Kaufmann, "König," cols. 999–1023, and "Königsbann," cols. 1023–25; C. Brühl, "Königsgastung," cols. 1032–34; A. Gauert, "Königspfalzen," cols. 1044–55; M. Herberger, "Krongut," cols. 1217–29; E. Kaufmann and H. Holzhauer, "Landfriede," cols. 1451–85.

6. See the impressive cartographical rendering of this in J. Engel, *Grosser historischer Weltatlas*, vol. II, *Mittelalter* (Munich, 1970), pp. 111–15; ibid., vol. III, *Neuzeit* (Munich, 1957), pp. 134f., 144.

7. W. Sellert, "Landeshoheit," HRG ii, cols. 1388–94.

8. Outlined in English in A. Mayhew, *Rural Settlement and Farming in Germany* (London, 1973), pp. 37–90; H. Aubin, "The Land East of the Elbe and German Colonization Eastwards," in *Cambridge Economic History*, vol. I, 2d ed. (Cambridge, 1966), pp. 449–86; Haverkamp, *Medieval Germany*, pp. 170–85, 294–311.

9. For these quarrels see K. J. Leyser, "The Polemics of the Papal Revolution," in B. Smalley (ed.), *Trends in Medieval Political Thought* (Oxford, 1965), pp. 42–64, and in his *Medieval Germany and its Neighbours, 900–1250* (London, 1982), pp. 138–60; I. S. Robinson, *Authority and Resistance in the Investiture Contest. The Polemical Literature of the Late Eleventh Century* (Manchester and New York, 1978), and "Pope Gregory VII, the Princes and the *Pactum* 1077–1080," *English Historical Review* 94 (1979): 721–56; Fuhrmann, *Germany*, pp. 51–95; Haverkamp, *Medieval Germany*, pp. 101–35.

10. A. Hofmeister, *Ottonis Episcopi Frisingensis Chronica sive Historia de duabus Civitatibus*, MGH Scriptores rerum Germanicarum in usum scholarum, vol. XLV, 2d ed. (Hanover and Leipzig, 1912), pp. 368f., 391, 400f., and 2 Cor. 1, 8–9. On Otto's views, see J. Spörl, "Die 'Civitas Dei' im Geschichtsdenken Ottos von Freising," in W. Lammers (ed.), *Geschichtsdenken und Geschichtsbild im Mittelalter. Ausgewählte Aufsätze und Arbeiten*, Wege der Forschung, vol. XXI (Darmstadt, 1965), pp. 298–320; J. Koch, "Die Grundlagen der Geschichtsphilosophie Ottos von Freising," ibid., pp. 321–49; H.-W. Goetz, *Das Geschichtsbild Ottos von Freising. Ein Beitrag zur historischen Vorstellungswelt und zur Geschichte des 12. Jahrhunderts*, Beihefte zum Archiv für Kulturgeschichte, vol. XIX (Cologne and Vienna, 1984); W. Lammers, *Weltgeschichte und Zeitgeschichte bei Otto von Freising*, Sitzungsberichte der wissenschaftlichen Gesellschaft an der Johann Wolfgang Goethe-Universität Frankfurt am Main, vol. XIV, part 3 (Wiesbaden, 1977), pp. 75–99; K. F. Morrison, "Otto of Freising's Quest for the Hermeneutic Circle," *Speculum* 55 (1980): 207–36.

11. For the political and social consequences of this, see the work of Karl Leyser in *Rule and Conflict in an Early Medieval Society. Ottonian Saxony* (London, 1979), pp. 49–62; "The German Aristocracy from the Ninth to the Early Twelfth Century: A Historical and Cultural Sketch," *Past and Present* 41 (1968): 25–53, and in his *Medieval Germany*, pp. 161–89; Leyser, "The Crisis of Medieval Germany," *Proceedings of the British Academy* 69 (1983): 409–43.

12. L. Falck, *Mainz im frühen und hohen Mittelalter*, Geschichte der Stadt Mainz, vol. II (Düsseldorf, 1972); B. Witte, *Herrschaft und Land im Rheingau*, Mainzer Abhandlungen zur mittleren und neueren Geschichte, vol. III (Meisenheim, 1959); M. Stimming, *Die Entstehung des weltlichen Territoriums des Erzbistums Mainz*, Quellen und Forschungen zur hessischen Geschichte, vol. III

(Darmstadt, 1915), and *Mainzer Urkundenbuch*, vol. I, *Die Urkunden bis zum Tode Erzbischof Adalberts I (1137)*, Arbeiten der Historischen Kommission für den Volksstaat Hessen (Darmstadt, 1932); P. Acht, *Mainzer Urkundenbuch*, vol. II, *Die Urkunden seit dem Tode Erzbischof Adalberts I. (1137) bis zum Tode Erzbischof Konrads (1200)*, part 1, *1137–1175*, part 2, *1176–1200*, Arbeiten der Hessischen Historischen Kommission Darmstadt (Darmstadt, 1968 and 1971); H. Büttner, "Das Erzstift Mainz und das Reich im 12. Jahrhundert," *Hessisches Jahrbuch für Landesgeschichte* 9 (1959): 18–36; W. Schöntag, *Untersuchungen zur Geschichte des Erzbistums Mainz unter den Erzbischöfen Arnold und Christian I. (1153–1183)*, Quellen und Forschungen zur hessischen Geschichte, vol. XXII (Darmstadt and Marburg, 1973), pp. 84–185; K.-H. Spiess, "Königshof und Fürstenhof. Der Adel und die Mainzer Erzbischöfe im 12. Jahrhundert," in E.-D. Hehl, H. Seibert, and F. Staab (eds.), *Deus qui mutat tempora. Menschen und Institutionen im Wandel des Mittelalters. Festschrift für Alfons Becker* (Sigmaringen, 1987), pp. 203–34.

13. See Abbot Markward of Fulda's complaints about this in G. Franz, *Quellen zur Geschichte des deutschen Bauernstandes im Mittelalter*, AQ, vol. XXXI (Darmstadt, 1967), no. 80, pp. 212–18 (1150–1165).

14. For guidance see G. W. Sante and A. G. Ploetz Verlag, *Geschichte der deutschen Länder. "Territorien Ploetz,"* vol. I, *Die Territorien bis zum Ende des alten Reiches* (Würzburg, 1964); F. Uhlhorn and W. Schlesinger, "Die deutschen Territorien," in H. Grundmann (ed.), *Gebhardts Handbuch der deutschen Geschichte*, vol. II, 9th ed. (Stuttgart, 1970), pp. 546–764; H. Patze (ed.), *Der deutsche Territorialstaat im 14. Jahrhundert*, VF, vol. XIII, 2 parts (Sigmaringen, 1970–1971); K. S. Bader, *Der deutsche Südwesten in seiner territorialstaatlichen Entwicklung* (Stuttgart, 1950); H. Büttner, *Schwaben und Schweiz im frühen und hohen Mittelalter*, VF, vol. XV (Sigmaringen, 1972); P. Fried (ed.), *Probleme und Methoden der Landesgeschichte*, Wege der Forschung, vol. CCCCXCII (Darmstadt, 1978).

15. W. Mohr, *Geschichte des Herzogtums Lothringen*, 3 vols., Saarbrücken (1974–1979); M. Parisse, "Les ducs et la duché de Lorraine au XIIe siècle, 1048–1206," *BDLG* III (1975): 86–102, and *La noblesse lorraine XIe–XIIIe siècles*, 2 vols. (Lille and Paris), 1976; L. Genicot, *Études sur les principautés lotharingiennes*, Recueil de travaux d'histoire et de philologie, 6th ser., vol. VII (Louvain, 1975); F. Steinbach, "Gibt es einen lotharingischen Raum?" in F. Petri and G. Droege (eds.), *Collectanea Franz Steinbach. Aufsätze und Abhandlungen* (Bonn, 1967), pp. 230–42; B. Schneidmüller, "Regnum und ducatus. Identität und Integration in der lothringischen Geschichte des 9. bis 11. Jahrhunderts," *RVB* 51 (1987): 81–114.

16. H. Patze, *Die Entstehung der Landesherrschaft in Thüringen*, MDF, vol. XXII (Cologne and Graz, 1962); H. Eberhardt, "Die Gerichtsorganisation der Landgrafschaft Thüringen im Mittelalter," *ZRGGA* 75 (1958): 108–80; W. Leist, *Landesherr und Landfrieden in Thüringen im Spätmittelalter 1247–1349*, MDF, vol. LXXVII (Cologne and Vienna, 1975); H. Patze and W. Schlesinger (eds.), *Geschichte Thüringens*, vol. II, 2 parts, *Hohes und Spätes Mittelalter*, MDF, vol. XLVIII, part 2 (Cologne and Vienna, 1973–1974).

17. K. Jordan, *Henry the Lion. A Biography*, trans. P. S. Falla (Oxford, 1986), pp. 160–82, and "Herzogtum und Stamm in Sachsen während des hohen Mittelalters," *Niedersächsisches Jahrbuch für Landesgeschichte* 30 (1958): 1–27; W.-D. Mohr-

mann, "Das sächsische Herzogtum Heinrichs des Löwen. Von den Wegen seiner Erforschung," in Mohrmann (ed.), *Henrich der Löwe,* Veröffentlichungen der Niedersächsischen Archivverwaltung, vol. XXXIX (Göttingen, 1980), pp. 44–84; B. Schwineköper, "Heinrich der Löwe und das östliche Herzogtum Sachsen," in ibid., pp. 127–50; W.-D. Mohrmann, *Lauenburg oder Wittenberg? Zum Problem des sächsischen Kurstreites bis zur Mitte des 14. Jahrhunderts,* Veröffentlichungen des Instituts für historische Landesforschung der Universität Göttingen, vol. VIII (Hildesheim, 1975); J. Leuschner, "Der Streit um Kursachsen in der Zeit Kaiser Siegmunds," in W. Wegener (ed.), *Festschrift für Karl Gottfried Hugelmann,* vol. I (Aalen, 1959), pp. 315–44.

18. H. Maurer, *Der Herzog von Schwaben. Grundlagen, Wirkungen und Wesen seiner Herrschaft in ottonischer, salischer und staufischer Zeit* (Sigmaringen, 1978), pp. 263–97.

19. M. Spindler, *Die Anfänge des bayerischen Landesfürstentums,* Schriftenreihe zur bayerischen Landesgeschichte, vol. XXVI, new ed. (Aalen, 1973), and "Grundlegung und Aufbau 1180–1314," in HBG ii, pp. 11–137; G. Flohrschütz, "Machtgrundlagen und Herrschaftspolitik der ersten Pfalzgrafen aus dem Haus Wittelsbach," in H. Glaser (ed.), *Die Zeit der frühen Herzöge. Von Otto I. zu Ludwig dem Bayern,* Beiträge zur bayerischen Geschichte und Kunst 1180–1350, vol. I, part 1 (Munich and Zürich, 1980), pp. 42–110; F. Genzinger, "Grafschaft und Vogtei der Wittelsbacher vor 1180," ibid. pp. 111–25; A. Kraus, "Das Herzogtum der Wittelsbacher: Die Grundlegung des Landes Bayern," ibid. pp. 165–200; P. Fried, "Vorstufen der Territorienbildung in den hochmittelalterlichen Adelsherrschaften Bayerns," in Fried and W. Ziegler (eds.), *Festschrift für Andreas Kraus zum 60. Geburtstag,* Münchener Historische Studien. Abteilung Bayerische Geschichte, vol. X (Kallmünz/Opf., 1982), pp. 33–44.

20. This is the principal theme of my forthcoming book *Princes and Territories.*

21. From the large literature on the upsurge of dynasties and their self awareness in the later eleventh and twelfth centuries, see K. Schmid, "Zur Problematik von Familie, Sippe und Geschlecht, Haus und Dynastie beim mittelalterlichen Adel. Vorfragen zum Thema Adel und Herrschaft im Mittelalter," *ZGOR* 105 (1957): 1–62, and "Über die Struktur des Adels im früheren Mittelalter," *JFLF* 19 (1959): 1–23; W. Störmer, *Früher Adel. Studien zur politischen Führungsschicht im fränkisch-deutschen Reich vom 8. bis 11. Jahrhundert,* Monographien zur Geschichte des Mittelalters, vol. VI, 2 parts (Stuttgart, 1973); F. Prinz, "Bayerns Adel im Hochmittelalter," *ZBLG* 30 (1967): 53–117, and "Die bayerischen Dynastengeschlechter des Hochmittelalters," in Glaser (ed.), *Zeit,* pp. 253–67; H. Patze, "Adel und Stifterchronik. Frühformen territorialer Geschichtsschreibung im hochmittelalterlichen Reich," *BDLG* 100 (1964): 8–81, and 101 (1965): 67–128; J. Fleckenstein, "Über die Herkunft der Welfen und ihre Anfänge in Süddeutschland," in G. Tellenbach (ed.), *Studien und Vorarbeiten zur Geschichte des grossfränkischen und frühdeutschen Adels,* Forschungen zur oberrheinischen Landesgeschichte, vol. IV (Freiburg im Breisgau, 1957), pp. 71–136; K. Schmid, "Welfisches Selbstverständnis," in J. Fleckenstein and K. Schmid (eds.), *Adel und Kirche. Gerd Tellenbach zum 65. Geburtstag* (Freiburg im Breisgau, Basel, and Vienna, 1968), pp. 389–416; O. G. Oexle, "Adeliges Selbstverständnis und seine Verknüpfung mit dem liturgischen Gedenken—das Beispiel

der Welfen," *ZGOR* 134 (1986): 47–75; J. B. Freed, *The Counts of Falkenstein: Noble Self-Consciousness in Twelfth-Century Germany,* Transactions of the American Philosophical Society, vol. LXXIV, part 6 (Philadelphia, 1984); H.-M. Maurer, "Die Entstehung der hochmittelalterlichen Adelsburg in Südwestdeutschland," *ZGOR* 117 (1969): 295–332; G. Althoff, "Anlässe zur schriftlichen Fixierung adligen Selbstverständnisses," ibid. 134 (1986): 34–46. Schmid's article of 1959 is translated in Reuter (ed.), *The Medieval Nobility,* pp. 37–59.

22. Compare the contributions to HRG i by M. Kobler, "Bayern," cols. 331–37, A. Erler, "Brandenburg," cols. 498–502, and H. H. Hofmann, "Franken," cols. 1192–1201; HRG ii by K. E. Demandt, "Hessen," cols. 127–38, M. Herberger, "Kolonisation," cols. 954–60, and "Landesausbau," cols. 1365–69; HRG iii by R. Hoke, "Lothringen," cols. 62–73, A. Cremer, "Niederlande," cols. 991–98, and W. Brauneder, "Österreich," cols. 1334–59; HRG iv by K. Jordan and W. Lammers, "Sachsen," cols. 1223–28, and the literatures cited there.

23. On the process, see R. Endres, "Die Eingliederung Frankens in den neuen bayerischen Staat," in P. Fried (ed.), *Probleme der Integration Ostschwabens in den bayerischen Staat,* Augsburger Beiträge zur Landesgeschichte Bayerisch-Schwabens, vol. II (Sigmaringen, 1982), pp. 93–113, and G. Schwaiger, *Die altbayerischen Bistümer Freising, Passau und Regensburg zwischen Säkularisation und Konkordat, 1803–1817,* Münchener theologische Studien, Historische Abteilung, vol. XIII (Munich, 1959).

24. H. Glaser (ed.), *Die Zeit der frühen Herzöge,* 2 vols., *Um Glauben und Reich. Kurfürst Maximilian I.,* 2 vols., *Krone und Verfassung. König Maximilian I. Joseph und der neue Staat,* 2 vols. (Munich and Zürich, 1980), the exhibitions held in Burg Trausnitz at Landshut, the Munich *Residenz,* and the Völkerkundemuseum at Munich, respectively.

25. M. Bloch, "A Contribution Towards a Comparative History of European Societies," in his *Land and Work in Medieval Europe. Selected Papers,* trans. J. E. Anderson (London, 1971), p. 71.

26. For the marked contrast of the agrarian structures, Engel, *Weltatlas,* vol. II, pp. 96f., and for the Hansa, p. 123. It is possible to refer only briefly here to one of the largest literatures in German medieval historiography; W. Schlesinger (ed.), *Die deutsche Ostsiedlung des Mittelalters als Problem der europäischen Geschichte,* 2 parts, VF, vol. XVIII (Sigmaringen, 1975); K. Zernack, "Landesausbau und Ostsiedlung," in *Die Zeit der Staufer. Katalog der Ausstellung im Württembergischen Landesmuseum,* vol. III (Stuttgart, 1977), pp. 51–57; H. Helbig and L. Weinrich (eds.), *Urkunden und erzählende Quellen zur deutschen Ostsiedlung im Mittelalter,* 2 parts, AQ, vol. XXVI (Darmstadt, 1968 and 1970); F. L. Carsten, *The Origins of Prussia* (Oxford, 1954), pp. 1–88; P. Dollinger, *The German Hansa,* trans. D. S. Ault and S. H. Steinberg (London, 1970); R. Sprandel (ed.), *Quellen zur Hanse-Geschichte,* AQ, vol. XXXVI (Darmstadt, 1982).

27. L. Petry, "Träger und Stufen mittelrheinischer Territorialgeschichte," in *Aus Geschichte und Landeskunde. Forschungen und Darstellungen für Franz Steinbach* (Bonn, 1960), pp. 71–91; H. Aubin, *Die Entstehung der Landeshoheit nach niederrheinischen Quellen,* 2d ed. (Bonn, 1961); O. Engels, "Grundlinien der rheinischen Verfassungsgeschichte im 12. Jahrhundert," *RVB* 39 (1975): 1–27; W. Janssen, "Die

niederrheinischen Territorien in der zweiten Hälfte des 14. Jahrhunderts," ibid. 44
(1980): 47–67; A. Gerlich, "Interterritoriale Systembildungen zwischen Mittelrhein
und Saar in der zweiten Hälfte des 14. Jahrhunderts," *BDLG* III (1975): 103–37;
R. Holbach, "Die Regierungszeit des Trierer Erzbischofs Arnold (II.) von Isen-
burg. Ein Beitrag zur Geschichte von Reich, Territorium und Kirche um die Mitte
des 13. Jahrhunderts," *RVB* 47 (1983): 1–66; M. Nikolay-Panter, "Terra und Territorium in Trier an der Wende vom Hoch- zum Spätmittelalter," ibid. 67–123;
W. Reichert, *Finanzpolitik und Landesherrschaft. Zur Entwicklung der Grafschaft
Katzenelnbogen vom 12. bis zum 14. Jahrhundert,* Kleine Schriften zur Geschichte und
Landeskunde, vol. I (Trier, 1985); R. Laufner, "Die Ausbildung des Territorialstaates der Kurfürsten von Trier," in Patze (ed.), *Territorialstaat,* vol. II, pp. 127–47;
W. Janssen, "Niederrheinische Territorialbildung. Voraussetzungen, Wege, Probleme," in E. Ennen and K. Fink (eds.), *Soziale und wirtschaftliche Bindungen im
Mittelalter am Niederrhein,* Klever Archiv. Schriftenreihe des Stadtarchivs Kleve,
vol. III (Cleves, 1981), pp. 95–113; G. Droege, "Pfalzgrafschaft, Grafschaften und
allodiale Herrschaften zwischen Maas und Rhein in salisch-staufischer Zeit," *RVB*
26 (1961): 1–21; L. G. Duggan, *Bishop and Chapter. The Governance of the Bishopric of
Speyer to 1552,* Studies presented to the International Commission for the History of
Representative Parliamentary Institutions, vol. LXXII (New Brunswick, 1978), and
G. Fouquet, *Das Speyerer Domkapitel im späten Mittelalter (ca. 1350–1540). Adlige
Freundschaft, fürstliche Patronage und päpstliche Klientel,* Quellen und Abhand-
lungen zur mittelrheinischen Kirchengeschichte, vol. LVII, 2 parts (Mainz, 1987);
W.-R. Berns, *Burgenpolitik und Herrschaft des Erzbischofs Balduin von Trier (1307–
1354),* Vorträge und Forschungen, Sonderband XXVII (Sigmaringen, 1980), and
F.-J. Heyen (ed.), *Balduin von Luxemburg. Erzbischof von Trier, Kurfürst des Reiches
1285–1354,* Quellen und Abhandlungen zur mittelrheinischen Kirchengeschichte, vol.
LIII (Mainz, 1985).

28. On the development of their power and status, see R. Laufner, "Das
rheinische Städtewesen im Hochmittelalter," in W. Rausch (ed.), *Die Städte Mit-
teleuropas im 12. und 13. Jahrhundert,* Beiträge zur Geschichte der Städte Mit-
teleuropas, vol. I (Linz, 1963), pp. 27–40; K. Schulz, *Ministerialität und Bürgertum
in Trier. Untersuchungen zur rechtlichen und sozialen Gliederung der Trierer Bürgerschaft vom ausgehenden 11. bis zum Ende des 14. Jahrhunderts,* Rheinisches Archiv,
vol. LXVI (Bonn, 1968); D. Demandt, *Stadtherrschaft und Stadtfreiheit im Span-
nungsfeld von Geistlichkeit und Bürgerschaft in Mainz (11.–15. Jahrhundert),* Geschichtliche Landeskunde, vol. XV (Wiesbaden, 1977); E. Maschke, "Die Stellung
der Reichsstadt Speyer in der mittelalterlichen Wirtschaft Deutschlands," *VSWG* 54
(1967): 435–55; T. Zotz, "Bischöfliche Herrschaft, Adel, Ministerialität und Bürgertum in Stadt und Bistum Worms (11.–14. Jahrhundert)," in J. Fleckenstein (ed.),
*Herrschaft und Stand. Untersuchungen zur Sozialgeschichte im 13. Jahrhundert,* Veröffentlichungen des Max-Planck-Instituts für Geschichte, vol. LI (Göttingen, 1977),
pp. 92–136; H. Mosbacher, "Kammerhandwerk, Ministerialität und Bürgertum in
Strassburg. Studien zur Zusammensetzung und Entwicklung des Patriziats im 13.
Jahrhundert," *ZGOR* 119 (1971): 33–173; E. Voltmer, "Ministerialität und Ober-
schichten in den Städten Speyer und Worms im 13. und 14. Jahrhundert," in F. L.
Wagner (ed.), *Ministerialität im pfälzer Raum,* Veröffentlichungen der pfälzischen

Gesellschaft zur Förderung der Wissenschaften, vol. LXIV (Speyer, 1975), pp. 23–33; A. Buschmann, "Der Rheinische Bund von 1254–1257. Landfriede, Städte, Fürsten und Reichsverfassung im 13. Jahrhundert," in H. Maurer (ed.), *Kommunaler Bündnisse Oberitaliens und Oberdeutschlands im Vergleich,* VF, vol. XXXIII (Sigmaringen, 1987), pp. 167–212; O. Engels, "Der Niederrhein und das Reich im 12. Jahrhundert," in his *Stauferstudien. Beiträge zur Geschichte der Staufer im 12. Jahrhundert* (Sigmaringen, 1988), pp. 177–99.

29. Especially the counts-palatine of the Rhine; see B. Brinken, *Die Politik Konrads von Staufen in der Tradition der rheinischen Pfalzgrafschaft,* Rheinisches Archiv, vol. XCII (Bonn, 1974); P. Spiess, "Pfalz, Kurpfalz," in HRG iii, cols. 1659–67; A. Gerlich, "Die rheinische Pfalzgrafschaft in der frühen Wittelsbacherzeit," in Glaser (ed.), *Zeit,* vol. I, pp. 201–22; H. Büttner, "Das Bistum Worms und der Neckarraum während des Früh- und Hochmittelalters," in his *Zur frühmittelalterlichen Reichsgeschichte an Rhein, Main und Neckar* (Darmstadt, 1975), pp. 207–36; M. Schaab, "Die Festigung der pfälzischen Territorialmacht im 14. Jahrhundert," in Patze (ed.), *Territorialstaat,* vol. II, pp. 171–97; H. Cohn, *The Government of the Rhine-Palatinate in the Fifteenth Century* (Oxford, 1965), pp. 43–74; M. Schaab, *Geschichte der Kurpfalz,* vol. I, *Mittelalter* (Stuttgart, etc., 1988); C. Frh. von Brandenstein, *Urkundenwesen und Kanzlei, Rat und Regierungssystem des pfälzer Kurfürsten Ludwig III. (1410–1436),* Veröffentlichungen des Max-Planck-Instituts für Geschichte, vol. LXXI (Göttingen, 1983).

30. On Cologne and its power, see H. Stehkämper (ed.), *Köln, das Reich und Europa,* Mitteilungen aus dem Stadtarchiv von Köln, vol. LX (Cologne, 1971); U. Lewald, "Köln im Investiturstreit," in J. Fleckenstein (ed.), *Investiturstreit und Reichsverfassung,* VF, vol. XVII (Sigmaringen, 1973), pp. 373–93; P. Strait, *Cologne in the Twelfth Century* (Gainesville, 1974); Haverkamp, *Medieval Germany,* pp. 337–39; J. Deeters, "Köln," in HRG ii, cols. 935–42; T. Zotz, "Städtisches Rittertum und Bürgertum in Köln um 1200," in L. Fenske, W. Rösener, T. Zotz (eds.), *Institutionen, Kultur und Gesellschaft im Mittelalter. Festschrift für Josef Fleckenstein* (Sigmaringen, 1984), pp. 609–38; K. Flink, "Köln, das Reich und die Stadtentwicklung im nördlichen Rheinland (1100–1250)," BDLG 120 (1984): 155–93. See also the consideration of economic regions based upon German cities in J. C. Russell, *Medieval Regions and Their Cities,* Studies in Historical Geography, (Newton Abbot, 1972).

31. G. Waitz and B. von Simson, *Ottonis et Rahewini Gesta Friderici I. Imperatoris,* MGH Scriptores rerum Germanicarum in usum scholarum, vol. XLVI, 3d ed. (Hanover and Leipzig, 1912), p. 97 (1151) and MGH Dipl. Frederick I, no. 795, p. 363 (1180); see G. Droege, *Landrecht und Lehnrecht im hohen Mittelalter,* Veröffentlichungen des Instituts für geschichtliche Landeskunde der Rheinlande (Bonn, 1969), pp. 142–52; H. Wolter, *Arnold von Wied, Kanzler Konrads III. und Erzbischof von Köln,* Veröffentlichungen der kölnischer Geschichtsverein, vol. XXXII (Cologne, 1973), pp. 53–65; E. Ewig, "Zum lothringischen Dukat der kölner Erzbischöfe," in *Aus Geschichte und Landeskunde,* pp. 210–46; G. Droege, "Lehnrecht und Landrecht am Niederrhein und das Problem der Territorialbildung im 12. und 13. Jahrhundert," ibid. pp. 278–307, and "Das kölnische Herzogtum Westfalen," in Mohrmann (ed.), *Heinrich der Löwe,* pp. 275–304. The consequent ambitions took

a long time to give up; see E. Ennen, "Erzbischof und Stadtgemeinde in Köln bis zur Schlacht von Worringen (1288)," in her *Gesammelte Abhandlungen zum europäischen Städtewesen und zur rheinischen Geschichte* (Bonn, 1977), pp. 388–404, and G. Droege, *Verfassung und Wirtschaft in Kurköln unter Dietrich von Moers (1414–1463)*, Rheinisches Archiv, vol. L (Bonn, 1957). See also G. Kallen, "Das Kölner Erzstift und der 'Ducatus Westfalie et Angarie' (1180)," in his *Probleme der Rechtsordnung in Geschichte und Theorie*, Kölner Historischer Abhandlungen, vol. XI (Cologne and Graz, 1965), pp. 223–53.

32. G. Waitz, *Chronica regia Coloniensis. Annales maximi Colonienses*, MGH Scriptores rerum Germanicarum in usum scholarum, vol. XVIII (Hanover, 1880); G. Jenal, *Erzbischof Anno II. von Köln (1056–1075) und sein politisches Wirken*, Monographien zur Geschichte des Mittelalters vol. VIII, 2 parts (Stuttgart, 1974–1975); W. Pötter, *Die Ministerialität der Erzbischöfe von Köln vom Ende des 11. bis zum Ausgang des 13. Jahrhunderts*, Studien zur kölner Kirchengeschichte, vol. IX (Düsseldorf, 1967); H. Stehkämper, "Der kölner Erzbischof Adolf von Altena und die deutsche Königswahl (1195–1205)," in T. Schieder (ed.), *Beiträge zur Geschichte des mittelalterlichen deutschen Königtums*, Historische Zeitschrift Beihefte II, new ser. (Munich, 1973); R. Reisinger, *Die römisch-deutschen Könige und ihre Wähler 1198–1273*, Untersuchungen zur deutschen Staats- und Rechtsgeschichte, new ser., vol. XXI (Aalen, 1977); F.-R. Erkens, *Der Erzbischof von Köln und die deutsche Königswahl*, Studien zur kölner Kirchengeschichte, vol. XXI (Siegburg, 1987); C. C. Bayley, "The Diplomatic Preliminaries of the Double Election of 1257 in Germany," *English Historical Review* 62 (1947): 457–83; H. Stehkämper, "Der Reichsbischof und Territorialfürst (12. und 13. Jahrhundert)," in P. Berglar and O. Engels (eds.), *Der Bischof in seiner Zeit. Bischofstypus und Bischofsideal im Spiegel der Kölner Kirche. Festgabe für Joseph Kardinal Höffner, Erzbischof von Köln* (Cologne, 1986), pp. 95–184; H. Hofmann, *Die Heiligen Drei Könige. Zur Heiligenverehrung im kirchlichen, gesellschaftlichen und politischen Leben des Mittelalters*, Rheinisches Archiv, vol. XCIV (Bonn, 1975), pp. 96–114; M. Groten, "Zur Entwicklung des Kölner Lehnshofes und der Kölnischen Ministerialität im 13. Jahrhundert," *BDLG* 124 (1988): 1–50.

33. L. Weinrich, *Quellen zur deutschen Verfassungs-, Wirtschafts- und Sozialgeschichte bis 1250*, AQ, vol. XXXII (Darmstadt, 1977), p. 266.

34. See the bishop of Chur's letter to King Rudolf I in MGH Consts. iii, no. 304, pp. 299f. For the significance of Tirol, see H. Wiesflecker, *Meinhard der Zweite. Tirol, Kärnten und ihre Nachbarländer am Ende des 13. Jahrhunderts*, Veröffentlichungen des Instituts für österreichische Geschichtforschung, vol. XVI (Innsbruck, 1955); H. Steinacker, *Staatswerdung und politische Willensbildung im Alpenraum*, Libelli CLII (Darmstadt, 1967), pp. 1–46; O. Stolz, "Zur Entstehung und Bedeutung des Landesfürstentums im Raume Bayern, Österreich, Tirol," *ZRGGA* 71 (1954): 339–53; F. Huter, "Tirol im 14. Jahrhundert," in Patze (ed.), *Territorialstaat*, vol. II, pp. 369–87; M. Bitschnau, *Burg und Adel in Tirol zwischen 1050 und 1300. Grundlagen zu ihre Erforschung*, Mitteilungen der Kommission für Burgenforschung und Mittelalter-Archäologie, vol. I, and Sitzungsberichte, Österreichische Akademie der Wissenschaften, phil.-hist. Klasse, vol. CCCCIII (Vienna, 1983). See also T. Mayer (ed.), *Die Alpen in der europäischen Geschichte des Mittelalters*, VF, vol. X (Constance and Stuttgart, 1965); O. Stolz, "Bauer und Landesfürst in Tirol und

Vorarlberg," in T. Mayer (ed.), *Adel und Bauern im deutschen Staat des Mittelalters*, new ed. (Darmstadt, 1976), pp. 170–212; S. Steinherz, "Margareta von Tirol und Rudolf IV," *MIöG* 26 (1905): 553–611; G. Sandberger, "Einige Beobachtungen zur Herkunft der älteren Grafen von Tirol," *ZBLG* 45 (1982): 419–26.

35. P. and A.-M. Bonenfant, "Du duché de Basse-Lotharingie au duché de Brabant," *Revue belge de philologie et d'histoire* 46 (1968): 1129–65; W. Kienast, *Der Herzogstitel in Frankreich und Deutschland (9. bis 12. Jahrhundert)* (Munich and Vienna, 1968), pp. 395–408; F. L. Ganshof, "Brabant," in HRG i, cols. 494–96.

36. On this province, B. Schmeidler, "Franconia's Place in the Structure of Mediaeval Germany," in G. Barraclough (ed.), *Mediaeval Germany 911–1250,* vol. II, *Essays by German Historians,* Studies in Mediaeval History, vol. II, new ed. (Oxford, 1961), pp. 71–93; K. Bosl, *Franken um 800. Strukturanalyse einer fränkischen Königsprovinz,* 2d ed. (Munich, 1969); Hofmann, "Franken," in HRG i, cols. 1192–1201; E. Schrader, "Vom Werden und Wesen des würzburgischen Herzogtums Franken," *ZRGGA* 80 (1963): 27–81; G. Zimmermann, "Vergebliche Ansätze zu Stammes- und Territorialherzogtum in Franken," *JFLF* 23 (1963): 379–408; M.-L. Crone, "Der Ducatus Orientalis Franciae. Ein Beitrag zur Kirchengeschichte Lothars III.," ibid. 41 (1981): 1–21; F.-J. Schmale, "Franken vom Zeitalter der Karolinger bis zum Interregnum (716/19–1257)," in HBG iii, pp. 27–112.

37. E. von Guttenberg, *Die Territorienbildung am Obermain,* Berichte des historischen Vereins zu Bamberg, vol. LXXIX (Bamberg, 1927); K. Bosl, "Würzburg als Reichsbistum," in *Aus Verfassungs- und Landesgeschichte. Festschrift für Theodor Mayer,* vol. I (Lindau and Constance, 1954), pp. 161–81; F. Merzbacher, *Judicium Provinciale Ducatus Franconiae. Das kaiserliche Landgericht des Herzogtums Franken-Würzburg im Spätmittelalter,* Schriftenreihe zur bayerischen Landesgeschichte, vol. LIV (Munich, 1956); A. Wendehorst, *Das Bistum Würzburg,* vol. I, *Die Bischofsreihe bis 1254,* vol. II, *Die Bischofsreihe von 1254 bis 1455,* Germania Sacra, new ser., vols. I and IV (Berlin, 1962 and 1969); F. Geldner, "Das Hochstift Bamberg in der Reichspolitik von Kaiser Heinrich II. bis Kaiser Friedrich Barbarossa," *Historisches Jahrbuch* 83 (1964): 28–42; S. Jenks, "Die Anfänge des Würzburger Territorialstaates in der späteren Stauferzeit," *JFLF* 43 (1983): 103–16; F. Geldner, "Bamberg," in R.-H. Bautier et al. (eds.), *Lexikon des Mittelalters,* vol. I (Munich and Zürich, 1980), cols. 1394–1401.

38. On its political importance, see A. Hofemann, *Studien zur Entwicklung des Territoriums der Reichsabtei Fulda und seiner Ämter,* Schriften des hessischen Landesamtes für geschichtliche Landeskunde, vol. XXV (Marburg, 1958); K. Lübeck, *Die Fuldaer Äbte und Fürstäbte des Mittelalters. Ein geschichtlicher Überblick,* Veröffentlichungen des Fuldaer Geschichtsvereins, vol. XXXI (Fulda, 1952); T. Franke, "Studien zur Geschichte der Fuldaer Äbte im 11. und frühen 12. Jahrhundert," *AD* 33 (1987): 55–238; R. Hoke, "Fulda," in HRG i, cols. 1328–31; W. Heinemeyer, *Chronica Fuldensis. Die Darmstädter Fragmente der Fuldaer Chronik,* AD Beihefte I (Cologne and Vienna, 1976); K. Lübeck, "Die Hofämter der Fuldaer Äbte," *ZRGGA* 65 (1947): 177–207.

39. F. Schwind, "Stamm—Territorium—Land. Kontinuität und Wandel im Namen 'Hessen,'" *BDLG* 121 (1985): 69–82; E. E. Stengel, "Der Stamm der Hessen und das Herzogtum Franken," in his *Abhandlungen und Untersuchungen zur hess-*

*ischen Geschichte,* Veröffentlichungen der Historischen Kommission für Hessen und Waldeck, vol. XXVI (Marburg, 1960), pp. 355–403; K. E. Demandt, "Hessen," in HRG ii, cols. 127–38; P. von Polenz, *Landschafts- und Bezirksnamen in frühmittelalterlichen Deutschland,* vol. I (Marburg, 1961), under "Hessiun." For the title, MGH Dipl. Frederick I, no. 38, p. 63 (1152). See also K. E. Demandt, *Geschichte des Landes Hessen,* 2d ed. (Kassel and Basel, 1972), pp. 93–168.

40. MGH Consts. iii, nos. 476–78, pp. 464–66.

41. J. Schultze, *Die Mark Brandenburg,* vol. I, *Entstehung und Entwicklung unter den askanischen Markgrafen* (Berlin, 1961); E. Schmidt, *Die Mark Brandenburg unter den Askaniern (1134–1320),* MDF, vol. LXXI (Cologne and Vienna, 1973), pp. 24–41; H.-D. Kahl, *Slawen und Deutsche in der brandenburgischen Geschichte des zwölften Jahrhunderts,* MDF, vol. XXX, parts 1–2 (Cologne and Graz, 1964); W. Podehl, *Burg und Herrschaft in der Mark Brandenburg,* MDF, vol. LXXVI (Cologne and Vienna, 1975); H.-J. Fey, *Reise und Herrschaft der Markgrafen von Brandenburg 1134–1319,* MDF, vol. LXXXIV (1981).

42. W. Hoppe, "Markgraf Konrad von Meissen, der Reichsfürst und der Gründer des wettinischen Staates," in his *Die Mark Brandenburg, Wettin und Magdeburg. Ausgewählte Aufsätze* (Cologne and Graz, 1965), pp. 153–206; H. Helbig, *Der Wettinische Ständestaat. Untersuchungen zur Geschichte des Ständewesens und der landständischen Verfassung in Mitteldeutschland bis 1485,* MDF, vol. IV (Münster and Cologne, 1955); H. Schieckel, *Herrschaftsbereich und Ministerialität der Markgrafen von Meissen im 12. und 13. Jahrhundert,* MDF, vol. VII (Cologne and Graz, 1956); R. Kötzschke, "Markgraf Dietrich von Meissen als Förderer des Städtebaues" and "Leipzig in der Geschichte der ostdeutschen Kolonisation," in his *Deutsche und Slawen im mitteldeutschen Osten. Ausgewählte Aufsätze* (Darmstadt, 1961), pp. 113–49, 170–214; W. Schlesinger, "Zur Gerichtsverfassung des Markengebietes östlich der Saale im Zeitalter der deutschen Ostsiedlung," in his *Mitteldeutsche Beiträge zur deutschen Verfassungsgeschichte des Mittelalters* (Göttingen, 1961), pp. 48–132, and "Zur Geschichte der Landesherrschaft in den Marken Brandenburg und Meissen während des 14. Jahrhunderts," in Patze (ed.), *Territorialstaat,* vol. II, pp. 101–26.

43. MGH Consts. ii, no. 197, pp. 263–65 (1235); Jordan, *Henry the Lion,* pp. 183–200; O. Engels, "Zur Entmachtung Heinrichs des Löwen," in P. Fried and W. Ziegler (eds.), *Festschrift für Andreas Kraus zum 60. Geburtstag,* Münchner Historische Studien. Abteilung Bayerische Geschichte, vol. X (Kallmünz/Opf., 1982), pp. 45–59; E. Boshof, "Die Entstehung des Herzogtums Braunschweig-Lüneburg," in Mohrmann (ed.), *Heinrich der Löwe,* pp. 249–74; H. Patze and K.-H. Ahrens, "Die Begründung des Herzogtums Braunschweig im Jahre 1235 und die 'Braunschweigische Reimchronik,'" *BDLG* 122 (1986): 67–89: L. Hüttebräuker, *Das Erbe Heinrichs des Löwen. Die territorialen Grundlagen des Herzogtums Braunschweig-Lüneburg von 1235,* Studien und Vorarbeiten zum historischen Atlas von Niedersachsen, vol. IX (Göttingen, 1927); S. Zillmann, *Die welfische Territorialpolitik im 13. Jahrhundert 1218–1267,* Braunschweiger Werkstücke, ser. A, vol. XII (Brunswick, 1975); H. Patze, "Die Welfen in der mittelalterlichen Geschichte Europas," *BDLG* 117 (1981): 139–66, and "Die welfischen Territorien im 14. Jahrhundert," in Patze (ed.), *Territorialstaat,* vol. II, pp. 7–99.

44. See n. 29 above.

45. General account in K. Lechner, *Die Babenberger. Markgrafen und Herzoge von Österreich 976–1246,* Veröffentlichungen des Instituts für österreichische Geschichtsforschung, vol. XXIII (Vienna, Cologne, and Graz, 1976).

46. Bader, *Der deutsche Südwesten,* pp. 72f., 95–105; H. E. Feine, "Die Territorialbildung der Habsburger im deutschen Südwesten vornehmlich im späten Mittelalter," *ZRGGA* 67 (1950): 176–308; U. Stutz, "Das habsburgische Urbar und die Anfänge der Landeshoheit," ibid. 25 (1904): 192–257; O. Redlich, *Rudolf von Habsburg. Das deutsche Reich nach dem Untergange des alten Kaisertums,* new ed. (Aalen, 1965), pp. 544–90; H.-G. Hofacker, *Die schwäbischen Reichslandvogteien im späten Mittelalter,* Spätmittelalter und Frühe Neuzeit. Tübinger Beiträge zur Geschichtsforschung, vol. VIII (Stuttgart, 1980), pp. 105–55.

47. The basic work on this manifestation was published by Hans Hirsch in 1922: *Die hohe Gerichtsbarkeit im deutschen Mittelalter,* 2d ed. (Graz and Cologne, 1958). See also F. Merzbacher, "Hochgerichtsbarkeit," "Landgericht," and "Landrichter," in *HRG* ii, cols. 172–75, 1495–1501, 1545–47.

48. A. C. Schlunk, *Königsmacht und Krongut. Die Machtgrundlage des deutschen Königtums im 13. Jahrhundert* (Stuttgart, 1988), pp. 179–202.

49. W. Petke, *Kanzlei, Kapelle und königliche Kurie unter Lothar III (1125–1137),* Forschungen zur Kaiser- und Papstgeschichte des Mittelalters. Beihefte zu J. F. Böhmer, Regesta Imperii, vol. V (Cologne and Vienna, 1985), p. 100: "Auf Grund seiner faktischen Machtstellung hat der Adel seit der fränkischen Zeit Ansprüche auf Mitherrschaft geltend gemacht."

50. As in MGH Consts. i, no. 106, p. 158, 1121: "Hoc est consilium in quod convenerunt principes de controversia inter domnum imperatorem et regnum."

51. Engel, *Weltatlas,* vol. II, pp. 111, 114.

# 2. The See of Eichstätt and Its Neighbors

The revised geographical and social outlines of the German regions that were emerging under the prelates and princes in the twelfth and thirteenth centuries fluctuated as the committed parties rose or fell in the regional competitions for political power and security. In the late Middle Ages, the border region of Bavaria, Swabia, and Franconia had come to be dominated by the bishopric of Eichstätt,[1] by that time one of the middle ranking German sees in terms of assets, territory, and political authority. But the rise to autonomy and self-government was the result of hard struggles, which we can begin to follow in some detail from the 1120s. For a long time it seemed likely that the bishopric's rights would be swallowed up by its advocates, the Bavarian comital dynasty of Hirschberg, just as the counts of Tirol were subjecting the see of Brixen, the margraves of Meissen the see of Merseburg, and the margraves of Brandenburg the see of Havelberg. Eichstätt was fortunate in that the Hirschberg line failed in 1305, the last count bequeathing nearly all his possessions to the bishopric. So the see was enabled to follow the precarious path of independence and expansion after all, even though much more powerful neighbors, the Wittelsbach dukes of Bavaria and the Zollern burgraves of Nuremberg, virtually encircled its arena of territorial operations in the fourteenth century.

Ducal Bavaria, the cathedral church of Eichstätt, and the Zollern burgravate were thus the fourteenth-century heirs of a more complicated configuration of regional authority in which the imperial crown had itself been a leading force in the eleventh and twelfth centuries. In eastern Franconia and in Bavaria north of the Danube, the province known as the Nordgau of Bavaria,[2] the Salian dynasty (1024–1125) possessed many forests, towns, manors, monastic advocacies, and castles garrisoned by *ministeriales*.[3] In economic terms these were undeveloped areas, but notable advances were made in the eleventh century. Nuremberg, which was to become one of the great cities of the medieval urban revival, was first mentioned in the 1050s,[4] and the royal forests were being assarted by the monastic orders, the aristocratic vassals of the crown, and the imperial *ministeriales*. As the preeminence of Saxony in the economy of the imperial court waned rapidly in the later eleventh century, so the more southerly possessions of the crown took on renewed significance: the upper Rhineland, "where the great resources of the kingdom are known to lie";[5] the Swabian and Alsatian patrimony of the Staufen emperors;[6] and the vast forests stretching across Franconia and the northern reaches of Bavaria to the Czech border and to the Thuringian marches. One of the earlier enterprises in developing the potential of these latter woodlands had been the foundation and endowment of the bishopric of Bamberg by Emperor Henry II in 1007.[7]

The crown's possessions in eastern Franconia and northern Bavaria were a legacy from the Carolingians.[8] Until the old duchy of Bavaria was abolished by Charlemagne and incorporated directly into his empire in 788,[9] the Franks had relied largely upon ecclesiastical outposts, Würzburg, Fulda, and Eichstätt, all founded in the 740s, to sustain their influence.[10] The Franks deliberately laid out the diocese of Eichstätt to include Bavarian as well as Franconian territory in roughly equal proportions, and then attached the see, not to the senior Bavarian diocese of Salzburg but to Mainz, which was being established under St. Boniface as the principal focus of Carolingian influence for the provinces lying east of the Rhine.[11] At first the establishment of Eichstätt merely indicated Frankish political and ecclesiastical intentions. The bishopric received a large *regio*, or territorial estate, but we are told that in this remote frontier land of the Carolingian realm, it was a total waste and contained nothing but the church of Eichstätt itself.[12] Indeed, the cathedral was run for a long time as a fortified monastic chapter,[13] but the region was not really an entirely trackless woodland either.

In the age that succeeded the passing of the Roman Empire in the west, the Alamannians and Bavarians considered it worthwhile to extend their colonization into this region traversed by the Jura range. The Alamannians settled to the west of the hills, and are often held to be traceable principally through the *-ingen* place name endings, the Bavarians to the east, supposedly traceable through the *-ing* ending.[14] Their settlements were not numerous, and gave ground before the Frankish colonization under the Merovingians, which was beginning to establish the medieval province of Franconia. The Carolingians promoted a second wave of Frankish settlement in the eighth century. With reservations, the Frankish colonization is often held to be traceable in the place name endings of *-heim, -dorf,* and *-bach.*[15] So this Frankish intermingling with Alamannic (Swabian) and Bavarian settlement appears to have provided the early demographic basis to the Eichstätt region's economy.

Although most of the detail is lost to us, clearly there was an impressive subdivision of the land between the king, the Church, and the Frankish aristocracy[16] in the decades before and after 788, when the cathedral church of Eichstätt, no doubt with relief to its incumbents, lost its status as a political outpost. One of the largest of all the imperial manors was established at Weissenburg im Sand, at about the midpoint on the road between two other important centers of Carolingian rule, the episcopal town of Augsburg and the manor of Forchheim, which was declared in 805 to be a frontier station for commerce with the Slavs.[17] Weissenburg and its forest remained one of the richest possessions of the crown until the early fourteenth century. As so frequently in medieval Europe, the pioneers of woodland clearance and agrarian settlement were the monasteries, and we can discern this in the Eichstätt region. The founder of the see, St. Willibald, and his immediate circle of friends and relations, as well as the royal dynasty and the Frankish nobles, had already established many houses by about 800, notably those of Herrieden, Gunzenhausen, Ansbach, Solnhofen, and Heidenheim.[18]

It was near to Weissenburg that Charlemagne ordered a canal to be excavated, in order to unite the Main and the Danube by means of their tributaries. The intention was to link the Rhineland markets, by haulage through these upper waters, with Regensburg in the east. The project was a failure, but it was well preserved in the popular memory. A twelfth-century source reports that in 793

a huge undertaking ordered by Charles was uselessly set about by the Bavarians, Franconians, and Swabians en masse, intending to divert by diggings the Rezat and Altmühl into the river Danube, so that a boat might pass up and down. But human sagacity and deliberation cannot prevail against the Lord. For several nights afterwards were heard around those trenches voices roaring, as well as mocking and chattering sounds mixed together.

More prosaically the *Annales regni Francorum* explained that the diggings kept subsiding because the ground was too marshy, and so the work had to be abandoned.[19]

The secular progress of the bishopric of Eichstätt depended upon a series of handsome gifts from the crown between the ninth and eleventh centuries, reminding us that in the imperial scheme of terrestrial rule, the temporalities entrusted to the Church were intended not only to sustain the ecclesiastical structure but were also regarded as investments for the crown's eventual use and benefit.[20] Apart from various properties, jurisdictions, and forest rights,[21] the bishops received the rights of toll and market at Eichstätt,[22] towns and forests,[23] and confirmation of the see's jurisdictional immunity from competitive secular interference by counts, dukes, or margraves.[24] By far the most substantial new endowment was the monastery of Herrieden and its extensive estates, conferred by King Arnulf in 888.[25] From the material point of view, this gift represented almost a second founding of the see in that the bishops, having expelled the monks and installed canons on much more restricted incomes, drew their principal economic support from the Herrieden lands down to the twelfth century.

In possession of its original endowment, of religious houses and monastic lands,[26] of towns with their increasingly profitable rights, and a retinue of vassals enfeoffed largely upon the Herrieden lands,[27] the bishopric of Eichstätt was enabled to make its contribution to the theocratic imperial regime of Otto the Great and his successors. We are informed that in 981 Bishop Reginald was required to send fifty *loricati,* or armored warriors, as reinforcements to Otto II's army in Italy. Comparing this with his episcopal neighbors, Regensburg and Salzburg provided seventy each, Würzburg sixty and Augsburg a hundred, Freising and Constance forty each.[28] Not long after this, Bishop Megingaud of Eichstätt had the temerity to voice objections to the method whereby ecclesiastical resources were exploited by the crown.

Irritated by Henry II's insistence that a portion of his diocese be surrendered to the new bishopric of Bamberg founded in 1007, the bishop turned off the customary demands for supplies to be sent to the itinerant imperial court with a jest, and apparently got away with what was tantamount to a refusal.[29] He was, admittedly, related to the emperor, and allowances could presumably be made for eccentric cousins. One of the more remarkable of the early bishops of Eichstätt was Gebhard I (1042–1057). A close associate of Henry III in his schemes for reforming the papal curia and the imperial Church, he succeeded to the papacy as Victor II in 1055 while retaining his see at Eichstätt.[30] Upon the emperor's early death in the following year, the Empire was entrusted to him. He saw to the infant Henry IV's installation as king, and to the appointment of the latter's mother as regent. Victor II himself died unexpectedly in the next year. Had he survived, it is possible that his pervasive influence could have ensured a more stable regency in Germany, as well as curtailing the harmful effects of the rivalry between Archbishops Anno of Cologne and Adalbert of Bremen, who subsequently wrested direction of the regency from Empress Agnes.[31]

We know very little about the initial impact of the demographic and economic upsurge beginning in these parts of Germany in the later eleventh century. But some of the results are plain to see in the new regional order entrenched by Bishop Gebhard II of Eichstätt (1125–1149) and his brother, Count Hartwig of Grögling. They established the bishopric of Eichstätt as a significant element in Franconian and Bavarian politics and set up a virtual condominium of the bishopric with the formidable Grögling-Hirschberg dynasty, a commensal arrangement lasting until the 1220s, and in some respects until 1305. We shall see why they were motivated to bring this about. The previous role of the secular aristocracy, and the patterns of their landowning in the Eichstätt region, are difficult to ascertain. We know that Frankish noblemen supported the foundation of Eichstätt and of the monasteries. Their descendants are recorded as counts exercising the *comitatus,* or comital jurisdiction, in the various *pagi,* or districts, both Franconian and Bavarian, which made up or bordered on the diocese.[32] They possessed, not counties in the later territorial sense, but military powers, judicial functions over free men, and oversight of royal property, which together made up the comital function.[33] They owned in addition their hereditary family lands, and held fiefs from the crown and Church. But it is hardly possible to construct convincing genealogies for the comital families generally before the beginning of the twelfth century, when the adoption of dynastic toponymics derived from castles became the norm, and provide us with much more reliable information than first name affiliations alone. One of the earliest examples of the new usage in the Eichstätt region was furnished by Count Henry of Lechsgemünd, who was killed at the Battle of Mellrichstadt in 1078 fighting for Henry IV against the rebel Saxons.[34]

By the twelfth century the comital dynasties can be listed with confidence, and their considerable authority shows the inroad that aristocratic claims as vassals had already made upon the possessions of the Church and crown. The most significant were the counts of Grögling and Dollnstein, who built a large new castle residence, much of it still standing, at Hirschberg about 1200 and subsequently took that name. Their origins have recently been elucidated.[35] In the eleventh century the counts of Ottenburg in Bavaria were advocates of the cathedral church of Freising, but they were compelled by their rivals, the counts of Scheyern and Wittelsbach, to relinquish their interests south of the Danube and to retire to their lands in the Eichstätt region. Ernest of Ottenburg died in 1096 as count of Grögling on the Altmühl and advocate of the cathedral church of Eichstätt, and it was his son Gebhard who became bishop in 1125. Many details are unclear. We do not know who the previous advocates or secular protectors of the bishopric may have been. It was common for bishops and abbots to enfeoff counts with this formidable and remunerative office in order that their secular jurisdictions might effectively be exercised,[36] and it is likely that members of the Ottenburg-Grögling kindred had already enjoyed it.

Another open question concerns the Grögling-Hirschberg lands. The dynasty always considered their extensive estates in the heart of the bishopric to be alodial, that is, possessed in full and unfettered proprietary right.[37] In addition, we know from thirteenth-century sources that the counts possessed extensive fiefs from Eichstätt in their capacity as advocates. Yet when the last of the Hirschberg counts was preparing to leave nearly all his lands to the see, he declared at the last moment that they were fiefs from Eichstätt after all.[38] The motive appears to have been to outwit the rival claimants, the dukes of Bavaria, with the contention that the Hirschberg estates were about to revert without question to their rightful lord, the bishop. However, in the two centuries for which we know something of the Grögling-Hirschberg lands, roughly 1120 to 1305, they were treated as alodial property. But it is also possible that the 1304 declaration echoes the absorption of ecclesiastical fief into dynastic, alodial possession in the decades before 1120, a process well attested elsewhere in Germany. By whatever method, inheritance or usurpation, the Grögling-Hirschberg dynasty was entrenched after 1100 at the center of the bishopric as landowner and advocate, dominating the affairs of Eichstätt for two hundred years, very often to the bishops' disadvantage. But the fortuitous demise of the dynasty in 1305 guaranteed Eichstätt's future as a reasonably secure territorial authority until 1802.[39]

By Bavarian standards the Grögling-Hirschberg dynasty was rich and powerful, but it also had formidable neighbors and rivals among the princes. On the eastern border of the diocese, the counts-palatine of Wittelsbach, who became dukes of Bavaria in 1180, were already the principal landowners, established there by inheritances that they had further extended by about 1200.[40] Although they were usually at enmity with the counts of Hirschberg, the Wittelsbach dukes were on good terms with the bishops of Eichstätt, from whom they and their knights held extensive fiefs.[41] Not until the dukes posed a threat to the transfer of Hirschberg to

Eichstätt (1291–1305) and fell out with the bishops over the see's official allegiance to the Avignon papacy (1327–1344), did the bishopric regard the ducal authority of the Wittelsbachs with some alarm. It is true that the *Landfriede* of 1281, proclaimed in Bavaria by King Rudolf I in conjunction with the dukes, included an ambitious list of bishoprics that were erroneously said to belong to "the land of Bavaria": the archbishopric of Salzburg and the sees of Regensburg, Freising, Passau, Bamberg, Eichstätt, Augsburg, and Brixen.[42] But this was not regarded directly as a program for absorbing the bishoprics into the Bavarian ducal territory, although the dukes certainly were on bad terms with Salzburg, Augsburg, and Regensburg, and had helped themselves to valuable portions of their ecclesiastical lands.

To the north, one of the richest dynasties of the Bavarian Nordgau, the counts of Sulzbach, died out in 1188.[43] The best part of their handsome possessions, including their enormous fiefs from the bishops of Bamberg, passed to the Staufen imperial house.[44] But the castle and dominion of Sulzbach, with a handful of other castles, estates, towns, and *ministeriales,* were inherited by the counts of Grögling-Hirschberg, whose close connections with the Sulzbachs are indicated by the forename Gebhard common to both houses, connoting a blood relationship extending back to the eleventh century. Toward the end of the twelfth century two other comital dynasties situated in this area also died out, and the heirs of both, the newly appointed burgraves of Nuremberg from the Swabian house of Zollern, were to become the major power on Eichstätt's and Hirschberg's northern flank in the course of the thirteenth century. The failed lines were the counts of Abenberg, and the counts of Raabs in Austria, who had been burgraves of Nuremberg since the 1130s.[45] The estates of the former gave the new Zollern burgraves a wide stake in the Franconian countryside to add to their royal fiefs, consisting of the castle, forests, and manors of Nuremberg. These burgraves also held fiefs of Eichstätt, and remained on very good terms with the bishops.

On the western frontier of the diocese,[46] where Eichstätt's principal possession was the large patrimony delivered with Herrieden in 888, the most powerful feoffee was the comital dynasty of Oettingen, resident in Wallerstein and other castles. Another noble family, the Hohentrüdingen, were not so significant. But one of them married an heiress of the ducal house of Andechs and Merania, and on the basis of her substantial inheritance in northeastern Franconia acquired after 1248, the Hohentrüdingen began to call themselves counts. To the southwest of Eichstätt the counts of Lechsgemünd, later called of Graisbach, were substantial landowning neighbors and vassals of the bishops.[47]

In the constellation of all these dynasties there existed many dangers for the bishops of Eichstätt. Not only did the Hirschbergs seriously abuse their advocacy in the thirteenth century, but the Oettingen had usurped their principal fiefs by the 1280s and attempted to deny episcopal overlordship for them. And after 1305 the Wittelsbach dukes tried to seize temporal, and to some extent spiritual jurisdiction in the see, to which they were by no means entitled. Also, the Staufen rulers of Germany, just in these districts of eastern Franconia and the Bavarian Nordgau, were interested in extending their own possessions, assarts, and jurisdictions through the activities of their knightly *ministeriales* enfeoffed with impressive castles, lands, and retinues of their own.[48] All this inhibited or retarded the bishops' advance as significant territorial princes in their own right. Yet Eichstätt did retain a few advantages: the visible temporal nucleus inherited from a distant past; the institutional continuity of a cathedral church and its rights; and a favorable agrarian economy that could be nurtured on the manors to the end of the thirteenth century at least. Eichstätt's circumstances did gradually change for the better in the century after 1250, as we shall see: dynasties collapsed, the purchasing power of money was shrewdly deployed, the advocacy of the Hirschbergs came to an end, enemies were beaten in the field or at sieges, and ancient rights were vindicated.

\*    \*    \*

The surviving sources for the history of the medieval diocese are uneven, and their quality and variety are not quite equal to the task of providing coherent explanations, but their scope may be extended, on occasion, by a legitimate tincture of human imagination. The chief narrative source is the episcopal *Liber Pontificalis* commissioned by Bishop Gundechar II at the beginning of the 1070s. As a record of the political, financial, and military enterprises of the bishops, it becomes much more valuable through its continuators who took up the story in biographies of the bishops from 1279 to the seventeenth century.[49] For 1306 to 1355 the continuator was a literary figure of some talent, the Eichstätt canon Henry Taube of Selbach, who wrote a general account of the popes and emperors of the times, as well as continuing the episcopal biographies.[50] Much more intriguing as a literary confection is the anonymous account of the early bishops of Eichstätt composed at Herrieden, at that time in all probability their principal residence, in the eleventh century.[51] Relying upon authentic tradition, this source assists in bridging the gap between Eichstätt's foundation story contained in the fine Carolingian biographies of the consortium of saints who set up the see, Willibald, Wynnebald, and Walburga,[52] and the *Liber Pontificalis*. Then, in support of the post-1279 continuators, the annals of Osterhofen and Niederaltaich abbeys furnish valuable information for the crucial transitional years in the diocese at the beginning of the fourteenth century.[53] The archive of the cathedral church for bishop and chapter is not very extensive, although it does preserve many important documents from the eleventh to the fourteenth centuries finely edited in Monumenta Boica, volumes 49 and 50.[54] Much of the material was preserved in the cartulary begun in the second decade of the fourteenth century as part of Eichstätt's current administrative reform, and was continued into the fifteenth century.[55]

The student is fortunate in that a far greater number of charters, now deposited in the Bavarian *Hauptstaatsarchiv* in Munich, has survived for the monasteries, towns, and knightly orders, especially the Teutonic Order, which had property in or near the diocese. From these it is possible to construct prosopography not only of the comital families and churchmen but also of the knights in their service over the generations. These rich collections are beginning to attract the labor of modern editing; for example, the Cistercian abbeys of Heilsbronn and Kaisheim,[56] the towns of Nördlingen and Nuremberg,[57] and the comital archive of Oettingen-Wallerstein.[58] The best guide to the medieval sources concerned with Eichstätt remains the remarkable digest called *Regesten der Bischöfe von Eichstätt* assembled by Canon Franz Heidingsfelder and published between 1915 and 1938. It is an accurate and informative collection consisting of over seventeen hundred references with commentaries, stretching from the foundation in the 740s to the death of Bishop Marquard of Hageln in 1324.[59]

Apart from the Wittelsbach dukes themselves, the history of the secular dynasties is much less thoroughly grounded. The best of the relevant publications is the lavish seven-volumed *Monumenta Zollerana* (1852–1861), which collects the early charters of the Swabian counts of Zollern and of the more significant burgravial line at Nuremberg down to 1417.[60] The history of the counts of Hirschberg is best represented in Monumenta Boica, volume 49, and in the second volume of Wittmann's classic collection of early sources for the dukes, *Monumenta Wittelsbacensia*, published in 1861.[61] It also happened that in the sixteenth century one of the priors of Plankstetten, the house monastery of the Hirschbergs, registered many of its early charters and this lucky means of survival has assisted in throwing light upon relations between the Grögling advocates and the cathedral church in the twelfth century.[62]

The scarcity of narratives is partially compensated for by two major sources originated by the bishop of Eichstätt's administration shortly after 1300, and deposited today in the Bavarian *Staatsarchiv* at Nuremberg. These are a cadastral survey of the see's possessions, and a register of fiefs recording all the episcopal vassals and their holdings, from the titled aristocracy to the castellans and *ministeriales,* both direct and subvassals, and to townsmen. The cadastre is an original parchment codex of fifty leaves in poor condition, but the disorderly nature of its entries with frequent erasures and insertions actually conveys some of the novelty and urgency that the attempt to organize the recent influx of important lands with their rights and revenues must have caused in the bishop's household.[63] It appears to have been written out as a single, somewhat hasty exercise shortly before the acquisition of Sandsee Castle and *officium,* or "district," in 1302. By contrast the book of fiefs was carefully copied in a clear hand into a new paper codex, with seven later registers dated 1365 to 1496, early in the sixteenth century, filling the first seventy-three leaves.[64] The original appears to have been assembled in sections at different times between 1305 and about 1320, with the portion (folios 2r–9v) on the counts, the freeborn lords, and the imperial *ministeriales* relying upon earlier information, probably a register of sorts compiled about 1270. The cadastre and register of fiefs coincide with the transition of most of the Hirschberg principality into Eichstätt's hands and are significant for elucidating the bishops' transformation, with new lands and retainers, into much more more powerful figures in the Empire in the first quarter of the fourteenth century.

## Notes

1. See my article "German Bishops and Their Military Retinues in the Medieval Empire," *German History* 7 (1989): 161–83.

2. This appears to have been a Frankish rather than a Bavarian designation for that area: see P. von Polenz, "Vorfränkische und fränkische Namenschichten in der Landschafts- und Bezirksbenemung Ostfrankens," *JFLF* 20 (1960): 173, and *Landschafts- und Bezirksnamen,* pp. 83ff; K. Reindel in HBG i, pp. 113f.; B. Heinloth, *Neumarkt,* Historischer Atlas von Bayern, Teil Altbayern, vol. XVI (Munich, 1967), pp. 11–15; A. Kraus, "Marginalien zur ältesten Geschichte des bayerischen Nord-

gaus," *JFLF* 34–35 (1975): 163–84; H. Sturm, *Nordgau—Egerland—Oberpfalz. Studien zu einer historischen Landschaft,* Veröffentlichungen des Collegium Carolinum, vol. XLIII (Munich and Vienna, 1984), pp. 9–24.

3. K. Bosl, *Die Reichsministerialität der Salier und Staufer. Ein Beitrag zur Geschichte des hochmittelalterlichen deutschen Volkes, Staates und Reiches,* Schriften der MGH, vol. X, part 1 (Stuttgart, 1950), pp. 32–112, and "Die Reichsministerialität als Träger staufischer Staatspolitik in Ostfranken und auf dem bayerischen Nordgau," *Jahresbericht des historischen Vereins für Mittelfranken* 69 (1941): 1–103. See also M. Herberger, "Krongut," in HRG ii, cols. 1217–29, and "Reichsgut," in ibid. iv, cols. 597–600; Engel, *Weltatlas,* vol. II, p. 78.

4. H. H. Hofmann, "Nürnberg. Gründung und Frühgeschichte," *JFLF* 10 (1950): 1–35; F. Schnelbögl, "Nürnberg im Verzeichnis der Tafelgüter des römischen Königs," ibid. 37–46; W. Schultheiss, "Nürnberg," in HRG iii, cols. 1114–19; MGH Dipl. Henry III, no. 253, pp. 366f., and no. 274, p. 375 (1050–1051).

5. Waitz and von Simson, *Ottonis et Rahewini Gesta,* p. 28.

6. Maurer, *Der Herzog von Schwaben,* pp. 218–68; Schlunk, *Königsmacht,* pp. 59–66; H. Heuermann, *Die Hausmachtpolitik der Staufer von Herzog Friedrich I. bis König Konrad III. (1079–1152)* (Leipzig, 1939); K. Schreiner, "Die Staufer als Herzöge von Schwaben," in *Die Zeit der Staufer,* vol. III, pp. 7–19. See also K. Schmid, "Probleme um den 'Grafen Kuno von Öhningen.' Ein Beitrag zur Entstehung der welfischen Hausüberlieferung und zu den Anfängen der staufischen Territorialpolitik im Bodenseegebiet," in his *Gebetsgedenken und adeliges Selbstverständnis im Mittelalter. Ausgewählte Beiträge* (Sigmaringen, 1983), pp. 127–79; H. Büttner, "Zum Städtewesen der Zähringer und Staufer am Oberrhein während des 12. Jahrhunderts," *ZGOR* 105 (1957): 63–88, and "Staufer und Welfen im politischen Kräftespiel zwischen Bodensee und Iller während des 12. Jahrhunderts," in his *Schwaben und Schweiz,* pp. 337–92; H. Werle, "Staufische Hausmachtpolitik am Rhein im 12. Jahrhundert," *ZGOR* 110 (1962): 241–370.

7. F.-J. Schmale, "Die Gründung des Bistums Bamberg," in HBG iii, pp. 56–60; E. von Guttenberg, *Das Bistum Bamberg,* part 1, *Das Hochstift Bamberg,* Germania Sacra, series 2, Die Bistümer der Kirchenprovinz Mainz, vol. I (Berlin and Leipzig, 1937), pp. 1ff., and *Territorienbildung am Obermain,* part 1, chap. 2; H. Nottarp, "Bamberg," in HRG i, cols. 292–98; MGH Dipl. Henry II, no. 143, pp. 169–72 (1007), and the extraordinary array of gifts that year in nos. 134f., pp. 160–62; nos. 144–71, pp. 172–203.

8. But not much is known about them: see F. Prinz in HBG i, pp. 288–90; Bosl, *Franken um 800,* pp. 9–31; F.-J. Schmale, "Franken als karolingische Königsprovinz (741–817)," in HBG iii, pp. 37–46.

9. K. Reindel, "Bayern im Karolingerreich," in H. Beumann (ed.), *Persönlichkeit und Geschichte,* Karl der Grosse. Lebenswerk und Nachleben, vol. I, 3d ed. (Düsseldorf, 1967), pp. 220–46, and in HBG i, pp. 127–33, 184–95.

10. A. Bauch, *Biographien der Gründungszeit,* Eichstätter Studien, new ser., Quellen zur Geschichte der Diözese Eichstätt, vol. XIX (Regensburg, 1984); F.-J. Schmale, "Christianisierung und kirchliche Organisation durch Bonifatius (716–741)," in HBG iii, pp. 29–39; S. Weinfurter, "Das Bistum Willibalds im Dienste des Königs. Eichstätt im frühen Mittelalter," *ZBLG* 50 (1987): 3–40.

G. Pfeiffer, "Erfurt oder Eichstätt? Zur Biographie des Bischofs Willibald," in H. Beumann (ed.), *Festschrift für Walter Schlesinger,* vol. II, MDF, vol. LXXIV, part 2 (Cologne and Vienna, 1974), pp. 137–61, revives the problem that St. Willibald may have been consecrated bishop of Erfurt, although he resided at Eichstätt; on this, see also G. Hirschmann, *Eichstätt (Beilngries, Eichstätt, Greding),* Historischer Atlas von Bayern, Teil Franken, series 1, vol. VI (Munich, 1959), pp. 19f., and Franz Heidingsfelder in his *Reg. Eichst.,* nos. 1–24, pp. 1–15.

11. J. M. Wallace-Hadrill, *The Frankish Church,* Oxford History of the Christian Church (Oxford, 1983), pp. 143–61; T. Schieffer, *Winfrid-Bonifatius und die christliche Grundlegung Europas,* new ed. (Darmstadt, 1980), pp. 199–286; E. Klebel, "Eichstätt zwischen Bayern und Franken," in *Probleme der bayerischen Verfassungs-geschichte,* Schriftenreihe zur bayerischen Landesgeschichte, vol. LVII (Munich, 1957), pp. 341–44; H. Löwe, "Bonifatius und die bayerisch-fränkische Spannung. Ein Beitrag zur Geschichte der Beziehungen zwischen dem Papsttum und den Karolingern," *JFLF* 15 (1955): 85–127; H. Büttner, "Bonifatius und die Karolinger," and "Das fränkische Mainz. Ein Beitrag zum Kontinuitätsproblem und zur fränkischen und mittelalterlichen Stadtgeschichte," in his *Zur frühmittelalterlichen Reichsgeschichte an Rhein und Neckar,* ed. A. Gerlich (Darmstadt, 1975), pp. 129–44, 145–57; R. Schieffer, "Über Bischofsitz und Fiskalgut im 8. Jahrhundert," *Historisches Jahrbuch* 95 (1975): 18–32.

12. *Reg. Eichst.* no. 1, pp. 3–7; Bauch, *Biographien,* p. 80: "illum regionem quod adhuc erat totum vastatum, ita ut nulla domus ibi erat nisi illa aecclesia sanctae Mariae."

13. *Reg. Eichst.,* no. 11, p. 11 (762) for *monasterium Achistadi,* and no. 63, p. 27 (c. 870) for *Eihstatense cenobium.* See R. Schieffer, *Die Entstehung von Domkapiteln in Deutschland,* Bonner Historische Forschungen, vol. XLIII (Bonn, 1976), pp. 187–90 on its early history.

14. There is a large literature on this controversial subject; see E. von Guttenberg, "Stammesgrenze und Volkstum im Gebiete der Rednitz und Altmühl," *JFLF* 8/9 (1943): 1–109; E. Klebel, "Baierische Siedlungsgeschichte," *ZBLG* 15 (1949): 75–82; H. Weigel, "Ostfranken im frühen Mittelalter," *BDLG* 95 (1959): 127–211; H. Dannheimer, *Die germanischen Funde der späten Kaiserzeit und des frühen Mittelalters in Mittelfranken,* Germanische Denkmäler der Völkerwanderungszeit, series A, vol. VII (Berlin, 1962), pp. 135–51; J. Werner, "Die Herkunft der Bajuwaren und der 'östlich-merowingische' Reihengräberkreis," and T. Gebhard, "Zur Frage der frühen dörflichen Siedlungen in Bayern," in *Aus Bayerns Frühzeit. Friedrich Wagner zum 75. Geburtstag,* Schriftenreihe zur bayerischen Landesgeschichte, vol. LXII (Munich, 1962), pp. 229–50, 351–69; H. Dannenbauer, "Bevölkerung und Besiedlung Alemanniens in der fränkischen Zeit," in W. Müller (ed.), *Zur Geschichte der Alemannen,* Wege der Forschung, vol. C (Darmstadt, 1975), pp. 91–125; P. Fried, "Zur Entstehung und frühen Geschichte der alamannisch-baierischen Stammes-grenze am Lech," in Fried (ed.), *Bayerisch-Schwäbische Landesgeschichte an der Universität Augsburg 1975–1977,* Augsburger Beiträge zur Landesgeschichte Bayerisch-Schwabens, vol. I (Sigmaringen, 1979), pp. 47–67; K. Reindel, "Landnahme und erste Siedlung," in HBG i, pp. 86–92; Heinloth, *Neumarkt,* pp. 5–11; W. Wiessner, *Hilpoltstein,* Historischer Atlas von Bayern, Teil Franken, series 1, vol. XXIV (Mu-

nich, 1978), pp. 1–24; see also A. Bach, *Deutsche Namenkunde,* vol. II, *Die deutsche Ortsnamen,* part 1 (Heidelberg, 1953), pp. 338–48 on *-ingen* and *-ing* endings: "Die leidenschaftlich betriebenen Versuche, hinter den Namen auf *-ingen* und *-heim* tiefgreifende Unterschiede wirtschaftlicher, siedlungstechnischer oder stammheit-licher Art zu erblicken, haben sich samt und sonders als unhaltbar erwiesen." This seems too strict. See also part 2 (Heidelberg, 1954) for discussion of *-ing* (pp. 315–22), *-heim* (pp. 323–30), and *-dorf* (pp. 349–55) endings. W. Mayerthaler's contention that early Bavarian was a fusion creole of Alamannic and Proto-Ladin has serious consequences for the identification of a Bavarian people and *Landnahme* separate from the history of the Alamannians; see the report by T. L. Markey, "Germanic in the Mediterranean: Lombards, Vandals, and Visigoths," in F. M. Clover and R. S. Humphreys (eds.), *Tradition and Innovation in Late Antiquity* (Madison and London, 1989), pp. 63f., 70f. The ethnogenesis of the Bavarians is currently the subject of new research; see the papers edited and published by the Austrian Academy of Sciences in the series *Veröffentlichungen der Kommission für Frühmittelalterforschung,* vols. VIII, XII, XIII (Vienna, 1985–1990).

15. H. Weigel, "Studien zur Eingliederung Ostfrankens in das merowingisch-karolingische Reich," *Historische Vierteljahrschrift* 28 (1934): 449–502; E. von Gut-tenberg, "Siedlungsgeschichte in Franken als Programm," *ZBLG* 15 (1949): 83–90, and "Grundzüge der fränkische Siedlungsgeschichte," ibid. 17 (1953–1954): 1–12; A. Gabler, *Die alamannische und fränkische Besiedlung der Hesselberglandschaft,* Ver-öffentlichungen der schwäbischen Forschungsgemeinschaft bei der Kommission für bayerische Landesgeschichte, series 1, vol. IV (Augsburg, 1961); H. Dann-heimer, "Reihengräber und Ortsnamen als Quellen zur frühmittelalterlichen Besiedlungsgeschichte Bayerns," in *Aus Bayerns Frühzeit,* pp. 251–86; Bosl, *Franken um 800,* pp. 9–38; E. Herrmann, "Zur mittelalterlichen Siedlungsgeschichte Ober-frankens," *JFLF* 39 (1979): 1–21; R. Wenskus, "Die deutschen Stämme im Reiche Karls des Grossen," in Beumann (ed.), *Persönlichkeit,* pp. 178–219; see also F.-J. Schmale, "Siedlung und Bevölkerung," and A. Layer, "Die alamannische Landnahme," "Siedlung und Bevölkerung in frühmittelalterlicher Zeit," in HBG iii, pp. 18f., 804–9, 824–30. On the Merovingian phase of these processes, see R. Butzen, *Die Merowinger östlich des mittleren Rheins. Studien zur Erfassung durch Königtum und Adel im 6. sowie 7. Jahrhundert,* Mainfränkische Studien, vol. XXXVIII (Würzburg, 1987).

16. For the aristocracy, G. Mayr, *Studien zum Adel im frühmittelalterlichen Bayern,* Studien zur bayerischen Verfassungs- und Sozialgeschichte, vol. V (Mu-nich, 1974); W. Störmer, *Adelsgruppen im früh- und hochmittelalterlichen Bayern,* Studien zur bayerischen Verfassungs- und Sozialgeschichte, vol. IV (Munich, 1972); Bosl, *Franken um 800,* pp. 63–114; E. Klebel, "Bayern und der fränkische Adel im 8. und 9. Jahrhundert," in T. Mayer (ed.), *Grundfragen der alemannischen Geschichte,* VF, vol. I (Lindau and Constance, 1955), pp. 193–208; F. Prinz, "Zur Herrschafts-struktur Bayerns und Alemanniens im 8. Jahrhundert," *BDLG* 102 (1966): 11–27; and in HBG i, pp. 270–88. See also D. Kudorfer, "Das Ries zur Karolingerzeit. Herr-schaftsmodell eines reichsfränkischen Interessengebiets," *ZBLG* 33 (1970): 470–541, and R. Endres, "Die Rolle der Grafen von Schweinfurt in der Besiedlung Nord-ostbayerns," *JFLF* 32 (1972): 1–43. On the flexibility and mobility of this phase in

the history of the aristocracy, see E. Hlawitschka, *Franken, Alemannen, Bayern und Burgunder in Oberitalien 774–962*, Forschungen zur oberrheinischen Landesgeschichte, vol. VIII (Freiburg im Breisgau, 1960), and H. Beumann and W. Schröder (eds.), *Die Transalpinen Verbindungen der Bayern, Alemannen und Franken bis zum 10. Jahrhundert,* Nationes, vol. VI (Sigmaringen, 1987). See also G. Streich, *Burg und Kirche während des deutschen Mittelalters. Untersuchungen zur Sakraltopographie von Pfalzen, Burgen und Herrensitze,* VF, Sonderband XXIX, part 1 (Sigmaringen, 1984), pp. 104–23.

17. A. Boretius, *Capitularia Regum Francorum,* MGH Legum sectio 2, vol. I (Hanover, 1883), no. 44, p. 123 (805). Early references to the *villa* of Weissenburg, *curtis et comitatus,* with its *silva et forestis,* in MGH Dipl. Louis the German, no. 122, pp. 171f. (867), and Arnolf, no. 72, p. 108 (889). See also F. Blendinger, "Weissenburg im Mittelalter," *Jahrbuch des historischen Vereins für Mittelfranken* 80 (1962–1963): 1–35, and F. B. Fahlbusch, "Weissenburg—Werden und Wachsen einer fränkischen Kleinstadt," *JFLF* 48 (1988): 19–38.

18. J. B. Kurz, *Die Eigenklöster in der Diözese Eichstätt* (Eichstätt, 1923), pp. 18–28; *Reg. Eichst.,* nos. 1, 5, 7–10, 12–13, 16, 26–27, pp. 3, 8–12, 16–18; *Vita Sualonis* in Bauch, *Biographien,* pp. 187–246; Bosl, *Franken um 800,* pp. 114–35; A. Bayer, *Sankt Gumberts Kloster und Stift in Ansbach,* Veröffentlichungen der Gesellschaft für fränkische Geschichte, series 9, vol. VI (Würzburg, 1948); M. Adamski, *Herrieden. Kloster, Stift und Stadt im Mittelalter,* Schriften des Instituts für fränkische Landesforschung an der Universität Erlangen, Historische Reihe, vol. V (Kallmünz/Opf., 1954). On the early establishment of parishes, Wiessner, *Hilpoltstein,* pp. 148–75.

19. *Annalium Salisburgensium additamentum,* MGH Scriptores, vol. XIII (Hanover, 1881), p. 237 for 793: "Eodem anno ingens opus iussu Karoli inutiliter fiebat a Wavarorum et Francorum et Swevorum multitudine, volentes flumen Ratensa et Alchmona dirivare per fossata in Danubium, ut navigio hac et illac posset transiri. Set nec prudencia nec consilium est contra Dominum. Postmodum circa easdem fossas per singulas noctes audite sunt voces mugiencium, set et ludencium et garriencium confusi strepitus." See also G. H. Pertz and F. Kurze, *Annales regni Francorum et Annales qui dicuntur Einhardi,* MGH Scriptores rerum Germanicarum in usum scholarum, vol. VI (Hanover, 1895), pp. 92f. See K. Schwarz, "Der 'Main-Donau Kanal' Karls des Grossen. Eine topographische Studie," in *Aus Bayerns Frühzeit,* pp. 321–28; H. H. Hofmann, "Fossa Carolina," in Beumann (ed.), *Persönlichkeit,* pp. 437–53.

20. For the Carolingian foundations of this program, see L. Santifaller, *Zur Geschichte des ottonisch-salischen Reichskirchensystems,* Sitzungsberichte der österreichischen Akademie der Wissenschaften, phil.-hist. Klasse, vol. CCXXIX (Vienna, 1954), pp. 15–21, 41–66; F. Prinz, *Klerus und Krieg im früheren Mittelalter. Untersuchungen zur Rolle der Kirche beim Aufbau der Königsherrschaft,* Monographien zur Geschichte des Mittelalters, vol. II (Stuttgart, 1971), pp. 73–146; C. Brühl, *Fodrum, Gistum, Servitium Regis. Studien zu den wirtschaftlichen Grundlagen des Königtums im Frankenreich und in den fränkischen Nachfolgestaaten Deutschland, Frankreich, und Italien,* Kölner Historische Abhandlungen, vol. XIV, 2 parts (Cologne and Graz, 1968), pp. 7–107.

21. MGH Dipl. Arnolf, no. 72, pp. 107–09 (889) and no. 135, pp. 202f. (895);

Louis the Child, nos. 21f., pp. 127f. (903); Conrad I, no. 3, pp. 3f. (912) and no. 36, pp. 33f. (918); Otto III, no. 424, pp. 857f. (1002). See Freiherr von Oefele, "Vermisste Kaiser- und Königsurkunden des Hochstiftes Eichstätt," in *Sitzungsberichte der historischen Classe der königlich bayerischen Akademie der Wissenschaften*, vol. I (Munich, 1893), pp. 288–301.

22. MGH Dipl. Louis the Child, no. 58, pp. 185–87 (908).

23. Ibid., Henry III, no. 303, pp. 411–13, and no. 306, pp. 415f. (1053); Henry IV, no. 323, pp. 424f. (1080). For the purposes of forest and its jurisdiction, see H. Rubner, "Forst," in HRG i, cols. 1168–80, and C. Hafke, "Jagd- und Fischereirecht," in ibid. ii, cols. 281–88.

24. MGH Dipl. Conrad I, no. 4, pp. 4f. (912). See D. Willoweit, "Immunität," in HRG ii, cols. 312–30.

25. MGH Dipl. Arnolf, no. 18, pp. 27–29, later improved by exchanges of property in no. 175, pp. 264f. (899) and Louis the Child, nos. 74f., pp. 211f. (910). See A. Glässer, "1200 Jahre Herrieden, Ursprung und Geschichte im christlichen Abendland," *Jahrbuch des Historischen Vereins für Mittelfranken* 92 (1984–1985): 1–33.

26. Eichstätt also received Monheim Abbey in the 890s; MB, vol. XLIX, no. 1, pp. 3–6.

27. This is revealed by the eleventh century source, *Anonymus Haserensis de episcopis Eichstetensibus*, MGH Scriptores, vol. VII, p. 256.

28. MGH Consts. i, no. 436, pp. 632f. On the background and implications of this source, see K. F. Werner, "Heeresorganisation und Kriegführung im deutschen Königreich des 10. und 11. Jahrhundert," in *Ordinamenti militari in Occidente nell'alto Medioevo*, Settimane di Studio del Centro Italiano di Studi sull'alto Medioevo, vol. XV (Spoleto, 1968), pp. 791–843. See also S. Weinfurter, "Sancta Aureatensis Ecclesia. Zur Geschichte Eichstätts in ottonisch-salischer Zeit," *ZBLG* 49 (1986): 3–40. On Würzburg, Regensburg, and Augsburg as Eichstätt's immediate diocesan neighbors, see A. Bigelmair et al. "Herbipolis Jubilans. 1200 Jahre Bistum Würzburg," *Würzburger Diözesangeschichtsblätter* 14–15 (1952–1953): 1–319; K. Hausberger, *Geschichte des Bistums Regensburg*, vol. I, *Mittelalter und frühe Neuzeit* (Regensburg, 1989), pp. 31–154; W. Volkert, *Die Regesten der Bischöfe und des Domkapitels von Augsburg*, vol. I, *Von den Anfängen bis 1152*, Veröffentlichungen der Schwäbischen Forschungsgemeinschaft bei der Kommission für Bayerische Landesgeschichte, series II B, vol. I (Augsburg, 1985).

29. *Anonymus Haserensis,* p. 260; *Reg. Eichst.*, no. 142, 147f., pp. 51–54; E. N. Johnson, *The Secular Activities of the German Episcopate 919–1024*, University of Nebraska Studies, vols. XXX–XXXI (Lincoln, 1932), pp. 46–48, 89f., 242–45. From the large literature on *servitia* owed by the Church to the crown, see the summary by W. Metz, *Das Servitium Regis. Zur Erforschung der wirtschaftlichen Grundlagen des hochmittelalterlichen deutschen Königtums*, Erträge der Forschung, vol. LXXXIX (Darmstadt, 1978), pp. 64–115, and for Eichstätt's contributions, his "Quellenstudien zum Servitium Regis (900–1250)," *AD* 24 (1978): 241–45.

30. H. Beumann, "Reformpäpste als Reichsbischöfe in der Zeit Heinrichs III.," in H. Ebner (ed.), *Festschrift Friedrich Hausmann* (Graz, 1977), pp. 21–37; K. G. Hugelmann, "Der Einfluss Papst Viktors II. auf die Wahl Heinrichs IV.," *MIöG* 27 (1906): 209–36; J. N. D. Kelly, *The Oxford Dictionary of Popes* (Oxford and New York, 1986), pp. 148f.

31. On this period see G. Meyer von Knonau, *Jahrbücher des deutschen Reiches unter Heinrich IV. und Heinrich V.,* vol. I, new ed. (Berlin, 1964), pp. 12–548.

32. E.g., Nordgau and Sulzgau in MB, vol. XLIX, no. 4, pp. 15f., (1068); Rudmarsberg and Sulzgau in MGH Dipl. Henry IV, no. 323, pp. 424f. (1080); Sualafeld and Ries in ibid. Henry III, no. 303, pp. 411–13 (1053), surviving as *provintiae* in MGH Consts. i, no. 319, p. 453 (1188), and as *Retia Suevie* in *Nürnberger Urkundenbuch,* Quellen und Forschungen zur Geschichte der Stadt Nürnberg, vol. I (Nuremberg, 1959), no. 53, p. 37 (1147–1152). The names Rudmarsberg and Sulzgau were still in use in the fourteenth century; MB, vol. XLIX, no. 344, p. 528 (1304); EL f21v; Bayr. Hsta. München, Kl. Seligenporten, fasc. 26 (1351).

33. From the extensive and controversial literature about the genesis and progress of comital jurisdiction in East Francia and Germany, see D. Willoweit, "Graf, Grafschaft," in HRG i, cols. 1775–85; H. K. Schulze, *Die Grafschaftsverfassung der Karolingerzeit in den Gebieten östlich des Rheins,* Schriften zur Verfassungsgeschichte, vol. XIX (Berlin, 1973); Bosl, *Franken um 800,* pp. 63–135; F. Prinz in HBG i, pp. 280–88; J. Prinz, "Pagus und comitatus in den Urkunden der Karolinger," *Archiv für Urkundenforschung* 17 (1941–1942): 329–58; A. Bauer, *Gau und Grafschaft in Schwaben. Ein Beitrag zur Verfassungsgeschichte der Alamannen,* Darstellungen aus der Württembergischen Geschichte, vol. XVII (Stuttgart, 1927); S. Krüger, *Studien zur sächsischen Grafschaftsverfassung im 9. Jahrhundert,* Studien und Vorarbeiten zum historischen Atlas Niedersachsens, vol. XIX (Göttingen, 1950); R. Schölkopf, *Die sächsischen Grafen 919–1024,* ibid., vol. XXII (1957); A. Waas, *Herrschaft und Staat im deutschen Frühmittelalter,* 2d ed. (Darmstadt, 1965), pp. 53–106, 153–226; W. Schlesinger, *Die Entstehung der Landesherrschaft. Untersuchungen vorwiegend nach mitteldeutschen Quellen,* new ed. (Darmstadt, 1973), pp. 130–265; R. Sprandel, "Gerichtsorganisation und Sozialstruktur Mainfrankens im früheren Mittelalter," *JFLF* 38 (1978): 7–38; U. Nonn, *Pagus und Comitatus in Niederlothringen. Untersuchungen zur politischen Raumgliederung im früheren Mittelalter,* Bonner Historische Forschungen, vol. XLIX (Bonn, 1983); and my forthcoming *Princes and Territories,* pp. 112–20.

34. H.-E. Lohmann, *Brunos Buch vom Sachsenkrieg,* MGH Deutsches Mittelalter. Kritische Studientexte des Reichsinstituts für älterer deutsche Geschichtskunde, vol. II (Leipzig, 1937), p. 92.

35. P. Fried, "Zur Herkunft der Grafen von Hirschberg," *ZBLG* 28 (1965): 82–98. See also F. Mader, *Geschichte des Schlosses und Oberamtes Hirschberg* (Eichstätt, 1940).

36. For functions and problems of advocacy in the southeastern quarter of the Empire, see Störmer, *Früher Adel,* vol. II, pp. 424–56; E. Klebel, "Eigenklosterrechte und Vogteien in Bayern und Deutschösterreich," *MIöG,* Ergänzungsband 14 (1939): 175–214; G. Tellenbach, *Die bischöflich passauischen Eigenklöster und ihre Vogteien,* Historische Studien, vol. CLXXIII (Berlin, 1928); F. Prinz in HBG i, pp. 370–73; MGH Dipl. Henry IV, nos. 482–84, pp. 657–60 (1104 [Augsburg]); ibid., Frederick I, no. 148, pp. 250f. (1156) and no. 160, pp. 274–76 (1157 [Tegernsee]); Otto of Freising, *Chronica sive Historia,* pp. 283f. (Freising); *Chounradi Schirensis Chronicon,* MGH Scriptores, vol. XVII, pp. 615–23 (Scheyern); *De advocatis Altahensibus,* ibid., pp. 373–76 (Niederaltaich). See also Hirsch, *Die hohe Gerichtsbarkeit,* pp. 111–33; R. Scheyhing, *Eide, Amtsgewalt und Bannleihe. Eine Unter-*

*suchung zur Bannleihe im hohen und späten Mittelalter,* Forschungen zur deutschen Rechtsgeschichte, vol. II (Cologne and Graz, 1960), pp. 200–23; A. Erler, "Ecclesia non sitit sanguinem," in HRG i, cols. 795–98.

37. On such right, H. Ebner, *Das freie Eigen. Ein Beitrag zur Verfassungsgeschichte des Mittelalters,* Aus Forschung und Kunst, vol. II (Klagenfurt, 1969); G. Köbler, "Eigen und Eigentum," *ZRGGA* 95 (1978): 1–33; D. von Gladiss, "Die Schenkungen der deutschen Könige zu privatem Eigen (800–1137)," *DA* 1 (1937): 80–137; H. Dubled, "Allodium dans les textes latins du moyen âge," *Le Moyen Age* 57 (1951): 241–46; W. Goez, "Allod," W. Ogris, "Dominium," and D. Schwab, "Eigen," in HRG i, cols. 120f. (755–757, 877–879).

38. In German custom certain castles represented the legal center of dominion, so that all the material assets pertaining to them took on their status either as alod or as fief; see my forthcoming *Princes and Territories,* pp. 217–19. This is spelled out with such force in the 1304 instrument for Hirschberg that some of the text is worth quoting; MB, vol. XLIX, no. 344, pp. 527f.: "castrum nostrum Hyrzperch, quod ab ipsa Eystetensi ecclesia tenemus et recognoscimus titulo feodali, cum omnibus iuribus et pertinentiis eiusdem . . . cum universis et singulis possessionibus ad ipsum castrum spectantibus . . . [place names follow] . . . necnon cum omnibus aliis eidem castro annexis oppidis, villis, molendinis ac locis aliis, quocumque nomine censeantur, agris, pratis, hortis, pascuis, silvis, nemoribus, piscationibus, cultis et incultis, viis, inviis, quesitis et inquirendis necnon cum omni iurisdictione, iudiciis que vulgariter dorferiht dicuntur, comodo et honore, quo nos omnia premissa tenuimus et tememus, sive ad nos titulo proprietatis pertineant sive a dicta ecclesia Eystetensi titulo feodali descendant." Although the statements about tenure in fief seem rebarbative, they emphasize that the assets derive their status from the (supposed) status of the castle as a fief from the see of Eichstätt.

39. Hirschmann, *Eichstätt,* pp. 24–66; H. H. Hofmann, "Territorienbildung in Franken im 14. Jahrhundert," in Patze (ed.), *Territorialstaat,* vol. II, pp. 255–300; A. Gerlich and R. Endres in HBG iii, pp. 289–92, 353–60; F.-X. Buchner, *Das Bistum Eichstätt. Historisch-statistische Beschreibung auf Grund der Literatur, der Registratur des bischöflichen Ordinariats Eichstätt sowie der pfarramtlichen Berichte,* 2 vols. (Eichstätt, 1937–1938).

40. Spindler, *Anfänge,* pp. 14–19, and in HBG ii, pp. 21–24; F. Genzinger, "Grafschaft und Vogtei," and A. Kraus, "Herzogtum," in Glaser (ed.), *Zeit,* pp. 111–25, 165–200.

41. EL ff. 2 r–v, 10r–14 v.

42. MGH Consts. iii, no. 278, p. 269. See also G. Schwertl, *Die Beziehungen der Herzöge von Bayern und Pfalzgrafen bei Rhein zur Kirche (1180–1294),* Miscellanea Bavarica Monacensia, vol. IX (Munich, 1968).

43. E. Klebel, "Die Grafen von Sulzbach, als Hauptvögte des Bistums Bamberg," *MIöG* 41 (1926): 108–28; J. Moritz, *Stammreihe und Geschichte der Grafen von Sulzbach,* 2 parts, Abhandlungen der historischen Classe der königlich bayerischen Akademie der Wissenschaften, vol. I (Munich, 1833); Heinloth, *Neumarkt,* pp. 17–21.

44. MGH Dipl. Frederick I, nos. 624f., pp. 117–20 (1167–1174).

45. W. Spielberg, "Die Herkunft der ältesten Burggrafen von Nürnberg,"

*MIöG* 43 (1929): 117–23; H. Dannenbauer, *Die Entstehung des Territoriums der Reichsstadt Nürnberg*, Arbeiten zur deutschen Rechts- und Verfassungsgeschichte, vol. VII (Stuttgart, 1928), pp. 67–77; R. Seigel, "Die Entstehung der schwäbischen und der fränkischen Linie des Hauses Hohenzollern," *Zeitschrift für Hohenzollerische Geschichte* 92 (1969): 9–44.

46. See H. Maurer, *"Confinium Alamannorum.* Über Wesen und Bedeutung hochmittelalterlicher 'Stammesgrenzen,'" in H. Beumann (ed.), *Historische Forschungen für Walter Schlesinger* (Cologne and Vienna, 1974), pp. 150–61, and MGH Dipl. Henry III, no. 303, pp. 411–13 (1053) for Eichstätt's forest in the Ries (Swabia) and Sualafeld (Franconia) "ubi duae provinciae dividuntur" ("where the two provinces separated").

47. On these dynasties and their possessions, see D. Kudorfer, *Die Grafschaft Oettingen. Territorialer Bestand und innerer Aufbau, um 1140 bis 1806*, Historischer Atlas von Bayern, Teil Schwaben, 2d ser., vol. III (Munich, 1985), and *Nördlingen*, ibid., 1st ser., vol. VIII (Munich, 1974); H. H. Hofmann, *Gunzenhausen-Weissenburg*, ibid., Teil Franken, 1st ser., vol. VIII (Munich, 1960); G. Grupp, *Oettingische Regesten* (Nördlingen, 1896–1908); R. Endres, "Die Bedeutung des Reichsgutes und der Reichsrechte in der Territorialpolitik der Grafen von Öttingen," *Jahrbuch des Historischen Vereins für Mittelfranken* 80 (1962–1963): 36–54; S. Englert, *Geschichte der Grafen von Truhendingen* (Würzburg, 1885); W. Kraft and E. von Guttenberg, "Gau Sualafeld und Grafschaft Graisbach," *JFLF* 8/9 (1943): 110–222, and 13 (1953): 85–127; A. Gerlich in HBG iii, pp. 314–16. For their fiefs from Eichstätt, EL ff. 2v–3r, 4r, 5r–v, and of their knights, ff. 31r–v, 43v–49v, 54r–55r, 66r–v. For the royal possessions in this area, the Castilian *pactum* of 1188 provides the best guide: MGH Consts., no. 319, pp. 452–57, and P. Rassow, *Der Prinzgemahl. Ein Pactum Matrimoniale aus dem Jahre 1188*, Quellen und Studien zur Verfassungsgeschichte des deutschen Reiches in Mittelalter und Neuzeit, vol. VIII, part 1 (Weimar, 1950).

48. See Bosl, "Reichsministerialität" (1941) and *Reichsministerialität* (1950–1951), pp. 157–62, 482–90.

49. *Gundechari Liber Pontificalis Eichstetensis*, MGH Scriptores, vol. VII, pp. 239–53, and the continuations to 1445 as *Gesta Episcoporum Eichstetensium continuata*, ibid., vol. XXV, pp. 590–609. See H. Wellmer, *Persönliches Memento im deutschen Mittelalter*, Monographien zur Geschichte des Mittelalters, vol. V (Stuttgart, 1973), pp. 1–10, and W. Wattenbach, R. Holtzmann, and F.-J. Schmale, *Deutschlands Geschichtsquellen im Mittelalter. Die Zeit der Sachsen und Salier*, part 2, *Das Zeitalter des Investiturstreites (1050–1125)*, new ed. (Cologne and Graz, 1967), p. 473. Illustrations of the bishops in the *Liber Pontificalis* are reproduced in S. H. Steinberg and C. Steinberg von Pape, *Die Bildnisse geistlicher und weltlicher Fürsten und Herren*, vol. I, *Von der Mitte des 10. bis zum Ende des 12. Jahrhunderts (950–1200)*, Die Entwicklung des menschlichen Bildnisses, vol. III, 2 parts (Leipzig and Berlin, 1931), part 2, pp. 14–16, 72–73, with commentary in part 1, pp. 29, 74, 120f., 132f. I have not been able to see the recent facsimile of the text (*Pontifikale Gundekarium*, Codex B4, Diözesenarchiv Eichstätt) or the *Kommentarband* edited by A. Bauch and E. Reiter. The continuations to the *Liber Pontificalis* are hereafter cited as *Gesta episc*.

50. H. Bresslau, *Die Chronik Heinrichs Taube von Selbach mit den von ihm verfassten Biographien Eichstätter Bischöfe*, MGH, Scriptores rerum Germanicarum, new ser., vol. I, 2d ed. (Berlin, 1964); E. E. Stengel, "Heinrich der Taube. Neue Nachrichten über den Eichstätter Chronisten," *MIöG* 71 (1963): 76–86. See also M. Haeusler, *Das Ende der Geschichte in der mittelalterlichen Weltchronisten*, Beihefte zum Archiv für Kulturgeschichte, vol. XIII (Cologne and Vienna, 1980), pp. 121–23.

51. *Anonymus Haserensis* in MGH Scriptores, vol. VII, pp. 253–66, on whom see Wattenbach, Holtzmann, and Schmale, *Geschichtsquellen*, p. 474. I have not seen E. M. Werner's thesis (Munich, 1966) on this author. See now Weinfurter's edition (1987), at Introduction, n. 41.

52. Bauch, *Biographien der Gründungszeit* and *Ein bayerisches Mirakelbuch aus der Karolingerzeit. Die Monheimer Walpurgis-Wunder des Priesters Wolfhard*, Quellen zur Geschichte der Diözese Eichstätt, vol. II, Eichstätter Studien, new ser., vol. XII (Regensburg, 1979). See also H. Holzbauer, *Mittelalterliche Heiligenverehrung. Heilige Walpurgis*, Eichstätter Studien, new ser., vol. V (Kevelaer, 1972), pp. 51–61.

53. *Annales Osterhoveneses*, MGH Scriptores, vol. XVII, pp. 537–58, and *Hermanni Altahensis continuatio tertia*, ibid. vol. XXIV, pp. 53–57.

54. MB, vols. XLIX and L, *Die Urkunden des Hochstifts Eichstätt* (Munich, 1910 and 1932).

55. W. Füsslein, "Das älteste Kopialbuch des Eichstätter Hochstiftes nebst einem Anhang ungedruckter Königsurkunden," *Neues Archiv* 32 (1906–1907): 605–46.

56. G. Schuhmann and G. Hirschmann, *Urkundenregesten des Zisterzienserklosters Heilsbronn*, part 1, *1132–1321*, Veröffentlichungen der Gesellschaft für fränkische Geschichte, ser. 3, vol. III (Würzburg, 1957); H. Hoffmann, *Die Urkunden des Reichsstiftes Kaisheim 1135–1287*, Schwäbische Forschungsgemeinschaft bei der Kommission für bayerische Landesgeschichte, ser. 2A, Urkunden und Regesten, vol. XI (Augsburg, 1972). See also his *Die ältesten Urbare des Reichsstiftes Kaisheim 1319–1352*, ibid., ser. 5, Urbare, vol. I, 1959.

57. K. Puchner and G. Wulz, *Die Urkunden der Stadt Nördlingen*, vol. I, *1233–1349*, vol. II, *1350–1399*, Schwäbische Forschungsgemeinschaft bei der Kommission für bayerische Landesgeschichte, ser. 2A, vols. I and V (Augsburg, 1952 and 1956); *Nürnberger Urkundenbuch* (1959).

58. R. Dertsch and G. Wulz, *Die Urkunden der fürstlichen Oettingischen Archive in Wallerstein und Oettingen 1197–1350*, Schwäbische Forschungsgemeinschaft bei der Kommission für bayerische Landesgeschichte, ser. 2A, vol. VI (Augsburg, 1959).

59. F. Heidingsfelder, *Die Regesten der Bischöfe von Eichstätt*, Veröffentlichungen der Gesellschaft für fränkische Geschichte, ser. 6, vol. I (Innsbruck, Würzburg, and Erlangen, 1915–1938). For the papal charters sent to the cathedral church and to the monasteries of the diocese down to the end of the twelfth century, see A. Brackmann, *Germania Pontificia*, vol. II, *Provincia Maguntinensis*, part 1, *Dioceses Eichstetensis, Augustensis, Constantiensis*, Regesta Pontificium Romanorum, new ed. (Berlin, 1960), pp. 1–25.

60. R. von Stillfried and T. Maercker, *Monumenta Zollerana. Urkunden der schwäbischen und fränkischen Linien*, 7 vols. (Berlin, 1852–1861). A further volume of materials and corrections was published by Grossmann and Scheins in 1890.

61. F. M. Wittmann, *Monumenta Wittelsbacensia. Urkundenbuch zur Geschichte des Hauses Wittelsbach,* vol. II, Quellen zur bayerischen und deutschen Geschichte, vol. VI (Munich, 1861).

62. Bayr. Hsta. München, Klosterliteralien Plankstetten 24, *Chronik des Priors Lukas Teyntzer.*

63. Bayerisches Staatsarchiv Nürnberg, Hochstift Eichstätt Literalien 165, *Isti sunt Redditus spectantes mense Episcopali Eystetensis.*

64. Ibid., Lehenbücher 1, *Liber Feudorum ad Collationem Episcopi Eystetensis spectantium,* ff. 1–73. On this and comparable sources, see my "German Bishops and Their Military Retinues in the Medieval Empire," pp. 175–79; K.-H. Spiess, "Lehnbuch, Lehnregister," in HRG ii, cols. 1686–88; H. Hoffmann, *Das älteste Lehenbuch des Hochstifts Würzburg 1303–1345,* Quellen und Forschungen zur Geschichte des Bistums und Hochstifts Würzburg, vol. XXV (Würzburg, 1972); H. Rothert, *Die mittelalterlichen Lehnbücher der Bischöfe von Osnabrück,* Osnabrücker Geschichtsquellen, vol. V (Osnabrück, 1932); G. Hertel, *Die ältesten Lehnbucher der Magdeburgischen Erzbischöfe,* Geschichtsquellen der Provinz Sachsen und angrenzender Gebiete, vol. XVI (Halle, 1883); K. Andermann, "Das älteste Lehnbuch des Hochstifts Speyer von 1343/47 beziehungsweise 1394/97," ZGOR 130 (1982): 1–70.

# 3. Counts, Bishops, and Knights, 1125–1245

In the first half of the twelfth century many parts of southern Germany were still in a perturbed state on account of the rivalries left over from the War of Investitures, which had engulfed the whole Empire after 1076. Then from 1139 the Bavarian aristocracy was involved in a new feud over the incumbency of the duchy between the Swabian prince Welf VI acting for his nephew Henry the Lion, the Welf claimant to Bavaria, and the Babenberg margraves of Austria successively appointed as dukes of Bavaria by their half-brother Conrad III. This dispute caused trouble until 1156, when Frederick Barbarossa confirmed Henry the Lion as duke.[1] The uneasy transition of the imperial crown from the Salian house to the Staufen was also marked by regional armed struggles between 1125 and 1147.[2] The diocese of Eichstätt was just sufficiently isolated to avoid devastation in these confrontations, bitterly chronicled by Eichstätt's near neighbor Bishop Otto of Freising (1138–1158), who considered himself to be one of the victims.[3] Instead, the churches and secular landowners of the Eichstätt region were able to take advantage of agrarian expansion and monastic foundation to entrench their local power. Although there is not much detail in the sources about ecclesiastical and comital lands and their administrations before the thirteenth century, it is clear that Bishop Gebhard II and his brother, Count Hartwig of Grögling, advocate of the cathedral church, were able to confirm their authority on the Franconian-Bavarian border, and like the adjacent sees of Würzburg, Bamberg, and Augsburg, firmly identified themselves with the rising fortune of the Staufen royal dynasty. This was recognized and rewarded by Frederick Barbarossa in 1159 when Bishop Conrad I of Eichstätt (1153–1171) accompanied the current imperial expedition to Italy. At Lodi the emperor confirmed the transfer of an extensive royal property on the River Altmühl to Eichstätt, and took under his protection the Augustinian canonry of Rebdorf, which had been founded upon it.[4]

In the great woodlands north of the Danube, the twelfth century was an era vigorous for assart, the establishment of manors, the erection of stone castles, and the foundation of religious houses. In 1129 the bishop of Eichstätt and his brothers founded their own abbey at Plankstetten.[5] But the principal evidence for the enterprise of Bishop Gebhard II and Count Hartwig lies in the enfeoffment of a new retinue of knightly *ministeriales*. It has often been shown how the ambitions of the secular aristocracy, the Church, and the crown were to a great degree sustained by the services of their armed retinues of *ministeriales*,[6] even though the more solid evidence for this stems from the thirteenth century rather than the twelfth.[7] Agrarian expansion, the enfeoffment of *ministeriales*, and castle building were allied processes that contributed to the consolidation of princely authority in the German regions.[8] The bishops of Eichstätt had possessed a retinue of *ministeriales* before Bishop Gebhard II's time, and no ecclesiastical prince could have survived for very long in German politics without one. In 1122 for example, Bishop Udalrich II (1112–1125) and Count Hartwig of Grögling visited Henry V's court at Bamberg with about two dozen *ministeriales* in their entourage.[9] As this retinue begins to emerge with clarity as to individual names in the 1120s, we find some twenty families with toponymics derived from their fiefs or fortified residences, in line with the aristocratic tendency of Bavarian *ministeriales* to follow the social pattern established by the freeborn nobility.[10] Most of these families were enfeoffed in the Bavarian half of the diocese, six of them in the Altmühl valley near to Grögling Castle, and six in Eichstätt's ancient *regio* between the cathedral town and the Danube.

This arrangement marks a contrast with the report provided by the *Anonymus Haserensis* during the eleventh century, from which we hear that the episcopal vassals were beneficed with the Herrieden lands in Franconia: "For the first time the bishopric of Eichstätt began to have *milites*, or vassals, since before that it had had none or very few. And today, of all the number of Eichstätt's vassals, three or four excepted, all are beneficed from the lands of this abbey."[11] In 1058 Bishop Gundechar II had stayed at Herrieden with a following of such *milites*, all of whom were *ingenue condicionis viri*, "men of freeborn status."[12] Between the 1050s and the 1120s we may therefore be observing a distinct shift in social structure from entourages of free vassals to the more tightly disciplined retinues of *ministeriales*, which the princes of Germany in any case needed for reasons of security during the large-scale disorders of the War of Investitures. What may have happened during the twelfth century to the legal status of the descendants of those free vassals of the church mentioned in 1058, we shall see shortly.

In the second quarter of the twelfth century, Bishop Gebhard II and Count Hartwig of Grögling used their resources to expand the retinue of *ministeriales* by enfeoffment to a total of about ninety families identifiable by toponymics. Many of the names were preserved in the witness lists for charters before 1150, and then corroborated by later evidence for fiefs and castles possessed by these families in the thirteenth century. Further important sources are Prior Lukas Teyntzer's cartulary,[13] and the book recording land gifts to the Augustinian priory at Berchtesgaden in the Bavarian Alps. Founded shortly after 1100 by the counts of Sulzbach on the basis of one of their many inheritances, the motive for involving the *ministeriales* of the Eichstätt diocese in a project so far away was undoubtedly the close relationship of the Grögling and Sulzbach dynasties. Reinforced by the marriage of Count Hartwig of Grögling's son Gerhard of Dollnstein to Sophia of Sulzbach, one of the residual heiresses of her house, this event probably took place a little later than the relevant entries in the Berchtesgaden *Traditionsbuch*.[14]

In some cases the sources reveal that the new *ministeriales* of this twelfth-century expansion in enfeoffment belonged to families that hitherto had been *liberi,* that is, of freeborn status. It is likely that they received new fiefs, castles, or offices at the same time as accepting their novel status as *ministeriales,* submitting to the strict rules over retinues that lords were requiring all over Germany. In 1147, for example, Conrad III confirmed to Abbot Wibald of Corvey that he might turn free men, *liberi homines,* into *ministeriales* of his church, and also encouraged him to promote persons from below, *liti* and *censuarii,* who previously had owed head taxes, into *ministeriales.*[15] Such recruitment from the lower order, *de infimo ordine,* is possibly what happened in the Eichstätt region as well, and is attested for neighboring provinces of southern Germany.[16] The process of converting *liberi* into *ministeriales* is probably what befell some of the vassals of free status who had joined Bishop Gundechar II at Herrieden in 1058, or to their descendants. But since we are not told of their family names, we cannot be certain about what proportion of free knightly families eventually accepted the status of *ministeriales.*

One motive for free knights submitting to what looks like a personal diminution of prestige was undoubtedly that they achieved security of tenure and secured new fiefs, better conditions of service, and hereditary rights within the retinue such as the bishop of Bamberg's *ministeriales* had confirmed to them in the 1060s.[17] For the nearby see of Freising, Conrad III confirmed in 1140 that the bishop's *ministeriales* were to enjoy the same *libertas,* privileged status, that the imperial *ministeriales* and those of the other cathedral churches possessed.[18] So the status of *ministerialis* under a cathedral church was an attractive proposition. It can be shown that at some time during the twelfth century, the following families of *liberi,* identifiable by toponymics, became the bishops of Eichstätt's *ministeriales:* Beilngries,[19] Buch,[20] Dachstetten,[21] Egweil,[22] Eichstätt,[23] Emskeim,[24] Enkering,[25] Konstein,[26] Lehmingen,[27] Thalmässing,[28] Trugenhofen,[29] and Walting.[30]

One result of such a process was that, by the thirteenth century, the bishops no longer retained any knightly vassals of free status in their entourage, and their advocates retained only one family, the knights of Absberg.[31] So we can perceive how a social and professional change, the marked decline of *liberi* and the numerical rise of *ministeriales* in the twelfth century, was in part engineered by bishop and count through their program of enfeoffment, and in part sustained the consolidation of their territorial authority. And between 1149, when Bishop Gebhard II died, and 1196, when the dynasty reproduced the same arrangement for the diocese with Hartwig of Dollnstein as bishop and his brother Count Gebhard I of Hirschberg as advocate,[32] the Eichstätt retinue of *ministeriales* had expanded by an additional fifty traceable toponymics.[33]

However, we should note a problem about tracing and adding up families of *ministeriales* before more prolific charter evidence becomes available from the thirteenth century, and that is the fluidity of toponymics. Not every new toponymic to be found in the sources necessarily testifies to a new lineage of *ministeriales* because the members of the same family might employ more than one place name among themselves. They might change their names when they changed castles as residences, or they might take the family names of prestigious heiresses upon marriage. The details of these confusing practices become much easier to follow in the second half of the thirteenth century as the sources grow more copious, as we shall see in Chapters 4 and 5. Nevertheless, the proliferation of toponymics since Bishop Udalrich II's visit to Bamberg in 1122 does point in a specific social direction: the expansion of enfeoffed military retinues with the toponymics of the members being derived from manors and castles that were conferred upon the *ministeriales* in question.

Military retinues well into three figures were by no means uncommon among the German bishops of the twelfth and thirteenth centuries. What was less usual was the cooperative nature of enfeoffment by bishops and advocates, persons more likely to be found at odds over their respective rights. In the bishopric of Eichstätt before 1150, the expansion of the retinue was facilitated by more than the blood relationship between Bishop Gebhard II and Count Hartwig of Grögling. The dynasty was in the process of building up its political significance in the diocese of Eichstätt, since its hereditary position in the diocese of Freising was waning before the claims of the palatine house of Scheyern-Wittelsbach.[34] Bishop Gebhard confirmed the hereditary jurisdictional authority of his brother as advocate of the cathedral church; their resources in landed property lay side by side; and forms of joint lordship over *ministeriales* were familiar in German custom, even though the strict ownership of rights over such vassals were kept distinct between the lords.[35] The enfeoffment of so many more *ministeriales* by about 1200 indicates the increasing wealth of the see, and we know that the Grögling-Dollnstein dynasty was enriched in 1188 as part heirs of the counts of Sulzbach. Apart from new manors, castles, *ministeriales* and towns, the most valuable item was probably the advocacy of Kastl Abbey, from which their own abbey at Plankstetten had partly been furnished with monks.[36] As a sign of their rising status in the Bavarian half of the diocese, Hirschberg Castle near Plankstetten was rebuilt as their chief residence about 1200, lying roughly halfway between Dollnstein Castle near Eichstätt and Sulzbach Castle near Kastl, which places marked the outer limit of their estates.

The establishment of *ministeriales* in substantial numbers is the best available indication of the increasing consequence of the bishops of Eichstätt and the counts of Hirschberg by the beginning of the thirteenth century. Very little can be ascertained about their administrative and military functions, but the bishops did appoint butlers, seneschals, chamberlains, and marshals to the chief offices in their household and administration during the twelfth century.[37] In this they followed the practice in the neighboring bishoprics, first made explicit in Bishop Gunther of Bamberg's custumal for *ministeriales* drawn up about 1060, where it was stated that they would be constrained to no other administrative duties than such honorable offices.[38] From the siting of *ministeriales'* castles, remains of which still stand, one can infer the function of their occupiers as castellans guarding manors, communications, and woodlands. Another military purpose was shown up in 1197 when Bishop Hartwig was accompanied to Sicily by a number of his *ministeriales,* to join Emperor Henry VI for the projected crusade. Some of them witnessed one of the emperor's last surviving written acts,[39] before his unexpected death at Messina in September.

*   *   *

The evidence from the Eichstätt region is not exceptional in revealing an increase in the number of families engaged as knights in the military, administrative, and social senses,[40] but enfeoffed as *ministeriales* and usually called by the latter term in the twelfth century. By the second half of the century, the written evidence from different regions of Germany had already achieved notable consistency in equating *miles,* or knight, with *ministerialis,* thereby indicating knightly functions combined with unfree legal status.[41] In the diocese of Salzburg, for example, Engelram of Hohenstein, *ministerialis* of Margrave Engelbert III of Kraiburg, was called *strenuus miles,* or "active knight,"[42] and other Bavarian sources equated *miles* with *ministerialis* in the same manner; the imperial knight Albert of Eitting and Margrave Berthold of Andechs' knight Hartung of Nordhof can stand as examples.[43] In the Salzburg writing office *miles,* or knight, also served another purpose. Between about 1120 and 1200 it was "the standard designation for the servile vassal of a count, noble or ministerial,"[44] but as we have just seen, this by no means excluded Bavarian *ministeriales* from being designated *milites,* or knights, as well.[45] Other twelfth-century cases of this kind of equivalence worth noting are provided by the sources for Count Sigehard of Burghausen's assassination at Regensburg in 1104. The *Annales Rosenveldenses,* a Saxon source, called the killers *milites regis,* "the king's knights," while Bishop Otto of Freising, writing in the 1140s, labeled them *ministeriales.*[46] One of Conrad III's *milites* Baldwin of Rüsselbach on the border of Bavaria and Franconia not far from Nuremberg was called *ministerialis* in 1140,[47] and a charter forged in the late twelfth century for Ottobeuren Abbey in Swabia mentions the abbot's *militares vel alio nomine ministeriales,* "knights otherwise called *ministeriales.*"[48]

Turning to Alsace, the Marbach Annals reported for 1187 that "a certain rich and active knight called Siegfried, from amongst the *ministeriales* of Count Albert of Dagsburg," was the first to volunteer in that province for the Third Crusade,[49] thus joining what the author of the *Historia de expeditione Friderici* termed the "dreaded and well-ordered array of *ministeriales* and other chosen knights."[50] Another twelfth-century Alsatian source, the chronicle of Ebersheimmünster, also equated *ministeriales* with *milites*, claiming that it was Caesar who had commended *minores milites*, the lesser knights, to the princes: "And so it happened that, contrary to the other nations, German knights were called tenants of the realm and *ministeriales* of the princes."[51]

Just as in Bavaria, Swabia, and Alsace, scribes in the archbishopric of Cologne were conversant with equating the descriptions *ministerialis* and *miles* in the twelfth century. In the lengthy custumal drawn up for the Cologne retinue under Archbishop Rainald, probably in 1165, the *ministeriales* are called *milites de familia sua*, "knights of his retinue," as well as *ministeriales beati Petri*, St. Peter being the patron saint of the cathedral church.[52] In section 4 of the custumal, one of these *ministeriales beati Petri* was the advocate of Cologne, designated as Gerhard *miles* of Heppendorf when he was enfeoffed with his office as a hereditary fief in 1169.[53] We are also told of the method by which the younger son of a *ministerialis* might be taken up by the archbishop as a full-time knight: "standing before his lord, he will avow himself to be the *miles*, knight, and *ministerialis* of St. Peter."[54]

The breadth and detail of the Cologne custumal about military functions and knightly lifestyle reveal why the word *ministerialis*, adopted by the writing offices because it conveyed the needed sense of servile legal status, could be equated with *miles*, meaning knight or vassal, in twelfth-century Germany. Hence a family of Corvey *ministeriales* was called a *gens militaris* or "knightly family" in 1176,[55] and in 1147 a Bavarian source called the *ministerialis* Gozpert of Harthof a *militaris vir* or "knightly vassal" upon the eve of his departure for the Second Crusade.[56] This kind of aristocratic distinction was already conveyed by using the title of *dominus*, or lord, for *ministeriales* in the twelfth century. In Bavaria it was applied, for example, to such *ministeriales* as Engelram of Hohenstein[57] whom we met above,[58] to the margrave of Vohburg's *ministerialis* Liebhard of Falkenstein,[59] and to Bishop Otto of Eichstätt's *ministeriales* Bruno of Bechtal and Ulrich of Emmendorf in 1189.[60]

Sources such as the chronicle of Ebersheimmünster, which claimed that *ministeriales* were noble and martial enough to be comparable to free vassals,[61] reveal why the *ministeriales* of Germany were able to take up aristocratic trappings, and the Eichstätt *ministeriales* were no exception. A charter of Bishop Otto's from 1185 called Rüdiger of Affental *quidam miles nobilis, ministerialis Eystetensis ecclesie*, "a certain noble knight, *ministerialis* of the church of Eichstätt,"[62] and after 1195 a charter of Bishop Hartwig's likewise distinguished Merboto of Pfünz as *quidam nobilis ecclesie nostre ministerialis*, "a certain noble *ministerialis* of our church."[63] With so much evidence of this kind to show, what is surprising is that clerks in Germany persisted in using *ministerialis* rather than *miles* as the preferred term for knight beyond the end of the twelfth century. They did so because *ministerialis* caused no confusion between knightly vassals who were of unfree status and knights who were *liberi*, or free born. This distinction was eroded or died out in many parts of Germany during the course of the thirteenth century. But for demographic and administrative reasons it continued to be enforced in the Eichstätt region well into the fourteenth century, as we shall see.

\*   \*   \*

At the end of the twelfth century the German crown, through the fiefs, castles, forests, and offices beneficed to its vassals, was still the principal landowner in the diocese of Eichstätt, and was very substantially endowed in the adjacent sees of Bamberg, Würzburg, and Regensburg as well. Its principal freeborn vassals were the burgraves of Nuremberg, from 1192 the Zollern dynasty; the chief imperial *ministeriales* were the marshals of Pappenheim, enfeoffed since 1197 with the large *officium*, or administrative district, of Neuburg, which covered ground on both sides of the Danube.[64] The names of other imperial *ministeriales* surviving from the twelfth century could possibly provide us with further guidance to fiscal administration, but no detail survives except from the ancient royal manor at Weissenburg im Sand, which was administered in the thirteenth century by the marshals of Pappenheim.[65]

In the Bamberg *Codex Udalrici*, finished in 1125, there survives a charter of Conrad II dated 1029 but substantially reworked to include some of the rights and duties of imperial *ministeriales* attached to Weissenburg. In effect it is a custumal, *iura beneficiorum nobis*, "the rules for our fiefs," phrased as a petition to the royal court and subsequently confirmed.[66] When compared with other custumals, it seems to provide a reasonably accurate view of terms for service in the twelfth century:[67] fiefs of three royal *mansi*, or measures of land; the provision of cash and equipment for Italian expeditions and other campaigns; and mobility of service, that is, *potestatem habeant ubivis terrarum degere*, should fiefs not be forthcoming. There is information about Weissenburg Forest, where *ministeriales* had rights to game and fish, bee swarms, and timber. Three *primi servitores*, or "principal retainers," supposed to have been attached to Weissenburg in the eleventh or possibly the tenth century are mentioned: Reginzo of Salach, Wizo of

Weimersheim, and Adelger *de Curte*. Their ascription to so distant a past is probably a fiction, but the families in question are not. The *ministeriales* of Salach, established in the thirteenth century in Burgsalach Castle across the forest to the east of the town,[68] were related to the marshals of Pappenheim,[69] and were from time to time entrusted with the administration of Weissenburg.[70] But the *ministeriales* of Weimersheim, just to the west of Weissenburg, do not appear to have outlived the twelfth century.[71] One of the Weissenburg or *de curte* families acquired the surname Kropf, possibly referring to a person afflicted with goiter.[72] Before the end of the twelfth century they were residing in a new castle at Emetzheim, and in the thirteenth, at Flüglingen Castle as well.[73] These fortifications were within sight of Weissenburg. In the vicinity of Weissenburg, imperial vassals of comparable standing were to be found at Hilpoltstein, Sulzbürg, Stauf, Kammerstein, and Wernfels castles, but there is no evidence to connect these *ministeriales* directly with Weissenburg and its administration.[74]

The longest attested and most favorably endowed imperial *ministeriales* in the diocese of Eichstätt were the marshals of Pappenheim. An ancient royal property,[75] Pappenheim appears to have been enfeoffed by Henry V to one of his most able military commanders, Henry Caput, who was appointed burgrave of Meissen before 1116 and was finally expelled from Saxony by the emperor's enemies in 1123.[76] The line of descent is obscure; a Henry of Pappenheim was marshal of the imperial court in the 1150s;[77] and toward the end of the century a Marshal Henry of Kalden and Pappenheim had emerged as one of the most talented generals under Frederick Barbarossa and Henry VI.[78] During the Third Crusade he was responsible for the successful assault upon the Balkan fortress of Skribention,[79] and was noted for his energy during military operations in Sicily in the 1190s.[80] According to the oldest Eichstätt book of fiefs (1305–1320),[81] the bishops had conferred many valuable fiefs upon the imperial *ministeriales* of the region, consisting of manors, tithes, portions of land, patronage of churches, vineyards, fisheries, and mills. It is likely that the practice went back to the twelfth century, since the crown expected bishops to rely upon support from imperial *ministeriales*.[82] This arrangement worked well in fair weather, but in troubled times such as the civil war between Philip of Swabia and Otto IV, and more particularly during the slow collapse of Staufen rule in Germany after 1240, it caused vexation to the bishops, as we shall see. Apart from the marshals of Pappenheim, the *ministeriales* thus attached to Eichstätt were the Kropf family at Emetzheim and Flüglingen, and later at Kipfenberg as well, whom we have already considered; the castellans of Burgsalach, Hilpoltstein, Kammerstein, Stauf, Sulzbürg, and Weissenburg; the Rindsmaul family at Grünsberg, Schönberg, and Wernfels castles; and the butlers of Königstein and Reicheneck.

About 1200 the configuration of authority in the Eichstätt region did not yet rely upon any sort of territorial design that could be shown by boundaries drawn on a map. The jurisdictions were enterprises shared between the bishops and their cathedral advocates, between the crown and its *ministeriales*, and between the bishops' vassals who were counts, imperial *ministeriales*, or their own knights. Apart from the legal distinction between alod and fief, the possession of the land was also marked by shared rights over manors, castles, woodlands, and towns. If the lists of Eichstätt and Hirschberg manors dating from the earliest years of the fourteenth century are anything to go by,[83] the episcopal and comital manors were not only interspersed but were quite often centered in the same villages. The imperial woodlands and castles were also intermingled with these possessions, but none of this was perceived as inconvenient until the powers began to fall out with each other in the thirteenth century.

During the conflicts between Philip of Swabia, Otto IV, and Frederick II over their titles to the German Empire, which lasted from 1198 to 1214, this kind of local rivalry was temporarily obviated by the judicious attitude of Marshal Henry of Kalden, whose political stature permitted him to remain at the center of German affairs as counsellor to the three rival kings in turn. In 1206 for example, he tried strenuously to reconcile Otto IV with Philip of Swabia, and in 1209 he avenged, with the support of all parties, King Philip's murder by personally tracking down the assassin, Count-Palatine Otto of Wittelsbach, to his hiding place in a barn beside the Danube, and decapitating him. At the same time he was instrumental in reconciling the Staufen party to Otto IV, surrendering the imperial insignia to him and handing over the royal castles and towns under his command.[84] The marshal's authority absolved the pro-Staufen see of Eichstätt from serious threat or damage during the civil wars. But not long after his death, probably in 1214, the diocese did fall victim to a long feud that broke apart the joint rule by bishops and cathedral advocates, which had been established by Bishop Gebhard II and Count Hartwig of Grögling in the second quarter of the twelfth century.

As so often in German regional politics, the specific quarrel of 1223 illustrated a deep issue underlying the confrontation, in this case the practical liberty of the Church in Germany. The dispute concerned the succession to the bishopric, which the counts of Grögling and Hirschberg had hitherto been able to regard virtually as a pocket appointment. When his brother died in 1223, Count Gebhard I directed a small committee of *ministeriales* and cathedral canons to elect a cleric of his own choosing, the cathedral's custodian and canon Frederick of Haunstadt, as the next bishop. It is probable that the four incumbents who occupied the see between the two Grögling-Dollnstein bishops, from 1149 to 1196,[85] had been installed by similar methods. But in 1223 a party among the canons protested, and an appeal was lodged at the papal curia. It proved successful. In 1225 the Hirschberg candidate was deposed and a series of four bishops committed to the freedom of the see followed him over the next twenty years.[86]

It is not hard to see why the counts of Hirschberg took this challenge seriously. It was a defeat for the traditional authority of the dynasty; it undermined their wider command over the diocese; and it might lead to the erosion or revocation of their advocacy with its profitable rights, fiefs, and jurisdictions. Before the feud came to an end by negotiation in 1245, the counts made further attempts to install candidates of their own in the see.[87] Nevertheless, these unsuccessful assaults upon the contemporary theory of unfettered episcopal elections within cathedral chapters[88] were not regarded by the legitimate bishops of Eichstätt in so serious a light as the local question at stake, the scope and limits of Hirschberg powers as cathedral advocates. Although the Fourth Lateran Council of 1215 had recently underlined the independence and dignity of the higher clergy, the papacy still considered that the functions of secular advocates in the temporalities of the German bishoprics continued to serve the purposes of the Church. The legal argument turned upon the possession of criminal jurisdiction by prelates. As the temporalities of the German Church were gradually consolidated into principalities, it was unthinkable that bishops and abbots could run them without a competent jurisdiction of this kind. But since churchmen were forbidden in canon law to concern themselves in matters involving capital penalties, technically the best solution was still the traditional enfeoffment of hereditary advocates drawn from the secular aristocracy.

In 1234, when Bishop Henry III of Eichstätt visited Italy to enlist papal and imperial support for his cause, the question of suspending or abolishing the Hirschberg advocacy does not therefore seem to have been discussed. He received encouragement from Pope Gregory IX, but it was to the imperial court at Foggia that he turned for specific assistance against the excesses of the advocates. In a sense Frederick II's enactment was a vindication of both parties in the quarrel, since the advocatial office of the counts of Hirschberg was not called into question. However, they were warned not to abuse their powers.[89] This they had done by far exceeding the normal exercise of advocatial jurisdiction and its customary remuneration by a third of the fines. In fact the counts as advocates claimed to be enfeoffed with the best part of the episcopal temporalities, or *regalia*, and interpreted this to their own advantage. Not only did they enforce judicial powers and tax rights in all the episcopal towns and manors, but they also sought to appoint officials of their own to administer the see's property and to collect the revenues. Since the Hirschberg castles and *ministeriales* were interspersed among the episcopal lands, it can be perceived that Eichstätt was quite in peril of altogether abdicating its temporal authority to the house of Hirschberg. During the struggle over these issues, the counts were able to wear out the resources of the bishopric: in recruiting episcopal *ministeriales* to the Hirschberg retinue; in subverting the allegiance of the towns, including Eichstätt itself; and in usurping the bishops' manors and castles. Not surprisingly the see was reduced to bankruptcy, and cathedral prebends had to be abolished.[90] Repeated excommunication of the anti-episcopal party had had little effect,[91] although Bishop Frederick II (1237–1246) requested that Conrad IV renew the royal enactment of 1234 allowing for excommunicates to be deprived of their fiefs.[92]

Not much is known about military operations during this feud, but the strategic importance of castles commanding or obstructing the approaches to Eichstätt itself is plain to see. The counts held strongholds at Dollnstein and Wellheim, so Bishop Henry I (1225–1228) endeavored to outflank them by rebuilding Mörnsheim Castle to their west.[93] More significant was Nassenfels Castle on the main road to Eichstätt from the south, the castellan Ulrich of Nassenfels being the bishopric's marshal and chief military officer of the household in the 1230s and 1240s.[94] By 1245 Count Gebhard II of Hirschberg, who had succeeded his father early in the 1230s, sought a military solution by laying siege to Nassenfels. Here he was assassinated for unknown reasons by his own jester.[95] His son, Count Gebhard IV (1245–c. 1275)[96] at once sued for peace, and the conflict of two decades came to an end. There is no suggestion that the bishop or his party had a hand in this murder.

The decision for peace was a wise one, since time had shown that the bishops were in no position to revoke the Hirschberg advocacy, and that the counts could no longer impose their own candidates as bishops. So these issues were passed over in silence, and the details of the treaty were concerned with their respective fiscal and juridical rights.[97] In drawing up their instrument, the parties prudently decided to eschew the services of the higher ecclesiastical and secular powers in Germany, since the royal court under Conrad IV and Eichstätt's metropolitan court under Archbishop Siegfried III of Mainz were at daggers drawn. This was, after all, the year of the First Council of Lyons when renewed papal denunciations of the Staufen regime were bound to cause some confusion in a traditionally pro-imperial diocese. Not even Duke Otto II of Bavaria or Bishop Hermann I of Würzburg as duke of eastern Franconia were consulted or requested to confirm decisions through their superior jurisdiction.[98] There were further reasons for this. The first was the rapid evolution at this time of the sense of local juridical autonomy in the hands of the German princes as confirmed by the imperial court in the *Reichslandfriede,* or peace legislation, of 1235 and reflected in the widespread description of bishops, dukes, and counts as *principes terrae,* or "princes of the land."[99] More important was the simplicity and effectiveness of local committees of arbitration, usually consisting of *ministeriales* and clergy, to settle disputes in the thirteenth and fourteenth centuries, and this was the method adopted at Eichstätt in 1245.

Under the presidency of Cathedral Provost Albert of Eichstätt, a court of ten *ministeriales* was given full powers to impose a settlement. Bishop Frederick II was represented by his household officer, Butler Henry of Hirschlach, and four other knights, Meinward of Muhr, Albert of Emmendorf, Reinboto of Wittesheim, and Henry of Rohrbach. Count Gebhard IV's representatives were his own butler, Albert of Töging, and the knights Godfrey of Altenburg, Reinboto of Meilenhart, Henry of Jettenhofen, and Ernest of Wemding. The choices do indicate some desire to involve neighboring princes, since Henry of Rohrbach was a *ministerialis* belonging to Duke Otto II of Bavaria, and Reinboto of Meilenhart to Count Berthold of Graisbach, who himself came to Eichstätt to witness the treaty.

The bishop was compelled to accept that the count's advocacy included the military defense of the towns, particularly Eichstätt and Berching; the inevitable division of urban taxes between them; and their collection by officials of both authorities. Nevertheless, the judicial immunity of the *urbs,* or fortified enclosure, at Eichstätt containing the cathedral, episcopal residence, and houses of the clergy was to be maintained under the bishop's jurisdiction, as was customary in the German cathedral towns.[100] Although the Eichstätt clerics, their court cases, and their households were subject to the episcopal court, it is clear that everywhere else the *iudicium seculare,* or secular jurisdiction, of the count and his judges prevailed, an early reference to the criminal jurisdiction later known as the *Landgericht,* or regional magistracy, of Hirschberg. The counts thus retained a large part of the profits of justice, assuming the normal advocatial entitlement to one third of fines. In the case of annual taxation upon the diocese, the count did better. He was permitted to levy tax every autumn in the country, of which one third was due to the bishop. In addition, "he will have those other taxes which the grandfather or father of this count had in the country." Only the bishop's officials and their dependents were exempt. The church of Eichstätt paid quite a high price for peace. Control of the towns, the administration of justice, and the best part of the extraordinary taxes were confirmed to the advocates. Bishop Frederick II did, however, gain a point upon which his predecessor Bishop Henry III had petitioned the emperor in 1234. The episcopal properties that had not been enfeoffed or were otherwise unencumbered would be exempt from administration and exactions by comital officials, and would stand in future under those "officiales domini episcopi . . . qui dicuntur ad quatuor officia pertinere," the four household officers of the bishop, and their agents, who were prudently exempted in 1245 from paying over any tax or revenues to the count.[101]

The feud from 1225 to 1245 had effectively ruined the bishops, as the rickety status of their see for the next thirty years was to show. The counts of Hirschberg remained the dominant force in the bishopric, with their rights of advocacy more or less intact, with unencumbered enjoyment of revenues from at least a hundred manors, and with the most extensive rights of taxation and justice in the diocese. The progressive enfeeblement of Eichstätt is reflected through the respective sizes of the military retinues that bishops and counts could afford to maintain in the thirteenth century. Just as in the twelfth, the numbers of enfeoffed *ministeriales* are our best indicator of the relative power of these princes. Bishop Hartwig of Eichstätt and his brother Count Gebhard I of Hirschberg still had about a hundred knights between them. Many of the toponymics disappear from the witness lists or other sources as the lines of knights, reckoned by patrilinear descent, quite frequently failed. Probably their fiefs passed to collateral heirs, or back to their lords who used them to enfeoff more *ministeriales*.

Although the evidence is bound to be incomplete, it is possible to count about a hundred and seventy toponymics in the Eichstätt and Grögling-Hirschberg retinues covering the century down to Bishop Hartwig's death in 1223,[102] of which some seventy were again disappearing from the sources.[103] When it came to taking sides in and after 1225, the counts won a definite advantage over the bishops, in that it appears that about two thirds of the *ministeriales* supported them, and about one third, including families with places in the cathedral chapter, supported the bishops.[104] The bishops' complaints against the *ministeriales,* notably at the metropolitan synod held at Erfurt in 1239, bear out their preference for the Hirschberg cause. There is evidence that Count Gebhard II poached knights from the bishops. In 1243, for example, he claimed that Gozwin of Obereichstätt "adtinet nobis nomine familiae" (belongs to our household), although sources earlier and later than this explicitly show this family to have been episcopal *ministeriales.*[105]

An obvious consequence of the events of 1225, the deposition of the Hirschberg nominee to the bishopric, was a clear division into two hostile retinues, but after peace was secured from 1245, the bishops continued to confer fiefs upon Hirschberg *ministeriales* down to 1305,[106] and to expect services from them. However, the advantage in terms of numbers of enfeoffed knights and castellans that the counts had gained over the bishops continued until the end of the Hirschberg dynasty in 1305. It indicates not only that as political figures in their own diocese, the bishops were weaker men than their advocates, but was also an instrument important to counts Gebhard IV and V for keeping the episcopal household administration and cathedral chapter acquiescent to the poor bargain struck in 1245. In the thirteenth century the progress of multiple vassalage as well as mobility of service among the knightly orders of Germany provided princes with fresh opportunities for enfeoffing new *ministeriales.* So important were the advantages that even the impoverished bishops of Eichstätt, with careful management, could continue the process of recruitment or at least replacement.[107]

Between 1150 and 1250 there had been roughly a hundred toponymics for the *ministeriales* attached to the advocates and the bishops at any one time. By 1300 this average had much increased; Count Gebhard V had about a hundred and twenty knights, the cathedral church about sixty. It appears that in the era of frequent disturbances in Germany, which followed upon Innocent IV's denunciation of the Staufen ruling house during the First Council of Lyons in 1245, all bishops were anxious to provide for the temporal security of their sees by fresh recruitment to their military retinues. In the diocese of Eichstätt the clerks appear to have reacted, for a time, by preferring the term knight, or *miles,* even for the most distinguished members of the bishops' retinue of *ministeriales,* possibly to emphasize once again the conditions of military service and allegiance for which *ministeriales* had been enfeoffed in the first place. The marshal of the bishop's household was called *ministerialis* in 1245 and *miles* in 1248;[108] in

1265 Henry *miles* of Brünsee was *"ministerialis* of our church";[109] in 1279 Conrad *miles* of Landershofen is grandiloquently called *"ministerialis* of our Lord Hildebrand, bishop of Eichstätt";[110] and the examples go on.[111] However, since the functions and meaning of *miles* and *ministerialis* had been almost identical in most of Germany since the early twelfth century,[112] these cases continue a Bavarian scribal tradition of equating *miles* with *ministerialis* that we can perceive in the twelfth-century cases of Engelram of Hohenstein, Albert of Eitting, Hartung of Nordhof, Baldwin of Rüsselbach, Gozpert of Harthof, and Rüdiger of Affental.[113]

\*    \*    \*

The reign of Emperor Frederick II in Germany (1212–1250) was frequently punctuated by political violence; the young ruler's initial struggle with Otto IV; the rebellion of his son Henry (VII) in 1234; the conspiracy of the Rhenish archbishops against his son Conrad IV in the years following 1241; and the revolt against Staufen rule inspired by the anti-kings Henry Raspe, landgrave of Thuringia (1246–1247), and William, count of Holland (1247–1256). But the Eichstätt region, with problems of its own created by the counts of Hirschberg in the 1220s, does not appear to have been much affected by the wider history of civil war in Germany until the disorders of the later 1240s. This does not mean that its own pattern of political violence between 1225 and 1245 was an exception or eccentricity within the German regional framework. There were harsh armed struggles over local rights and resources taking place between bishops and counts everywhere: the counts of Guelders and Holland, for example, against the bishops of Utrecht;[114] the counts of Hals against the bishop of Passau;[115] or the archbishops of Cologne at odds with many of the adjacent secular magnates, of whom the counts of Jülich were the most tenacious and violent enemies.[116]

Among other things, this era of violence has illuminated, in the social history of our region in particular and of the Empire in general, armed knighthood in its heyday.[117] In the first place, the enfeoffed retinues of knightly *ministeriales* represented the defensive mainstay of princely local rule,[118] as we have just seen. Second, armed knighthood in its religious guise was becoming an instrument of German expansion through the Baltic crusades undertaken by the Teutonic Order, which recruited its principal membership from families of *ministeriales*.[119] And third, the growing importance of knighthood in a war-ridden society like medieval Germany was made manifest through new cultural forms,[120] but it was undoubtedly in the first aspect that knighthood was most important in the Eichstätt region. Actually, it was thought until recently that Wolfram von Eschenbach, the most distinguished of the epic poets, was a *ministerialis* with residence and vassalic connections in the Eichstätt region, but Joachim Bumke has shown how the identification of Wolfram either as a *ministerialis* or as stemming from the region are in all likelihood groundless fancies.[121]

Without constant attention to their retinues of *ministeriales,* the bishops of Eichstätt and the counts of Hirschberg could not have functioned as politically effective princes. And their concerns about recruitment, maintenance, and integration grew more, not less, significant as the thirteenth century wore on, as we shall see in Chapter 5.

## Notes

1. See K. Reindel, "Das welfische Jahrhundert in Bayern," in HBG i, pp. 246–67; A. Kraus, "Heinrich der Löwe und Bayern," in Mohrmann (ed.), *Heinrich der Löwe,* pp. 151–214; H. Büttner, "Das politische Handeln Friedrich Barbarossas im Jahre 1156," *BDLG* 106 (1970): 54–67.

2. W. Giese, "Das Gegenkönigtum des Staufers Konrad 1127–1135," *ZRGGA* 95 (1978): 202–20; K. Schmid, "De regia stirpe Waiblingensium. Bemerkungen zum Selbstverständnis der Staufer," *ZGOR* 124 (1976): 63–73, and in his *Gebetsgedenken* (1983), pp. 454–66.

3. Otto of Freising, *Chronica sive Historia,* pp. 347–52.

4. MGH Dipl. Frederick I, no. 279, pp. 90f.

5. *Reg. Eichst.,* nos. 327f., pp. 105–07.

6. See my *German Knighthood 1050–1300* (Oxford, 1985), pp. 100–39, 184–224.

7. This is the inference to be drawn from Wolfgang Metz's conclusions in *Staufische Güterverzeichnisse. Untersuchungen zur Verfassungs- und Wirtschaftsgeschichte des 12. und 13. Jahrhunderts* (Berlin, 1964), esp. pp. 140–42; see also the cautious approach of Gero Kirchner in "Staatsplanung und Reichsministerialität. Kritische Bemerkungen zu Bosls Werk über die staufische Reichsministerialität," *DA* 10 (1953–1954): 446–74.

8. On agrarian expansion near Eichstätt, see F. Eigler, *Die Entwicklung von Plansiedlungen auf der südlichen Frankenalb,* Studien zur bayerischen Verfassungs- und Sozialgeschichte, vol. VI (Munich, 1975), pp. 5–46. On the difficult problems of assessing population growth, see B. Herrmann and R. Sprandel (eds.), *Determinanten der Bevölkerungsentwicklung im Mittelalter,* Acta et humaniora (Weinheim, 1987). On the general build up of material resources, see my forthcoming *Princes and Territories,* pp. 152–85.

9. *Reg. Eichst.,* no. 311, p. 101, and Meyer von Knonau, *Jahrbücher,* vol. VII, pp. 217f.

10. W. Störmer, "Adel und Ministerialität im Spiegel der bayerischen Namengebung bis zum 13. Jahrhundert. Ein Beitrag zum Selbstverständnis der Führungsschichten," *DA* 33 (1977): 84–152. Apart from *Reg. Eichst.*, no. 311, see MB, vol. XLIX, no. 5B, p. 22 (1119), and *Reg. Eichst.*, no. 327, p. 105 (1129).

11. *Anonymus Haserensis*, p. 256: "Tunc primum Aureatensis episcopatus milites habere coepit, cum antea aut nullum aut perpaucos habuisset. Nam hodieque ex tanta Aureatensis militiae multitudine tribus tantum seu quatuor exceptis ceteri omnes beneficiati sunt ex huius abbatiae bonis."

12. *Reg. Eichst.*, no. 221, p. 78.

13. Lukas Teyntzer, *Chronik*, ff. 6r–10v.

14. K. A. Muffat, *Schenkungsbuch der ehemaligen gefürstete Probstei Berchtesgaden*, Quellen und Erörterungen zur bayerischen und deutschen Geschichte, vol. I, part 3 (Munich, 1856), pp. 225–364; see especially the examples at no. 74, pp. 276f., no. 92, p. 289, and no. 108, p. 303 from the 1130s and 1140s. On Berchtesgaden see MGH Dipl. Frederick I, no. 140, pp. 234–36 (1156); K. Bosl, "Forsthoheit als Grundlage der Landeshoheit in Bayern. Die Diplome Friedrich Barbarossas von 1156 und Heinrichs VI. von 1194 für das Augustinerchorherrenstift Berchtesgaden," in Bosl (ed.), *Zur Geschichte der Bayern*, Wege der Forschung, vol. LX (Darmstadt, 1965), pp. 443–509; F. Prinz in HBG i, p. 392. On the Bavarian *Traditionsbücher*, see H. Wanderwitz, "Traditionsbücher bayerischer Klöster und Stifte," *AD* 24 (1978): 359–80, and J. Widemann, "Die Traditionen der bayerischen Klöster," *ZBLG* 1 (1928): 225–43. See also P. Johanek, "Zur rechtlichen Funktion von Traditionsnotiz, Traditionsbuch und früher Siegelurkunde," in P. Classen (ed.), *Recht und Schrift im Mittelalter*, VF, vol. XXIII (Sigmaringen, 1977), pp. 131–62.

15. MGH Dipl. Conrad III, no. 181, pp. 325–28. Very little is known about Corvey's *ministeriales* before Abbot Wibald's time; see H. H. Kaminsky, *Studien zur Reichsabtei Corvey in der Salierzeit*, Abhandlungen zur Corveyer Geschichtsschreibung, vol. IV (Cologne and Graz, 1972), pp. 171–73.

16. See discussion of both processes in my *German Knighthood*, pp. 37–46.

17. Jaffé, *Monumenta Bambergensia*, pp. 51f.

18. MGH Dipl. Conrad III, no. 46, pp. 77f. See G. Flohrschütz, "Die Freisinger Dienstmannen im 12. Jahrhundert," *Oberbayerisches Archiv* 97 (1973): 32–339.

19. *Reg. Eichst.*, no. 311, p. 101 (1122); no. 364, p. 116 (1136–1143); no. 494, p. 157 (1191).

20. Ibid. no. 442, p. 139 (1166); no. 703, p. 215 (1238): Bayr. Hsta. München, Kl. Plankstetten, Lit. 1, f. 157 (1209).

21. Schuhmann and Hirschmann, *Urkundenregesten . . . Heilsbronn*, no. 16, p. 10 (1165); *Reg. Eichst.*, no. 539, p. 173 (1208).

22. T. Bitterauf, *Die Traditionen des Hochstifts Freising*, vol. II, *926–1283*, Quellen und Erörterungen zur bayerischen und deutschen Geschichte, new ser., vol. V (Munich, 1909), no. 1507, p. 347 (1104); MB, vol. XLIX, no. 5 B, p. 22 (1119); *Reg. Eichst.*, no. 491, p. 156 (1189).

23. *Reg. Eichst.*, no. 311, p. 101 (1122); no. 433, p. 137 (1162); no. 442, p. 139 (1166); no. 455, p. 145 (1180).

24. Ibid., no. 348, p. 111 (1137); no. 497, p. 158 (1194); no. 511, p. 166 (1198).

25. MB, vol. XLIX, no. 5 B, pp. 22 (1119); *Reg. Eichst.*, no. 442, p. 139 (1166); no. 486, p. 155 (1189); no. 538, p. 172 (1206).

26. *Reg. Eichst.*, no. 474, p. 151 (1186); no. 508, p. 165 (1197); nos. 511 and 513, p. 166 (1198).

27. Ibid., no. 443, p. 139 (1167); no. 539, p. 173 (1208).

28. Ibid., no. 442, p. 139 (1166); no. 487, pp. 155f. (1189).

29. J. Widemann, *Die Traditionen des Hochstifts Regensburg und des Klosters S. Emmeram,* Quellen und Erörterungen zur bayerischen Geschichte, new ser., vol. VIII (Munich, 1943), no. 355, p. 255 (1028), and *Reg. Eichst.*, no. 311, p. 101 (1122).

30. Ibid., no. 433, p. 137 (1162); no. 486, p. 155 (1189); no. 497, p. 158 (1194); no. 532, p. 170 (before 1204). There are several other cases in which family toponymics stand with known *liberi* in early twelfth-century witness lists, and with the *ministeriales* in the late twelfth- or early thirteenth-century lists. However, I have cited only those cases where the affiliation to status is made explicit in the source itself. See also the knights who became *ministeriales* of the local counts, by similar processes: Meilenhart, *Reg. Eichst.*, no. 264, p. 89 (1087), and Hoffmann, *Urkunden . . . Kaisheim,* no. 73, p. 53 (1237); Möckenlohe, *Reg. Eichst.*, no. 264, p. 89 (1087), and Bayr. Hsta. München, Kl. Rebdorf 8 (1238); and Pfalzpaint, MB, vol. XLIX, no. 5 B, p. 22 (1119), and *Reg. Eichst.*, no. 511, p. 166 (1198), and EL ff. 34r–v.

31. EL f. 32r, and their status as *liberi* in MB, vol. XLIX, no. 46, p. 86 (1245), and *Reg. Eichst.*, no. 838, p. 261 (1267). By the early fourteenth century Henry of Absberg had married Irmengard of Wolfstein, technically turning their descendants into *ministeriales* of the crown, itself a desirable status; see Chapter 4.

32. The counts changed residence and toponymic three times between Ernest of Ottenburg (d. 1096), Hartwig of Grögling, brother of Bishop Gebhard II, Gerhard of Dollnstein (d. before 1188), the father of Bishop Hartwig, and Gebhard I of Hirschberg (fl. 1190–1230).

33. Teyntzer's cartulary and the Berchtesgaden *Traditionsbuch* continue to furnish names; see also the charters in MB, vol. XLIX, nos. 9–11, pp. 27–30 (1149–1158); no. 13, pp. 33–35 (1180); no. 19, p. 43 (1185); nos. 22–24, pp. 50–55 (1189); and Bayr. Hsta. München, Kl. Rebdorf 4 (c. 1180–1190).

34. Hartwig still had residual comital rights near Freising; MGH Dipl. Lothar III, no. 27, pp. 42f. (1130).

35. See my *German Knighthood,* pp. 107–10; MB, vol. XLIX, no. 27, p. 60 (1208) has "Laici autem ministeriales Eystetensis ecclesie et vassaldi, quorum nomina hec sunt subnotata."

36. F. Prinz, "Klöster und Stifte," in HBG i, p. 388. On Kastl see Heinloth, *Neumarkt,* pp. 116–29, and K. Bosl, "Das Nordgaukloster Kastl," *Verhandlungen des Historischen Vereins von Oberpfalz und Regensburg* 89 (1939): 3–186 of which pp. 6–56 were reprinted as "Das Nordgaukloster Kastl. Gründung und Gründer," in his *Oberpfalz und Oberpfälzer. Geschichte einer Region. Gesammelte Aufsätze,* eds. K. Ackermann and E. Lassleben (Kallmünz/Opf., 1978), pp. 100–49. See corrections by J. Wollasch in *Mönchtum des Mittelalters zwischen Kirche und Welt,* Münstersche Mittelalter-Schriften, vol. VII (Munich, 1973), p. 110 n. 338, and p. 115.

37. *Reg. Eichst.*, no. 350, p. 112 (1147); no. 380, p. 119 (1138–1149); no. 474, p. 151 (1186); nos. 486f., pp. 151f. (1189).

38. P. Jaffé, *Monumenta Bambergensia,* Bibliotheca rerum Germanicarum, vol. V (Berlin, 1869), pp. 51f., and my *German Knighthood,* pp. 80f. For these *ministeriales* see F. Joetze, "Die Ministerialität im Hochstifte Bamberg," *Historisches*

*Jahrbuch* 36 (1915): 516–97, 748–98, and Guttenberg, *Territorienbildung am Obermain*, pp. 299–358, 395–456.

39. *Reg. Eichst.*, no. 506, p. 164.

40. See my *German Knighthood*, pp. 23–52.

41. As explained in ibid., pp. 53–75.

42. R. Höppl, *Die Traditionen des Klosters Wessobrunn*, Quellen und Erörterungen zur bayerischen Geschichte, new ser., vol. XXXII, part 1 (Munich, 1984), no. 65, p. 99 (1173).

43. Widemann, *Traditionen des Hochstifts Regensburg*, no. 827, pp. 395f. (c. 1147), and no. 979, p. 497 (c. 1185); P. Acht, *Die Traditionen des Klosters Tegernsee 1003–1242*, Quellen und Erörterungen zur bayerischen Geschichte, vol. IX (Munich, 1952), no. 332, pp. 252f. (1173–1180).

44. J. B. Freed, "Nobles, Ministerials, and Knights in the archdiocese of Salzburg," *Speculum* 62 (1987): 587.

45. As Professor Freed correctly observes (ibid., pp. 587f., 596f.), other authentic contemporary sources did style *ministeriales* as *milites* in twelfth-century Bavaria, for which Salzburg was the metropolitan see.

46. MGH Scriptores, vol. XIV, p. 102; Hofmeister, *Ottonis . . . Chronica sive Historia*, p. 318.

47. MGH Dipl. Conrad III, no. 50, p. 84.

48. MGH Dipl. Charlemagne, no. 219, pp. 292–94.

49. H. Bloch, *Annales Marbacenses qui dicuntur*, MGH Scriptores rerum Germanicarum in usum scholarum, vol. IX, Hanover and Leipzig, 1907, p. 58: "quidam miles nomine Syfridus dives et strenuus de ministerialibus comitis Alberti de Tagesburch."

50. A. Chroust, *Quellen zur Geschichte des Kreuzzuges Kaiser Friedrichs I.*, MGH Scriptores, new ser., vol. V, 2d ed. (Berlin, 1964), p. 22: "Ministerialium vero et aliorum electorum militum terribilem et ordinatam aciem."

51. *Chronicon Ebersheimense*, MGH Scriptores, vol. XXIII, p. 432; "Inde accidit, quod preter nationes ceteras Germani milites fiscales regni et ministeriales principum nuncupantur." On this source, see W. Wattenbach and F.-J. Schmale, *Deutschlands Geschichtsquellen im Mittelalter: Vom Tode Kaiser Heinrichs V. bis zum Ende des Interregnums*, vol. I (Darmstadt, 1976), pp. 332–38.

52. Weinrich, *Quellen*, no. 70, pp. 266–78.

53. T. J. Lacomblet, *Urkundenbuch für die Geschichte des Niederrheins*, vol. I, *779–1200*, new ed. (Aalen, 1966), nos. 433–34, pp. 302–04 (1169).

54. Weinrich, *Quellen*, pp. 276–78: "coram domino suo stans se militem esse et ministerialem beati Petri profitebitur."

55. H. A. Erhard, *Regesta Historiae Westfaliae accedit Codex Diplomaticus*, vol. II, *Vom Jahre 1126 bis 1200*, new ed. (Osnabrück, 1972), no. 380, pp. 132f.

56. C. Mohr, *Die Traditionen des Klosters Oberalteich*, Quellen und Erörterungen zur bayerischen Geschichte, new ser., vol. XXX, part 1 (Munich, 1979), no. 68, pp. 138–40 (1147).

57. K. Dumrath, *Die Traditionsnotizen des Klosters Raitenhaslach*, Quellen und Erörterungen zur bayerischen Geschichte, new ser., vol. VII (Munich, 1938), no. 24, p. 22 (1180s).

58. See n. 42 above.

59. Mohr, *Traditionen des Klosters Oberalteich,* no. 104, pp. 216–20 (1180).

60. MB, vol. XLIX, no. 22, p. 51.

61. *Chronicon Ebersheimense,* MGH Scriptores, vol. XXIII, p. 433: "Prima ministerialis, que etiam militaris directa dicitur, adeo nobilis et bellicosa, ut nimirum libere condicionis comparetur."

62. MB, vol. XLIX, no. 19, p. 43.

63. Ibid., no. 25, pp. 55–57 (after 1195). For further uses of *nobilis* for *ministerialis* in the twelfth century, see my *German Knighthood,* pp. 71–73 and n. 116–19, 129.

64. W. Kraft, *Das Urbar der Reichsmarschälle von Pappenheim,* Schriftenreihe zur bayerischen Landesgeschichte, vol. III, new ed. (Aalen, 1974).

65. Metz, *Staufische Güterverzeichnisse,* pp. 88–93. See also W. Kraft, "Über Weissenburg und den Weissenburger Wald in ihren Beziehungen zu den Marschällen von Pappenheim," *Jahrbuch des Historischen Vereins für Mittelfranken* 66 (1930): 145–74, and F. Eigler, "Weissenburger Reichsforst und Pappenheimer Mark. Ausgangspunkte für die früh- und hochmittelalterliche Besiedlung der südlichen Frankenalb," *ZBLG* 39 (1976): 353–77.

66. MGH Dipl. Conrad II, no. 140, pp. 188–91, and MGH Consts. i, no. 451, pp. 678f. (dated to 1029).

67. See my *German Knighthood,* pp. 76–94, and F.-J. Jakobi, "Ministerialität und 'ius ministerialium' in Reichsabteien der frühen Stauferzeit," in K. Hauck, et al. (eds.), *Sprache und Recht. Beiträge zur Kulturgeschichte des Mittelalters. Festschrift für Ruth Schmidt-Wiegand,* vol. I (Berlin and New York, 1986), pp. 321–52.

68. *Reg. Eichst.,* no. 392, p. 124 (1150); MB, vol. XLIX, no. 33, pp. 67f. (1212), and no. 76, p. 121 (1264); EL f.8r for their ecclesiastical fiefs.

69. Dertsch and Wulz, *Urkunden . . . Oettingen,* no. 22, p. 9 (1251); Hoffmann, *Urkunden . . . Kaisheim,* no. 142, p. 92 (1256); Bayr. Hsta. München, Ritterorden 1281 (1269).

70. Bayr. Hsta. München, Brandenburg-Ansbach/Weissenburg 1849 (1250) and Ritterorden 1948 (1307).

71. Reference to them in *Reg. Eichst.,* no 386, p. 120 (1146–1149).

72. *Nürnberger Urkundenbuch,* no. 65, p. 44, n. 3 (1138–1147); M. Lexer, *Mittelhochdeutsches Handwörterbuch,* vol. I (Leipzig, 1872), col. 1749 for "kropf, kroph."

73. *Reg. Eichst.,* no. 480, p. 153 (1187), and no. 690, p. 209 (1235).

74. Possibly there were imperial *ministeriales* enfeoffed at Landeck and Obermässing (e.g., Wiessner, *Hilpoltstein,* pp. 86–92), but the evidence has never been quite conclusive. For Landeck, Schlunk, *Königsmacht,* pp. 412f., prefers *Grundbesitzrechte,* or landed property, of the Empire, and Bosl, *Reichsministerialität* (1950–1951) finds imperial *ministeriales* of Landeck in the Rhineland and in the Saxon Marches, but not in the Bavarian-Franconian borderland, pp. 100, 235, 539. For Obermässing the reference is MB, vol. XLIX, no. 46, p. 86 (1245) to Henry of Mässing as *ministerialis imperii,* but the other references award this family to the church of Eichstätt and to the counts of Hirschberg as lords; *Reg. Eichst.,* no. 311, p. 101 (1122); no. 348, p. 111 (1137); MB, vol. XLIX, no. 50, p. 92 (1248). So Henry of Mässing's ascription may represent a division of offspring from a marriage involving more than one *familia* of *ministeriales;* on this system, see my *German Knighthood,*

pp. 162–69. When Berthold of Mässing left all his property to the Teutonic Order in 1281, it was not from the Empire but from the count of Hirschberg as lord that confirmation had to be sought; MB, vol. XLIX, no. 110, pp. 166–68 (1281) and no. 156, pp. 251f. (1287), so this indicates affiliation to the Hirschberg *familia*.

75. MGH Dipl. Henry III, no. 119, p. 150 (1044).

76. Meyer von Knonau, *Jahrbücher*, vol. VI, pp. 158, 277, 304; vol. VII, pp. 24f., 255.

77. MGH Dipl. Frederick I, no. 153, pp. 263f. (1155–1156).

78. On him and his family, see W. Kraft, "Das Reichsmarschallamt in seiner geschichtlichen Entwicklung," *Jahrbuch des Historischen Vereins für Mittelfranken* 78 (1959): 1–36, and 79 (1960–1961): 38–96; H. Graf zu Pappenheim, *Regesten der frühen Pappenheimer Marschälle vom XII. bis zum XVI. Jahrhundert* (Würzburg, 1927); K. Klohss, *Untersuchungen über Heinrich von Kalden, staufischen Marschall, und die ältesten Pappenheimer* (Berlin, 1901); P. Schubert, "Die Reichshofämter und ihre Inhaber bis um die Wende des 12. Jahrhunderts," *MIöG* 34 (1913): 465–72; G. Beckmann, "Die Pappenheim und die Würzburg des 12. und 13. Jahrhunderts," *Historisches Jahrbuch* 47 (1927): 1–62; K. Pfisterer, *Heinrich von Kalden. Reichsmarschall der Stauferzeit*, Quellen und Studien zur Geschichte und Kultur des Altertums und des Mittelalters, vol. VI (Heidelberg, 1937); Bosl, *Reichsministerialität* (1950–1951), pp. 483–88; and my *German Knighthood*, pp. 210, 212.

79. A. Chroust, *Quellen zur Geschichte des Kreuzzuges Kaiser Friedrichs I.*, MGH Scriptores, new ser., vol. V (Berlin, 1928), pp. 45, 141.

80. A. Hofmeister, *Ottonis de Sancto Blasio Chronica*, MGH Scriptores rerum Germanicarum in usum scholarum, vol. XLVII (Hanover and Leipzig, 1912), p. 60, and G. B. Siragusa, *Liber ad honorem Augusti di Pietro da Eboli*, Fonti per la storia d'Italia (Rome, 1906), p. 84. On the marshal in Henry VI's entourage, see I. Seltmann, *Heinrich VI. Herrschaftspraxis und Umgebung*, Erlanger Studien, vol. XLIII (Erlangen, 1983), pp. 140–46.

81. EL ff. 7r–9v.

82. On the interconnections of crown, Church, and *ministeriales*, a point made emphatically by Karl Bosl, see his "Die Reichsministerialität als Element der mittelalterlichen deutschen Staatsverfassung im Zeitalter der Salier und Staufer," in his *Frühformen der Gesellschaft im mittelalterlichen Europa* (Munich and Vienna, 1964), pp. 327–56.

83. ES for Eichstätt; Wittmann, *Mon. Wittelsb.*, vol. II, 222, pp. 134–41 (1305) for Hirschberg.

84. Waitz, *Chronica regia Coloniensis*, p. 224; O. Holder-Egger and B. von Simson, *Die Chronik des Propstes Burchard von Ursberg*, MGH Scriptores rerum Germanicarum in usum scholarum, vol. XVI, 2d ed. (Hanover and Leipzig, 1916), pp. 90f.; Hofmeister, *Ottonis de Sancto Blasio Chronica*, pp. 82–84; *Chounradi Schirensis Annales*, MGH Scriptores, vol. XVII, pp. 631f.; O. Holder-Egger, *Monumenta Erphesfurtensia saec. XII. XIII. XIV.*, MGH Scriptores rerum Germanicarum in usum scholarum, vol. XLII (Hanover and Leipzig, 1899), p. 206.

85. *Reg. Eichst.*, nos. 389–502, pp. 121–62, and HBG iii, p. 1449 for Bishops Burchard (1149–1153), Conrad I (1153–1171), Egelolf (1171–1182), and Otto (1182–1196).

86. *Reg. Eichst.*, no. 603, pp. 187f.; no. 607, pp. 190ff.

87. Ibid., no. 670, p. 203 (1233); no. 706, p. 216 (1239).

88. As confirmed by the Fourth Lateran Council in 1215. See F. Merzbacher, "Bischof," HRG i, col. 441: "Während das Decretum Gratiani noch das *consilium religiosorum virorum* bei der Wahl des Bischofs forderte, vermochten sich die Domkapitel endgültig mit dem 4. Laterankonzil von 1215 (c. 24) das ausschliessliche Bischofswahlrecht (*eligendi potestas*) zu sichern." And this was obviously the principle to which the Eichstätt canons appealed in 1223–1225.

89. MGH Consts. ii, no. 187, pp. 228f. (1234).

90. For meager detail about finance see *Reg. Eichst.*, no. 656, p. 198 (1225–1228); no. 672, p. 205 (1233); nos. 687–89, pp. 208f (1235); MB, vol. XLIX, nos. 41f., pp. 80f. (1234–1235).

91. *Reg. Eichst.*, no. 696, p. 212 (1236); no. 706, p. 216 (1239).

92. MGH Consts. ii, no. 330, p. 442 (1237).

93. *Reg. Eichst.*, no. 657, p. 198.

94. See MB, vol. XLIX, no. 29, p. 63 (1210) for "Arnoldus de Nazinuels et filius eius Volricus" and no. 49, p. 91 (1248) for "Ul. marschalcus de Nazzenvels," also in *Reg. Eichst.*, no. 703, p. 215 (1238).

95. Ibid. no. 737, p. 226 (1245). Court fools and jesters had just been banned by the Bavarian *Landfriede* of 1244; Wittmann, *Mon. Wittelsb.*, vol. I, no. 36, chap. 61, p. 87.

96. A cousin counted as Gebhard III was dead by 1245, or shortly after.

97. MB, vol. XLIX, no. 46, pp. 85–87 (1245).

98. In similar circumstances, the treaty of 1236 negotiated by Bishop Liudolf of Münster between the counts of Tecklenburg and the church of Osnabrück, the bishop declared: "Litteras etiam tam papales quam inperiales super predictas controversias (hinc) inde optentas judicamus nullius esse valoris"; F. Philippi, *Osnabrücker Urkundenbuch,* vol. II, *1201–1250* (Osnabrück, 1896), no. 351, pp. 271–73.

99. MGH Consts. ii, no. 196, pp. 241–47 (1235); see no. 305, p. 420 (1231) for *princeps terre;* the counts of Hirschberg were referred to as "magnates ac potentiores quidam de terra" in *Reg. Eichst.*, no. 706, p. 216 (1239); Bishop Henry IV of Eichstätt was called *princeps terrae* in ibid., no. 780, p. 243 (1255).

100. B. Diestelkamp, "Bischofstadt" in HRG i, cols. 446–49, and D. Willoweit, "Immunität," in HRG ii, cols. 312–30.

101. Gebhard IV confirmed this in 1250; MB, vol. XLIX, no. 55, p. 97.

102. See my thesis *"Ministeriales* and the Development of Territorial Lordship in the Eichstätt Region, 1100–1350" (Oxford, 1972), pp. 125f., 129–31, 135f., 355–61.

103. We should recall that not every toponymic necessarily represents a separate lineage, so the figures have to be treated with due caution.

104. For the episcopal entourage, see *Reg. Eichst.*, no. 662, p. 200 (1229); no. 691, p. 211 (1235); no. 703, p. 215 (1238); no. 721, pp. 219f. (1241); no. 724, p. 221 (1243); no. 733, p. 225 (1244); nos. 736–38, pp. 226f. (1245). For the chapter, see no. 664, p. 201 (1230) to no. 733, p. 225 (1244). For Hirschberg *ministeriales,* see especially Bayr. Hsta. München, Kl. Rebdorf 8, 11–14 (1238–1244).

105. Ibid. 13 (1243). For ascription to the episcopal *familia,* see *Reg. Eichst.*, no. 445, p. 140 (1166–1168); EL ff. 15v–16r.

106. EL ff. 32r–41v.

107. For evidence of this process, see MB, vol. XLIX, no. 68, p. 112 (1262), and

no. 77, pp. 121f. (1265); no. 45, p. 84 (1243) is a treaty with the bishop of Würzburg about the division of lordship over *ministeriales'* offspring, which would bring a proportion of them into the Eichstätt *familia*. On conditions for recruitment in the diocese of Salzburg, see J. B. Freed, "Devotion to St James and Family Identity: the Thurns of Salzburg," *Journal of Medieval History* 13 (1987): 207–22.

108. MB, vol. XLIX, no. 46, p. 86 (1245); no. 49, p. 91 (1248).

109. Ibid., no. 77, pp. 121f.

110. Ibid., no. 101, p. 153.

111. Ibid., no. 46, pp. 86f (1245) and no. 94, pp. 144f. (1274) for the knights of Zandt; no. 50, p. 92 (1248) and no. 60, p. 103 (1254) for the knights of Wemding.

112. But not in all parts of the diocese of Salzburg; see ns. 44–45 above.

113. See ns. 42–43, 47, 56, and 62 above.

114. A good view of their complicated interrelation is to be found in *Gesta episcoporum Traiectensium*, MGH Scriptores, vol. XXIII, pp. 400–26.

115. MGH Consts. ii, no. 278, pp. 391f. (1222).

116. Waitz, *Chronica regia Coloniensis,* pp. 274–85, and *Annales Sancti Pantaleonis Coloniensis,* MGH Scriptores, vol. XXII, pp. 529–47.

117. See as introductions J. Fleckenstein, "Das Rittertum der Stauferzeit," and O. Gamber, "Die Bewaffnung der Stauferzeit," in *Die Zeit der Staufer. Katalog der Ausstellung im Württembergischen Landesmuseum Stuttgart 1977,* vol. III, *Aufsätze* (Stuttgart, 1977), pp. 103–12, 113–18, and the essays in A. Borst (ed.), *Das Rittertum im Mittelalter,* Wege der Forschung, vol. CCCXLIX (Darmstadt, 1976).

118. See my *German Knighthood*, pp. 100–39, 184–203. On the integration of knightly and ministerial forms, see J.-P. Ritter, *Ministérialité et chevalerie. Dignité humaine et liberté dans le droit médiéval* (Lausanne, 1955); P. Kluckhohn, *Die Ministerialität in Südostdeutschland vom zehnten bis zum Ende des dreizehnten Jahrhunderts,* Quellen und Studien zur Verfassungsgeschichte des Deutschen Reiches im Mittelalter und Neuzeit, vol. IV, part 1 (Weimar, 1910); J. M. van Winter, "The ministerial and knightly classes in Guelders and Zutphen," *Acta Historiae Neerlandica* 1 (1966): 171–86; W. Störmer, "Adel und Ministerialität im Spiegel der bayerischen Namengebung bis zum 13. Jahrhundert. Ein Beitrag zum Selbstverständnis der Führungsschichten," *DA* 33 (1977): 84–152; and the comments by J. Fleckenstein in "Die Entstehung des niederen Adels und das Rittertum," in Fleckenstein (ed.), *Herrschaft und Stand,* pp. 17–39.

119. From the vast literature on these phenomena, see especially D. Wojtecki, *Studien zur Personengeschichte des Deutschen Ordens im 13. Jahrhundert,* Quellen und Studien zur Geschichte des östlichen Europas (Wiesbaden, 1971), and "Der Deutsche Orden unter Friedrich II." in J. Fleckenstein (ed.), *Probleme um Friedrich II.,* VF, vol. XVI (Sigmaringen, 1974), pp. 187–224; E. Christiansen, *The Northern Crusades. The Baltic and the Catholic Frontier 1100–1525,* New Studies in Medieval History (London, 1980), pp. 70–104; M. Hellmann, "Bemerkungen zur sozialgeschichtlichen Erforschung des Deutschen Ordens," *Historisches Jahrbuch* 80 (1961): 126–42; G. Labuda, "Die Urkunden über die Anfänge des Deutschen Ordens im Kulmerland und in Preussen in den Jahren 1226–1243," in J. Fleckenstein and M. Hellmann (eds.), *Die geistlichen Ritterorden Europas,* VF, vol. XXVI (Sigmaringen, 1980), pp. 299–316.

120. The best guides remain J. Bumke, *Studien zum Ritterbegriff im 12. und 13.*

*Jahrhundert,* Beihefte zum Euphorion, vol. I (Heidelberg, 1964), trans. by W. T. H. and Erika Jackson, *The Concept of Knighthood in the Middle Ages,* AMS Studies in the Middle Ages, vol. II (New York, 1982); and H. G. Reuter, *Die Lehre vom Ritterstand. Zum Ritterbegriff in Historiographie und Dichtung vom 11. bis zum 13. Jahrhundert,* Neue Wirtschaftsgeschichte, vol. IV (Cologne and Vienna, 1971). See also G. Kaiser, "Minnesang, Ritterideal, Ministerialität," in H. Wenzel (ed.), *Adelsherrschaft und Literatur,* Beiträge zur älteren deutschen Literaturgeschichte, vol. VI (Bonn and Frankfurt, 1980), pp. 181–208, and J. Fleckenstein (ed.), *Das ritterliche Turnier im Mittelalter. Beiträge zu einer vergleichenden Formen- und Verhaltensgeschichte des Rittertums,* Veröffentlichungen des Max-Planck-Instituts für Geschichte, vol. LXXX (Göttingen, 1985); for the thirteenth-century phase especially the papers by L. Fenske, "Adel und Rittertum im Spiegel früher heraldischer Formen und deren Entwicklung," J. Fleckenstein, "Das Turnier als höfisches Fest im hochmittelalterlichen Deutschland," and W. Rösener, "Ritterliche Wirtschaftsverhältnisse und Turnier im sozialen Wandel des Hochmittelalters," in ibid., pp. 75–160, 229–56, 296–338.

121. J. Bumke, *Die Wolfram von Eschenbach Forschung seit 1945. Bericht und Bibliographie* (Munich, 1970), pp. 69–72, and *Ministerialität und Ritterdichtung. Umrisse der Forschung* (Munich, 1976), pp. 59f. See also his *Mäzene im Mittelalter. Die Gönner und Auftraggeber der höfischen Literatur in Deutschland 1150–1300* (Munich, 1979), p. 28.

# 4. The Bishopric and Its Neighbors after the Treaty of Eichstätt in 1245

In the scenes of cooperation, compromise, and confrontation between count and bishop that were examined in Chapter 3, we can discern a pattern for the whole history of the involvement of the German Church with temporal concerns during the Staufen era, the Interregnum, and the subsequent reigns. Early in the thirteenth century Caesarius of Heisterbach had claimed in a well-known phrase that with some peril to their souls "Nearly all the bishops of Germany wield a double sword . . . ," meaning their secular as well as their spiritual authority.[1] At times their temporal power was put down by their enemies in the field: the bishop of Utrecht's before Coevorden Castle in 1227;[2] the archbishop of Magdeburg's at the River Biese in 1240;[3] the bishop of Strasbourg's at the Battle of Hausbergen in 1262;[4] or the archbishop of Cologne's at the Battle of Worringen in 1288.[5] Between 1225 and 1245 the bishops of Eichstätt had not done so badly as this in their field operations, and in 1245 the Treaty of Eichstätt restored the rights of the bishopric on the basis of a charter, which the cathedral advocates, in spite of temptations, never dared to overthrow. In principle the see of Eichstätt was guaranteed its rightful independence, but its position within the current configuration of Bavarian and Franconian politics was unfavorable. Why was this so?

For the present the answer lay chiefly in the relatively greater strength of the neighboring secular authorities as territorial powers. As Abbot Conrad of Scheyern had already reported of Duke Louis I of Bavaria (1183–1231): "He became richer than the rich, more powerful than the powerful, and resolution maintained him as sole prince of the princes in his land, who respected his authority."[6] This position was created by the acquisition of many rich inheritances, and in spite of the division of the duchy of Bavaria in 1255, Duke Louis II of Upper Bavaria, who succeeded in 1253, was by far the greatest man in the Eichstätt region. Eichstätt's neighbors to the north, the burgraves of Nuremberg, were also about to be enriched enormously as principal heirs to the Franconian lands of Duke Otto VIII of Merania, who died in 1248. The Treaty of Eichstätt had actually regularized the authority of the counts of Hirschberg in the heart of the bishopric. And in spite of the difficulties that the crown faced in Germany at the hands of its enemies since the excommunication of Emperor Frederick II in 1239, it was still a substantial landowner in Swabia, Franconia, and the Bavarian Nordgau, its rights provisionally protected by the imperial *ministeriales* from their castles. Of these the most notable were the marshals of Pappenheim with their advocacies at Weissenburg im Sand and at Neuburg on the Danube, and the *buticularius,* or butler, of Nuremberg with powers in that city and its environs. At this juncture the bishopric of Eichstätt was still too insignificant to make much of a showing compared with the Hirschberg counts, the Wittelsbach dukes, and the Zollern burgraves.

Even the downfall of the marshals of Pappenheim at the hands of the dukes of Bavaria between the 1240s and the 1270s, events to which we will shortly turn, made the tribulations of Eichstätt in its poverty seem relatively unimportant. Nevertheless, the resilience of the cathedral church as a legal and religious corporation surviving the decades and centuries proved its worth. As a perceptive critic of affairs in this region has observed, there were "dramatic turns of fortune which occurred at several points" after 1245, these being the dangers that the bishops proved capable of circumventing and opportunities at which they were able to grasp. Again the best explanation lies in the personalities of the bishops who reigned between the Treaty of Eichstätt and the Hirschberg testament of 1291, which held out the prospect of a substantial principality being bestowed upon the see. So we now need to investigate how Eichstätt's authority managed to survive among the territorial dynasties whose rights and possessions surrounded the see.

The feud between the counts of Hirschberg and the bishops of Eichstätt had worked out to the advantage of the former. Cathedral and chapter may have gained their ecclesiastical liberty by 1245, but at the cost of an economic collapse. The Hirschberg advocacy was a heavy encumbrance upon the Bavarian half of the diocese, while in the Franconian half the counts of Oettingen were in the process of despoiling Eichstätt of the best part of its Herrieden lands.[7] As a result, the regime of Bishops Henry IV of Württemberg (1247–1259), Engelhard of Dolling (1259–1261), and Hildebrand of Möhren (1261–1279) was constrained to practice strict measures to survive upon what was left to the episcopal *mensa,* the household lands directly administered by the church.

Although Bishops Henry IV and Hildebrand came from different backgrounds, they were similar in their prudent handling of the see's economic affairs. Bishop Henry IV was installed at the instigation of Pope Innocent IV through his legate in Germany, Bishop Philip of Ferrara[8] as part of plans following the First Council of Lyons to build up the pro-papal party in the German Church. As an outsider in a traditionally pro-imperial bishopric, Bishop Henry was unpopular. Bishop Engelhard was a local man and had been a cathedral canon at Eichstätt, and Bishop Hildebrand of Möhren had been archdeacon of Eichstätt before his election as the see's pastor.[9] He belonged to a rich local family consisting both of free lords and *ministeriales* who served in the entourage of the counts of Oettingen.[10] But under these bishops the see of Eichstätt was forced politically into virtual immobility while Count Gebhard IV of Hirschberg cut a figure in Bavarian affairs as brother-in-law of Dukes Louis II and Henry XIII. One result of the bishopric's insignificance was to facilitate the expansion of ducal Bavaria into the Eichstätt region, since the dukes successfully claimed inheritance of the substantial Staufen possessions in the vast stretch of country from the Swabian border to the Böhmerwald, a landscape of which the diocese formed a part.

In the Eichstätt treaty of 1245 the church regained the unfettered right to administer its own lands under the four household officers, although even this appears to have been called into question by the advocate and his advisers. In 1250 Count Gebhard IV again was asked to renounce any claims to revenues or services from the persons under the four officers' administration.[11] There is no detail about these offices, but the names of the *ministeriales* appointed by the bishops have survived: Hermann of Landershofen was chamberlain;[12] Ulrich and then Henry of Nassenfels were marshals;[13] Henry of Hirschlach, Henry of Arberg, and Gebhard of Kottingwört were butlers;[14] and Bruno of Immeldorf, Gebhard of Burggriesbach, and Albert of Pfünz were seneschals.[15] A report dated 1249 indicated how the church lands "had been much devastated by pillage, arson, and many other means,"[16] and one can infer from the chapter's complaint recorded ten years later what measures Bishop Henry IV had had to take in order to recover from this state of affairs. This plaint comes in the form of an electoral capitulation that the chapter intended to impose by oath upon Bishop Henry's successor.[17] The bishop had run up debts in Rome, neglected the cathedral's fabric, levied impositions upon the chapter's dependents throughout the diocese, halved the value of some of the Herrieden prebends, and had kept for himself the annual cash offerings dedicated to the cathedral. Such transgressions indicate an empty episcopal treasury, and that the resources from the see's own lands, or *mensa,* were inadequate for sustaining the bishop's household.

Worse still, ecclesiastical possessions had improperly been alienated in order to pay Bishop Henry's way, and the assart tithes, which should have pertained to the parish churches, were specifically mentioned. However, the process of enfeoffing the laity with material rewards of this nature was essential for securing the military, administrative, and political services required by churches, and the chapter had itself been obliged to authorize such grants of tithes.[18] The canons were also concerned that the principal fiefs of the church, those with annual revenues of more than twenty marks, should only be conferred upon consultation between bishop and chapter. That the affairs of the chapter were also in a disorderly state is indicated by a second electoral capitulation of 1265, to be imposed upon the next provost.[19] The canons were anxious about the neglected state of their prebends, and twice referred to the proper and acceptable administrative precepts for the provost's office introduced by Bishop Hartwig of Dollnstein sixty years before.

It is unlikely that these election oaths, even if they were ever extracted, would have had much effect upon Eichstätt's protracted economic difficulties. It is possible that Bishop Henry IV's ruthlessness paid dividends since the see's fortunes took a slight turn for the better under Bishop Hildebrand of Möhren. An explanation is that since Bishop Henry IV had been a pro-papal prelate in an imperialist diocese, this gave grounds to the laity for the continued spoliation of ecclesiastical possessions, rights, and incomes. It is certainly the case that the nunnery of Seligenporten, for which the bishop had just issued letters of protection, was burned down by imperialist agents in 1249.[20] Bishop Hildebrand found himself on much better terms with the secular lords and began to receive worthwhile gifts and legacies from them. In 1262 the freeborn lord Ulrich of Wahrberg gave Dürrwangen Castle and its knights called, in the text itself, *ministeriales nobiles.*[21] In 1264 the duke of Bavaria's magistrate in Ingolstadt, the knight Henry of Egweil, bequeathed all his alods and fiefs, retaining life tenure.[22] The imperial *ministeriales* Ulrich and Burchard of Weissenburg gave all their alodial possessions at Mischelbach including the castle just constructed there, to be held as fief.[23] In 1265 Burgrave Frederick of Nuremberg gave back the *officium,* or manorial complex, of Habersdorf, which he had held in pledge for the large sum of £130 granted to one of Bishop Hildebrand's predecessors, Bishop Henry IV being the likely candidate.

The burgrave would, however, keep Habersdorf for life on condition that he improve it by recuperating the portions currently alienated from the estate.[24] In 1269 the imperial *ministerialis* Ulrich of Sulzbürg converted his manor of Stockach into an Eichstätt fief; in 1276 Count Berthold of Graisbach resigned the tithes at Ettenstatt; and in 1279 the imperial *ministerialis* Henry of Hilpoltstein gave three manors to Eichstätt.[25] Further evidence for the see's recovery is shown in that property could now be purchased for the *mensa* by the bishop.[26]

At the same time, there is evidence for renewed efforts to gather renders from far-flung possessions acquired by Eichstätt in the Rhineland, the Main valley, Austria, and the Alps. Like so many of the major churches in Germany, Eichstätt was not exceptional in having received gifts in places geographically remote from the cathedral or abbatial foundation.[27] The most significant of such legacies was a portion of the property of Otto of Schweinfurt, duke of Swabia (1048–1057). It consisted of extensive possessions on the upper Main that had passed to his grandson Bishop Eberhard of Eichstätt (1099–1112) and included the town of Schweinfurt. The bishop left his inheritance to his see.[28] But Eichstätt was not powerful enough to retain direct control of so distant a prize, which in any case lay under another diocesan jurisdiction, that of Würzburg. It demonstrates how Eichstätt was politically weaker than one of its neighbors, the see of Bamberg, which directly ruled its distant Carinthian territories, notably Villach, which was situated in the diocese of Aquileia,[29] and Wolfsberg in the diocese of Salzburg. Schweinfurt was permanently enfeoffed to the crown,[30] and the lands chiefly to the counts of Henneberg, Wildberg, and Hohenlohe. From 1250 the bishops sought to renew their rights in these regions, rearranged the tenures, and also sent procurators to their Alpine possessions in pursuit of their incomes.[31]

All the transactions we have reviewed since the accession of Bishop Henry IV in 1247 were quite insignificant compared with the progress of Eichstätt's secular neighbors. With the Hirschberg alodial lands, the cathedral advocacy, a staunch retinue, and the Sulzbach dominion behind him, Count Gebhard IV's career as a Bavarian prince was a success. Apart from Kastl, he was also advocate of the dynastic mausoleum, Plankstetten Abbey, and of two foundations belonging to the see, Rebdorf and Monheim. Enriched by tithes and woodlands held of the church, he also commanded all the fisheries in the River Altmühl, the principal stretch of water in the diocese.[32] Before 1253 he was able to buy Rosenberg Castle, in sight of Sulzbach, from the imperial butler Walter of Klingenberg, it being one of the many possessions of the butler's wife, Elizabeth of Königstein.[33] In 1253 the count contracted a good marriage to an heiress, Elizabeth of Tirol. Her sister had married Count Meinhard I of Görz and Tirol, and the latter took the larger share of this ample Alpine county, keeping the title of count. So Gebhard IV was known as "lord of the Inn valley," his portion including the country from Landeck down to Innsbruck, the lucrative route over the Brenner Pass, and the cathedral advocacy of Brixen.[34]

Although this inheritance provided valuable revenues to Count Gebhard and his son, they were not able to exploit its political possibilities on the spot. The initiative passed to Count Meinhard II of Görz and Tirol (1258–1295) who resided in the county. In the 1280s he persuaded Count Gebhard V to give up all his rights in exchange for a substantial cash payment.[35] In any case the Görz claims were much stronger, since Elizabeth of Tirol had died childless in 1256 and Gebhard V was the offspring of his father's subsequent marriage to Sophia of Bavaria. Like the bishops of Eichstätt, Count Gebhard IV's household and estates were administered by *ministeriales* who were the appointed officials: the Gerhard and Gebhard who were in evidence as the comital chamberlains,[36] the seneschals Frederick of Sulzbach and Henry of Dollnstein,[37] and Albert and Berthold, butlers of Töging.[38] By the 1270s new *ministeriales* had been appointed butlers, Henry of Hofstetten and Godfrey of Altenburg and Flügelsberg.[39]

\*    \*    \*

Beyond the diocesan core occupied by Eichstätt and Hirschberg, the princes most closely involved in the politics of the region were the counts of Oettingen, the burgraves of Nuremberg, and the dukes of Upper Bavaria.[40] In the city of Nuremberg itself, just beyond the diocesan border to the north, the authority of the burgraves was in decline, outfaced by the city council, which gained its autonomy in 1219 and was to become one of the great urban powers in the Empire during the course of the thirteenth and fourteenth centuries.[41] But as a rural authority the burgravial dynasty made huge gains between 1248 and 1263 as principal heirs of the Andechs dukes of Merania, the best part of whose enormous estates in the dioceses of Würzburg, Bamberg, and Regensburg they were able to secure after a severe feud with the bishops of Bamberg.[42] The Andechs-Merania inheritance saved the burgraves from the townsmen bent upon expelling them from Nuremberg Castle. In 1273 King Rudolf I confirmed their burgravial title with the *Landgericht,* or regional magistracy, of Nuremberg, which completely surrounded the city.[43] The burgraves and some of their knights were associated with the bishopric of Eichstätt as its feoffees,[44] but the princes poised for making the greatest gains in the diocese, on the basis of their close relationship with the imperial dynasty, were the dukes of Bavaria. As an indication of their growing interest in this region, they married off their younger sister Sophia to Gebhard IV of Hirschberg, recently a childless widower, in 1257 or 1258.

During the reign of King Conrad IV (1237–1254), the German crown was still operating as an effective landowner in the Eichstätt region through its feoffees, the imperial *ministeriales*.[45] The marshals of Pappenheim administered Weissenburg im Sand with its attendant manors, castles, and forest. The imperial butler Walter of Klingenberg was the most substantial of the knightly vassals of the crown through his marriage to the heiress Elizabeth of Königstein, whose parents had founded an important reformist nunnery at Engelthal in 1240.[46] Henry of Hilpoltstein, another prominent imperial *ministerialis,* divided authority with the burgraves of Nuremberg in that he administered the royal estates attached to the castle of Nuremberg as their *buticularius,*[47] this title apparently being a variant upon *pincerna,* for butler, as one of the imperial household offices. Comparable with these three families were the *ministeriales* of Sulzbürg, founders of Seligenporten Abbey early in the 1240s,[48] and owners of several castles.[49] Apart from the offices, castles, and woodlands they held from the crown, the authority of these *ministeriales* can be gauged from their own substantial retinues of knights holding fiefs and fortifications.

According to the Neuburg cadastral survey of the 1220s, the marshals of Pappenheim had over seventy vassals on both sides of the Danube,[50] but only a few were knights and of these the majority were *ministeriales* owing primary allegiance to other lords. Sources a generation later show up about twenty families of Pappenheim knights and castellans identifiable by toponymics.[51] Apart from the extensive Königstein lands that Walter of Klingenberg took over in right of his wife in the 1250s, he or his sons Conrad and Walter, who entitled themselves butlers of Reicheneck,[52] also renewed the extensive Eichstätt fiefs that Ulrich of Königstein had held as rear tenant of the counts of Hirschberg.[53] This relationship stemmed from the proximity of Reicheneck, Königstein, and Engelthal to the Hirschberg dominion of Sulzbach. Like the marshals of Pappenheim, Walter of Klingenberg appears to have had about twenty knights in his retinue.[54]

At the time that the imperial *buticularius* Henry of Hilpoltstein retired from Nuremberg in the mid-1260s, his military retinue of this type[55] was considerably smaller than that of his immediate neighbors, the *ministeriales* of Sulzbürg. However, the Sulzbürg brothers Godfrey and Conrad[56] had recently partitioned their resources, and since Henry arranged for his two youngest sons to marry Conrad's joint heiresses, the Hilpoltsteins acquired several families of Sulzbürg knights for their retinue.[57] Godfrey's sons Ulrich of Sulzbürg and Godfrey of Wolfstein[58] retained about ten remaining families identifiable by toponymics.[59] Although it may be stating the obvious, it should be pointed out that since these knights and castellans were the rear tenants of men who themselves were possessed by the crown, the families pertaining to these imperial *ministeriales* were ipso facto of servile legal status.

The military and fiscal resources of the crown that might have been drawn from the diocese of Eichstätt were therefore not negligible, had it proved possible to mobilize them effectively for the defense of the imperial dynasty against the papacy and its supporters in the 1240s and 1250s. When Frederick II fell out with the pope in 1239, the towns of Nuremberg, Weissenburg, and Greding, the latter a royal fief held by the counts of Hirschberg, raised forces that were sent to the emperor's assistance in Italy. In 1240 Pope Gregory IX therefore instructed Bishop Frederick II of Eichstätt to excommunicate these places.[60]

The following year Weissenburg was assessed in the great tax round by which Conrad IV intended to place the Staufen cause upon a sound war footing.[61] But not long after this, the serious divisions revealed in Germany by the elections of anti-kings in 1246 and 1247 also began to surface in the diocese of Eichstätt. When Bishop Frederick II died in 1247 his pro-papal metropolitan, Archbishop Siegfried III of Mainz, and the papal legate in Germany installed, as we have seen, Bishop Henry IV (1247–1259),[62] a scion of the counts of Württemberg who were among the party of Swabian princes supporting the anti-king, Henry Raspe of Thuringia. With some success the new bishop began the work of converting his diocese away from its strongly imperialist tradition. By 1249 Count Gebhard IV of Hirschberg had temporarily entered the papal camp,[63] and what was worse, Godfrey of Sulzbürg had backed King Henry Raspe from the start.[64] Godfrey then persuaded the butler of Klingenberg to betroth his infant daughter to the Sulzbürg heir Ulrich. But this turned out to be the limit of a pro-papal party. Walter of Klingenberg changed his mind and returned to the Staufen cause "like a dog to its vomit," as the pope noted with disgust to Bishop Henry IV.[65]

The see's continued prostration after the treaty of Eichstätt in 1245 ensured that Bishop Henry could not do much to assist the papal party in a realistic fashion. In any case, the predatory attention of Duke Otto II of Bavaria was focused upon the Eichstätt region in 1246, the very year in which he became the mainstay of the Staufen party in Germany by marrying his elder daughter Elizabeth to Conrad IV. The duke was roused to action by the following circumstances. Ever since 1208 the Wittelsbachs had been at enmity with the powerful Bavarian dynasty of Andechs, whose secular titles included duke of Merania, count-palatine of Burgundy, and margrave of Istria.[66] When Duke Otto VIII of Merania (1234–1248) was casting around for allies against Duke Otto II, he attracted to his cause Marshal Henry of Pappenheim, who felt that a threat to his lands and advocacies south of the Danube lay in the proximity of ducal Bavaria's increasing political authority. This alliance turned out to be a great mistake. Duke Otto VIII and Marshal Henry were defeated on their campaign of 1246 to 1247; the duke fled to Franconia where he died childless in 1248; and Henry of Pappenheim disappeared into the duke of Bavaria's custody.[67] Conrad IV could do nothing for the marshal, although he was a Staufen vassal. The Pappenheim possessions had to be abandoned to the revenge of Conrad's new father-in-law. The fortress and advocacy of Neuburg were handed over to Otto II; the Pappenheim estates were ravaged; and the valuable manor and castle of Gaimersheim were transferred to the Wittelsbachs.[68]

After the fall of Henry of Pappenheim, Conrad IV and the duke of Bavaria did not consider the pro-papal stance of Eichstätt to be a threat sufficient to warrant any further military operations in that region. However, one consequence of the Staufen-Wittelsbach alliance of 1246 was Conrad IV's increasing reliance upon the Bavarian dukes as a source of supply, and the use of the remaining imperial lands north of the Danube as surety. After the king's death in 1254 the dukes continued as the principal supporters of their nephew Conradin, who declared them his rightful heirs in 1263 and again in 1266.[69] The results of this were made plain after Conradin's fatal expedition to Italy in 1268, when dukes Louis II and Henry XIII claimed the reversion of all their nephew's lands that they were near enough to occupy.[70] Thus they effectively replaced the crown as the greatest landowner adjacent to the possessions of the bishops of Eichstätt and the counts of Hirschberg. The process of ducal penetration into the Eichstätt region began with the punishment of the Pappenheims; made headway through Conrad IV's marriage to Elizabeth of Bavaria; and resulted in the transfer of the Staufen lands in 1269. This was confirmed by their other brother-in-law Count Gebhard IV of Hirschberg,[71] who had given up his pro-papal attitude long before his marriage to Sophia of Bavaria in 1257 or 1258.

Apparently neither Count Gebhard nor Bishop Hildebrand of Eichstätt, who had succeeded in 1261, regarded the occupation of these crown lands by Bavaria with any sense of disquiet. The north bank of the Danube was secured to the dukes by the fortress of Ingolstadt; the seizure of Neuburg from the marshals of Pappenheim; and the acquisition of Donauwörth from Conradin. Their chief gain in the diocese of Eichstätt itself was the large imperial *officium,* or district, of Neumarkt, the principal town with its manors on the main road from Nuremberg to Regensburg.[72] This huge estate set the term to Eichstätt's and Hirschberg's possessions in the east and north of the diocese. Similar gains centered upon the town of Amberg virtually encircled the Hirschberg dominion of Sulzbach, while Lauf and Hersbruck brought Duke Louis II within striking distance of Nuremberg itself.[73]

The relatively peaceful advance of the Wittelsbachs is indicated by the fiefs that the dukes of Upper Bavaria were willingly granted by the bishops of Eichstätt, and by the enfeoffment of about forty of their knights by the bishops toward the end of the thirteenth century.[74] The dukes, however, still bore a grudge against the marshals of Pappenheim. As soon as Conradin had left for Italy, they ravaged the Pappenheim lands, burned down Weissenburg im Sand,[75] and seized the marshals' castles of Druisheim and Donnsberg. This was uncharacteristic of Duke Louis II's attitude toward the imperial *ministeriales,* whose allegiance he was seeking as vassals of Bavaria in addition to their connection to the Empire. In a moment of doubt that occurred to him in 1276, "since the days of man are short," he ordered the castles to be returned to the marshals.[76] But this instruction was not carried out. In any case the marshals, abandoned by Conrad IV and ruined by the Wittelsbachs, were finished as a significant force in regional politics. The brothers Henry and Hildebrand of Pappenheim acrimoniously divided their remaining lands, castles, and retinue in 1279,[77] Hildebrand taking Biberbach Castle and the depleted lands south of the Danube, Henry keeping Pappenheim and the advocacy of Weissenburg. The latter office was lost to this branch before the end of the thirteenth century, probably confiscated by King Rudolf I. It was transferred to the *Landvogtei,* or advocacy, of Nuremberg, and then pledged to the counts of Oettingen by 1300.[78]

The dominion of Pappenheim itself survived as an autonomous territorial fragment, and in 1356 Charles IV's Golden Bull on imperial elections confirmed the family in their hereditary title of marshals of the Empire.[79] In keeping with their increasing stranglehold upon the crown's resources as the price of support for Conrad IV and Conradin, the Bavarian dukes were also interested in gaining the fealty of the imperial *ministeriales*. This was not in question for the marshals of Pappenheim who were their foes or the *ministeriales* of Sulzbürg who were papalists. The Rindsmauls, however, acknowledged their castles of Grünsberg and Schönberg as ducal fiefs in 1255 and 1274, respectively.[80] In 1276 the *ministeriales* of Stauf also turned their castle, with King Rudolf's consent, into a fief from Duke Louis II.[81]

*   *   *

Although it seems clear that by the 1270s the German crown had little future as a significant landowner in the Eichstätt region, this was found hard to accept by the successive incumbents of the German throne until Duke Louis IV of Bavaria squared the circle by himself securing the royal title in 1314. Although King Rudolf I was obliged to confirm Bavaria's right to Conradin's inheritance in 1274,[82] the crown was not entirely shorn of possessions. The marshals of Pappenheim were still advocates of Weissenburg, and the office of *buticularius* still existed at Nuremberg for the fisc in the vicinity of the town. Unfortunately for the king, it was necessary to confirm the right of the burgraves to the *Landgericht,* or the regional magistracy, of Nuremberg as well as to the extensive *officium de foresto,* or group of woodlands, all around, and to other fiefs.[83] Not much was left for the *buticularius,* but the office continued to function until 1298.[84]

The resumptions that King Rudolf favored therefore had to await a new political opportunity, and this occurred under his son, Albert I (1298–1308).[85] It was provided by Duke Rudolf I of Upper Bavaria (1294–1317) who imprudently supported Adolf of Nassau (1292–1298) as king.[86] When the latter was defeated and killed, Albert I confiscated much of Duke Rudolf's property and appointed a new official at Nuremberg to reactivate crown rights to the fisc. This was the Swabian *ministerialis* Dietegen of Kastel, with the title of *Landvogt,* or advocate, of Nuremberg.[87] At about this time a land register, the *Reichssalbüchlein* of Nuremberg, was drawn up in order to show what ought by right to belong to the crown.[88] It is an impressive list of property stretching from Donauwörth in Swabia, recently burned out as a punishment to Duke Rudolf, over to the Egerland in the east, enfeoffed to the king of Bohemia, and mentions the places such as Neumarkt, Amberg, and Hersbruck recently surrendered by Duke Rudolf I.

The *Reichssalbüchlein* bears comparison with the twelfth-century list of royal *curiae,* or manors, known as the king of the Romans' *Tafelgüterverzeichnis,*[89] which records Nuremberg, Weissenburg, Greding, Neuburg on the Danube, and Neumarkt *cum mille mansis,* "with a thousand homesteads," among the Bavarian properties of the crown. So the titles recorded in the *Reichssalbüchlein* had the long tradition of the fisc behind them, but the problem for Dietegen of Kastel as *Landvogt* was the rights of the feoffees. Nuremberg, as we have seen, was principally under the control of the town council and the burgraves, although it did provide generous annual cash subsidies to the crown from the citizens, the mint, and the Jews. Apart from much other property pledged to the burgraves,[90] Weissenburg with its *officium* and forest had been pledged to the counts of Oettingen, and Greding with its woodland was enfeoffed hereditarily to Count Gebhard V of Hirschberg. Furthermore, by no means all the Bavarian gains of 1269 could be taken back, and are listed in the *Reichssalbüchlein* as ducal fiefs. The reason for this is that in 1294 Duke Rudolf I was joint heir to Upper Bavaria with his younger brother Louis IV,[91] whose rights were to be preserved because his household had supported Albert I, not Adolf of Nassau.

The effectiveness of the policy of resumption in the Nuremberg *Landvogtei* was therefore called into question by these restrictions and exemptions. The test case was provided by Greding, which Dietegen of Kastel claimed for the crown when Gebhard V of Hirschberg died childless in 1305. This valuable estate had apparently been enfeoffed to his ancestors late in the twelfth century, but the church of Eichstätt put in a counter claim on the basis of Henry IV's authentic gift of this *predium,* or property, to the bishop in 1091.[92] King Albert prevaricated. It was advisable to reward the allegiance of Eichstätt, so Dietegen of Kastel was promoted to the *Landvogtei* of Swabia and the bishop was awarded some villages and manorial jurisdictions while the main case was pending.[93] The new *Landvogt* of Nuremberg, the imperial *ministerialis* and *magister coquinae* (master of the king's kitchen) Henry of Nordenberg, who was also a vassal of Eichstätt,[94] was permitted to make further concessions to the bishop.[95] The next king, Henry VII (1308–1313), regarded the conciliation of princes in this part of Germany to be more desirable than the recuperation of lands listed in the Nuremberg *Reichssalbüchlein.* Neumarkt and other properties were restored to Dukes Rudolf I and Louis IV; Greding was abandoned to

Bishop Philip of Eichstätt in 1311; and the Nuremberg *Landvogtei* was deprived of any further effective power.[96]

The *Reichssalbüchlein* of Nuremberg also reveals that the imperial butlers of Reicheneck, the descendants of Walter of Klingenberg and Elizabeth of Königstein, had tenaciously maintained their advocacy over crown property,[97] just as the marshals of Pappenheim had clung to their rightful administration of Weissenburg until quite late in the thirteenth century. But although they were quite powerful in castles and retinues, the imperial *ministeriales* were not up to the task of preserving the Staufen fisc. Undoubtedly they desired to usurp crown resources for their own advantage, but the main reason was the disappearance of a prestigious royal court once Conrad IV began to lose the struggle against the papal party in Germany in the mid-1240s.

In the Eichstätt region there were object lessons that cannot have inspired much confidence in the imperial *ministeriales* as to their future function as royal agents. Conrad IV was obliged to drop the Pappenheims in 1246 and to accept the loss of Neuburg on the Danube; the deliberate destruction of Weissenburg by fire in 1268 went unpunished; and part of King Rudolf I's election settlement constrained him in 1273 and 1274 to recognize the huge gains made by the dukes of Bavaria and the burgraves of Nuremberg at the expense of the fisc. It is not therefore surprising to find imperial *ministeriales* turning to multiple vassalage and accepting service under the bishops of Eichstätt and the counts of Hirschberg and Oettingen, as well as the burgraves and dukes. Nevertheless, they were shrewd and tenacious men with a strong sense of their dignity and esprit de corps as "*ministeriales* of the imperial court,"[98] and eluded direct submission under the territorial jurisdiction of the princes. The man most aware of the need for solidarity among imperial knights was Henry of Hilpoltstein who had been the *buticularius* of Nuremberg in the 1250s and 1260s,[99] as we have seen, and was therefore as well informed as anyone about the real eclipse of crown rights in Franconia and Bavaria.

Hilpoltstein was by no means a poor dominion.[100] Its resources were improved by the foundation of a new town, Freystadt, "upon our own ground," or "in proprio fundo nostro,"[101] and a number of knights were enfeoffed around Hilpoltstein and acted as castellans there.[102] The ex-*buticularius* also assembled four heiresses from among the adjacent imperial *ministeriales* to improve the standing of his house. By 1260 his son Hermann had married the daughter of Walter of Klingenberg and Elizabeth of Königstein,[103] and they were endowed with the castle of Breitenstein next door to Königstein. Hermann was therefore brother-in-law of the butlers of Reicheneck, and featured in the *Reichssalbüchlein* as a partner in the Reicheneck advocacies.[104] Next, Hermann's brother Henry was married to the heiress of Haimburg,[105] a castle defended by her father in 1247 from siege by the party of King Henry Raspe.[106] About 1265 their younger brothers Hilpolt and Henry were married to Petrissa and Adelheid of Sulzbürg, from the notable family of imperial *ministeriales* who were the immediate neighbors of Hilpoltstein.[107]

This was an attractive bargain because the castles, estates, and retinue had already been partitioned in the previous generation, so that Hilpolt and Henry came into half the Sulzbürg possessions in right of their wives and this included the main *castrum Solzburch* under the command of six castellans.[108] All four brothers adopted their wives' toponymics, and in the same year that the marshals of Pappenheim decided to divide their dominions, Henry of Hilpoltstein summoned his sons back to their home *aput Lapidem in castro*, "at Stein in the castle," to dispose of his assets before retiring upon a final penitential pilgrimage to Rome: "With the unanimous consent of my sons Henry of Haimburg, Hermann of Breitenstein, Henry and Hilpolt of Sulzbürg and with previous and proper deliberation, I give and bequeath freely and absolutely [manors to the Church] for the salvation of my soul and to recompense those I have injured."[109] The deed was appropriately dated to the feast of St. Paul's conversion, and his grandsons Henry of Haimburg and Henry of Breitenstein came forward as witnesses, possibly to impress the senior and better endowed lines that the original Hilpoltstein dominion was to go to the younger brothers called of Sulzbürg. The prudence of Henry *senior de Lapide*, "lord of Stein" as he was addressed in this source, had thus used the politics of marriage to elevate his family more or less to the eminence of the crown's household officers in the region, the butlers of Reicheneck and the marshals of Pappenheim. His sons' descendants were prominent enough to command prestigious careers in the Empire under Louis IV the Bavarian.

Once the Bavarian dukes had, by the 1270s, made such significant territorial advances north of the Danube, the possible resumption of crown lands proved to be an unfounded fancy. The dukes were enriched by their Staufen inheritance (1251–1269); the burgraves of Nuremberg by their share of the Andechs-Merania inheritance (1248–1263) and their gains from the royal fisc confirmed in 1273; and the counts of Hirschberg by the successful outcome of their feud with Eichstätt in 1245, and by the accession of revenues from their Sulzbach and Tirol inheritances. The lesser feoffees of

Eichstätt, the counts of Oettingen, Graisbach, and Hohentrüdingen, were also able to hold their own in the mid-thirteenth century, as we shall see in Chapter 7.

The bishops of Eichstätt, however, appeared to have the most meager future in terms of political authority based upon landowning. It was unfortunate for Eichstätt that the regional authority of the neighboring princes was enhanced by the eclipse of the Staufen dynasty, not because they usurped royal powers, but because they could acquire reasonably effective title to handsome portions of its fisc, which Eichstätt was unable to do until as late as 1311. Apart from the abasement of the Pappenheims, all this had proceeded in a relatively orderly fashion, punctuated by war with Duke Rudolf I of Bavaria from 1299 to 1301.

In spite of this contretemps, the lion's share still went to the Wittelsbachs, not only because they were so closely related to Conrad IV and Conradin, but also because they were actually stronger than possible competitors, the burgraves of Nuremberg and the dukes of Merania as well as the bishops of Bamberg and the crown officials at Nuremberg, ever since they began in the 1190s to consolidate their ducal jurisdiction and territorial authority by means of a remarkable series of comital inheritances all over Bavaria.[110] Towns, imperial *ministeriales,* and churches did not do nearly so well out of the scramble for the imperial fisc. Even the autonomy of Nuremberg, which had not yet acquired its later territorial glacis,[111] was still quite seriously at risk from the burgraves and the dukes in the thirteenth and fourteenth centuries, finally expelling the former in 1427. The obscurity of Eichstätt seems to have been taken for granted after 1245, although the bishops did not lose sight of their prestigious title of chancellor of the see of Mainz.[112] Then, about 1280, the regime of prudent management began to pay; the secular princes ran into financial crises; and Bishops Reinboto (1279–1297) and Conrad II (1297–1305) were able to redesign their see as a formidable principality on the Bavarian border. In these two churchmen we will again discern dominant personalities whose talent and enterprise in the political sphere were matched by their administrative initiative and expertise in secular as well as ecclesiastical affairs.

*Notes*

1. A. Hilka, *Die Wundergeschichten des Caesarius von Heisterbach,* vol. I, Publikationen der Gesellschaft für rheinische Geschichte, vol. XLIII (Bonn, 1933),

p. 127: "Duplicem habent gladium pene omnes episcopi Alemannie, unde et magnus eis timor incumbit."

2. *Gesta episcoporum Traiectensium,* MGH Scriptores, vol. XXIII, pp. 413–15.

3. *Gesta archiepiscoporum Magdeburgensium,* MGH Scriptores, vol. XIV, p. 422.

4. *Ellenhardi bellum Waltherianum,* MGH Scriptores, vol. XVII, pp. 105–14; A. Hessel, "Die Beziehungen der Strassburger Bischöfe zum Kaisertum und zur Stadtgemeinde in der ersten Hälfte des 13. Jahrhunderts," *Archiv für Urkundenforschung* 6 (1916–1918): 266–75.

5. *Gestorum abbatum Trudonensium continuatio tertia,* MGH Scriptores, vol. X, p. 405. Most of the papers in *BDLG* 124 (1988) are devoted to the Battle of Worringen, its causes, and aftermath, and are published simultaneously as *Mitteilungen aus dem Stadtarchiv Köln* 72 (1988) and by W. Janssen and H. Stehkämper (eds.), *Der Tag bei Worringen, 5. Juni 1288,* Veröffentlichungen der staatlichen Archive des Landes Nordrhein-Westfalen, series C, Quellen und Forschungen, vol. XXVII (Düsseldorf, 1988). On this period and the event, see also F.-R. Erkens, *Siegfried von Westerburg (1274–1297). Die Reichs- und Territorialpolitik eines Kölner Erzbischofs im ausgehenden 13. Jahrhundert,* Rheinisches Archiv, vol. CXIV (Bonn, 1982), pp. 180–259.

6. *Chounradi Schirensis Chronicon,* MGH Scriptores, vol. XVII, p. 621.

7. See Chapter 7.

8. *Reg. Eichst.,* no. 746, pp. 229–32.

9. Ibid., no. 791, p. 247; no. 804, pp. 250f.

10. E.g., Bayr. Hsta. München, Kl. Kaisheim, 283 (1288).

11. MB, vol. XLIX, no. 55, p. 97.

12. Ibid., no. 50, p. 92 (1248), and *Reg. Eichst.,* no. 769, p. 239 (1253).

13. MB, vol. XLIX, no. 49, p. 91 (1248); and A. Weissthanner, *Die Traditionen des Klosters Schäftlarn 760–1305,* Quellen und Erörterungen zur bayerischen Geschichte, new ser., vol. X, part 1 (Munich, 1953), no. 439 A, p. 428 (1263).

14. MB, vol. XLIX, no. 50, p. 92 (1248); *Reg. Eichst.,* no. 769, p. 239 (1253); Bayr. Hsta. München, Ritterorden 1291 (1273).

15. MB, vol. XLIX, no. 50, p. 92 (1248); no. 99, p. 150 (1278); no. 118, pp. 181f. (1282).

16. Ibid., no. 52, p. 94.

17. Ibid., no. 66, pp. 109–11 (1259).

18. Ibid., no. 65, pp. 108f. (1256).

19. Ibid., no. 80, pp. 124–26.

20. *Reg. Eichst.,* no. 754, p. 234 and *Nürnberger Urkundenbuch,* no. 339, p. 205.

21. MB, vol. XLIX, no. 68, p. 112.

22. Ibid., no. 72, pp. 114f.

23. Ibid., no. 73, pp. 116f. (1264).

24. Ibid., no. 81, pp. 126–28.

25. Ibid., no. 87, p. 134 (1269); no. 96, p. 146 (1276); no. 100, pp. 151f. (1279).

26. Ibid., no. 86, pp. 132f. (1269); no. 95, p. 145 (1275); see also ES ff. 37r and 43r.

27. E. Klebel, "Eichstätt und Herrieden im Osten," *JFLF* 14 (1954): 87–95.

28. *Reg. Eichst.*, no. 297, p. 97 (before 1112).

29. See H. Koller, "Bamberg und Villach," in A. Haidacher and H. E. Mayer (eds.), *Festschrift Karl Pivec zum 60. Geburtstag gewidmet,* Innsbrucker Beiträge zur Kulturwissenschaft, vol. XII (Innsbruck, 1966), pp. 223–33.

30. EL f. 2r.

31. MB, vol. XLIX, no. 54, p. 96 (1250); no. 75, p. 119 (1264); no. 92, pp. 142f. (1272). For the Alpine possessions, see also nos. 128f., pp. 196–98 (1282); no. 205, pp. 319f. (before 1295); no. 217, pp. 333f. (1295); properties at Pinzagen near Brixen.

32. EL f. 3v.

33. MB, vol. XLIX, no. 58, pp. 100f. (1253).

34. Wiesflecker, *Meinhard der Zweite,* p. 30, and *Reg. Eichst.,* no. 838, p. 261 (1267), where Gebhard's title is given as "dei gratia comes de Hirzberc advocatus Brixie et Aistetensis."

35. Wiesflecker, *Meinhard der Zweite,* pp. 99f., and *Reg. Eichst.,* no. 947, p. 293 (1282).

36. MB, vol. XLIX, no. 64, p. 107 (1256); Bayr. Hsta. München, Ritterorden 1291 (1273).

37. MB, vol. XLIX, no. 58, p. 100 (1253); no. 60, p. 103 (1254); no. 64, p. 107 (1256).

38. Ibid., no. 46, p. 85 (1245), and no. 58, p. 100 (1253).

39. Bayr. Hsta. München, Kl. Rebdorf 26f. (1270–1278) and Kl. Bergen 2 (1273).

40. For the Oettingen, see Chapter 7. Bavaria was divided into two, an upper and a lower duchy, in 1255: M. Spindler, "Die erste Teilung des Landes (1255) unter Ludwig II. (1253–1294) und Heinrich XIII. (1253–1290)," in HBG ii, pp. 69–72.

41. B. Diestelkamp, "Quellensammlung zur frühgeschichte der deutschen Stadt," in C. van de Kieft and J. F. Niermeijer (eds.), *Elenchus fontium historiae urbanae. Acta collegii historiae urbanae societatis historicum internationalis,* vol. I (Leiden, 1967), no. 124, pp. 197f., and *Nürnberger Urkundenbuch* 178, pp. 111–14 (1219); Dannenbauer, *Entstehung;* W. Schultheiss, "Nürnberg," in HRG iii, cols. 1114–19; E. Schremmer, "Die Wirtschaftsmetropole Nürnberg," in HBG iii, pp. 478–97; H. H. Hofmann, "Nobiles Norimbergenses. Beobachtungen zur Struktur der reichsstädtischen Oberschicht," in T. Mayer (ed.), *Untersuchungen zur gesellschaftlichen Struktur der mittelalterlichen Städte in Europa,* VF, vol. XI (Constance and Stuttgart, 1966), pp. 53–92; E. Pitz, *Die Entstehung der Ratsherrschaft in Nürnberg im 13. und 14. Jahrhundert,* Schriftenreihe zur bayerischen Landesgeschichte, vol. LV (Munich, 1956); G. Pfeiffer, "Die Offenhäuser der Reichsstadt Nürnberg," *JFLF* 14 (1954): 153–79; A. Schlunk, "Stadt ohne Bürger? Eine Untersuchung über die Führungsschichten der Städte Nürnberg, Altenburg und Frankfurt um die Mitte des 13. Jahrhunderts," in U. Bestmann, F. Irsigler, and J. Schneider (eds.), *Hochfinanz, Wirtschaftsräume, Innovationen. Festschrift für Wolfgang von Stromer,* vol. I (Trier, 1987), pp. 189–243.

42. On this period and its background in Franconia, see F.-J. Schmale, "Das staufische Jahrhundert in Franken," in HBG iii, pp. 72–92.

43. MGH Consts. iii, no. 17, pp. 20f., confirmed in no. 286, pp. 291f. (1281); see G. Pfeiffer, "Comicia burcgravie in Nurenberg," *JFLF* 11–12 (1953): 45–52.

44. EL ff. 3v–4r, 41v–43r.

45. For evidence of crown property, Heinloth, *Neumarkt,* pp. 31–51; Wiessner, *Hilpoltstein,* pp. 42–50; Schlunk, *Königsmacht,* pp. 51–58.

46. H. Grundmann, *Religiöse Bewegungen im Mittelalter. Untersuchungen über die geschichtlichen Zusammenhänge zwischen der Ketzerei, den Bettelorden und der religiösen Frauenbewegungen im 12. und 13. Jahrhundert,* Historische Studien, vol. CCLXVII, new ed. (Darmstadt, 1970), pp. 223–28; *Reg. Eichst.,* no. 730, p. 224; *Nürnberger Urkundenbuch,* no. 295, pp. 173–76 (1240). The family relationship is explained ibid., no. 319, p. 194 (1244): Ulrich of Königstein's "uxor mea" Adelheid, Elizabeth "unica filia mea," Walter "maritus prefate filie mee."

47. Dannenbauer, *Entstehung,* pp. 92f.; see *Nürnberger Urkundenbuch,* no. 352, p. 214 (1254); no. 376, p. 229 (1258); no. 415, p. 255, and no. 420, pp. 258f. (1266); see J. F. Niermeyer, *Mediae latinitatis lexicon minus* (Leiden, 1954–1976), p. 110, on the origins of *buticularius* as a court office. See also the duke of Merania's *putegelaer* Hermann in W. Schlögl, *Die Traditionen und Urkunden des Stiftes Diessen 1114–1362,* Quellen und Erörterungen zur bayerischen Geschichte, new ser., vol. XXII, part 1 (Munich, 1967), no. 36 A, pp. 48–51 (1231), and the Nuremberg *Buttigularius* in P. Zinsmaier, "Ungedruckte Stauferurkunden des 13. Jahrhunderts," *MIöG* 45 (1931): 203. On the Hilpoltstein family, see Wiessner, *Hilpoltstein,* pp. 55–78.

48. See *Reg. Eichst.,* no. 754, p. 234 (1249), for confirmation by its diocesan, Bishop Henry IV of Eichstätt; also Heinloth, *Neumarkt,* pp. 136–46.

49. Schuhmann and Hirschmann, *Urkundenregesten . . . Heilsbronn,* no. 98, pp. 53f. (1256), on Bürglein; and the castellans there in *Nürnberger Urkundenbuch,* no. 410, pp. 251f. (1265).

50. Kraft, *Urbar,* pp. 85–91, 135–37.

51. Bayr. Hsta. München, Ritterorden 1272f. (1250); ibid. 1916 (1253); ibid. 1920 (1255); ibid. 1295 (1276); Kl. St. Walburg in Eichstätt, 7 (1259); Hoffmann, *Urkunden . . . Kaisheim,* no. 87, pp. 61f. (1240); no. 121, p. 80 (1251); no. 127, p. 83 (1254); no. 142, pp. 91f. (1256); no. 165, pp. 103f. (1261); K. Puchner, *Die Urkunden des Klosters Oberschönenfeld,* Schwäbische Forschungsgemeinschaft bei der Kommission für bayerische Landesgeschichte, ser. 2 A, vol. II (Augsburg, 1953), no. 9, p. 4 (1256); EL ff. 58v–59r.

52. The castle was up by 1229 and the toponymic was already used by their grandfather, Ulrich of Königstein; see *Nürnberger Urkundenbuch,* no. 288, p. 170 (1238), and no. 332, p. 201 (1246). For Conrad and Walter, see ibid., no. 705/1, p. 414, (1286), and no. 822/1, p. 489 (1290–1291).

53. EL ff. 9r, 64v–65r; Ulrich of Königstein died in the 1250s, and the survival of his toponymic indicates the use of some earlier list of fiefs in assembling EL, where the name Reicheneck, which is actually contemporary with the text (1305–1320), is used at ff. 8v, 60r.

54. Bayr. Hsta. München, Kl. Kastl 15 (c. 1230); ibid. 18f. (1252–1253); ibid. 21 (1262), and Reichsstadt Nürnberg 29 (1260); *Nürnberger Urkundenbuch,* no. 288, p. 170 (1238); no. 317 A/B, p. 193 (1243); no. 409, p. 251 (1265); *Reg. Eichst.,* no. 729, p. 223 (1244); MB, vol. XLIX, no. 58, pp. 101f. (1253) and no. 76, p. 121 (1264).

55. Bayr. Hsta. München, Kl. Seligenporten 8 (1260), Ritterorden 1282 (1269), 1294 (1275); *Nürnberger Urkundenbuch,* no. 399, p. 243 (1263); no. 402, pp. 244f. (1264); no. 420, p. 259 (1266).

56. Godfrey and Conrad had long careers (e.g., Godfrey attested in Schuhmann and Hirschmann, *Urkundenregesten* . . . *Heilsbronn*, no. 45, p. 29 [1218], and Conrad in Wittmann, *Mon. Wittelsb.*, vol. I, no. 9, p. 28 [1224]). Conrad married the heiress of Bürglein, after which he was also called; *Nürnberger Urkundenbuch*, no. 420, p. 259 (1266).

57. Ibid. no. 410, p. 252 (1265) and no. 433, p. 267 (1268); Bayr. Hsta. München, Ritterorden 1282 (1269); EL ff. 56r–v, 58r.

58. Ulrich inherited *Obersoltzpurch* (as in *Nürnberger Urkundenbuch*, no. 742, pp. 432f. [1286]); Godfrey rebuilt Wolfstein as his residence (as in ibid., no. 677, pp. 397f. [1283]).

59. Ibid. no. 433, p. 267 (1268); no. 464, p. 288 (1274); no. 739, p. 432 (1286); MB, vol. XLIX, no. 87, p. 134 (1269); *Reg. Eichst.*, no. 837, p. 261 (1267); Bayr. Hsta. München, Kl. Seligenporten 34f. (1286), 58 (1294).

60. *Reg. Eichst.*, no. 709, p. 217.

61. MGH Consts. iii, pp. 1–6; Metz, *Staufische Güterverzeichnisse*, pp. 98–115; G. Kirchner, "Die Steuerliste von 1241. Ein Beitrag zur Entstehung des staufischen Königsterritoriums," *ZRGGA* 70 (1953): 64–104; A. Dreher, "Über die Herkunft zweier Güterverzeichnisse der späteren Stauferzeit," *Zeitschrift für württembergische Landesgeschichte* 29 (1970): 321–25.

62. *Reg. Eichst.*, no. 746, pp. 229–32.

63. Ibid., no. 758, p. 236.

64. He was rewarded in 1247; *Nürnberger Urkundenbuch*, no. 335, p. 203, confirmed in MB, vol. XXX/A, no. 797, p. 323 (1255).

65. *Reg. Eichst.*, no. 773, pp. 240f. (1254).

66. For this family see K. Bosl, "Europäischer Adel im 12.–13. Jahrhundert. Die internationalen Verflechtungen des bayerischen Hochadelsgeschlechtes der Andechs-Meranier," *ZBLG* 30 (1967): 20–52.

67. M. Spindler, "Das Ende der grossen Geschlechter," in HBG ii, pp. 44f.; Metz, *Staufische Güterverzeichnisse*, pp. 92f.

68. On the rise of the Wittelsbachs in the thirteenth century, see especially Spindler, *Anfänge*, pp. 14–182, and "Grundlegung und Aufbau (1180–1314)," parts 1 to 3, in HBG ii, pp. 7–103; P. Fried, "Verfassungsgeschichte und Landesgeschichtsforschung in Bayern. Probleme und Wege der Forschung," in Bosl (ed.), *Zur Geschichte der Bayern*, pp. 528–64; A. Kraus, "Das Herzogtum," in Glaser (ed.), *Zeit*, pp. 165–200; see also H. Patze, "Die Wittelsbacher in der mittelalterlichen Politik Europas," *ZBLG* 44 (1981): 33–79, and J.-M. Moeglin, "Die Genealogie der Wittelsbacher: Politische Propaganda und Entstehung der territorialen Geschichtsschreibung in Bayern im Mittelalter," *MIöG* 96 (1988): 33–54, and his *Les Ancêtres du prince. Propagande politique et naissance d'une histoire nationale en Bavière au moyen âge (1180–1500)*, École Pratique des Hautes Études, series 5, Études médiévales et modernes, vol. LIV (Geneva, 1985), pp. 3–46.

69. Wittmann, *Mon. Wittelsb.*, vol. I, no. 80, pp. 193ff., and no. 90, pp. 219ff.

70. Spindler, *Anfänge*, p. 41, and "Ludwig II. im Dienste des Reichs. Das Schicksal Konradins," in HBG ii, pp. 73–79.

71. Wittmann, *Mon. Wittelsb.*, vol. I, no. 99, pp. 234ff. Their widowed sister Queen Elizabeth married Count Meinhard II of Görz and Tirol in 1259.

72. Heinloth, *Neumarkt*, pp. 212–30.

73. The Bavarian land register drawn up c. 1280, MB, vol. XXXVI A, pp. 135–44, 146–48, 155–71, 314–22, 333f., 339–63, 395, 403–10, reviews all the new Wittelsbach lands in a huge arc from Donauwörth to Auerbach. Some were fiefs from the bishops of Bamberg; Wittmann, *Mon. Wittelsb.*, vol. I, no. 91, pp. 221f. (1266); nos. 97–99, pp. 231–35 (1269); no. 113, p. 270 (1274). On Amberg; Sturm, *Nordgau—Egerland—Oberpfalz*, pp. 64–112.

74. EL ff. 2r–v, 10r–14v.

75. Spindler, *Anfänge*, p. 56 (and n. 2) dates this event after Conradin's execution on 29 October 1268.

76. Wittmann, *Mon. Wittelsb.*, vol. I, no. 125, pp. 307f.

77. Hoffmann, *Urkunden . . . Kaisheim*, no. 320, pp. 182f.

78. Metz, *Staufische Güterverzeichnisse*, pp. 88f.; MGH Consts. iii, no. 644, p. 629 (c. 1300).

79. W. D. Fritz, *Die Goldene Bulle Kaiser Karls IV. vom Jahre 1356*, MGH Fontes iuris Germanici antiqui in usum scholarum, vol. XI (Weimar, 1972), pp. 85f.

80. R. Geiger and G. Voit, *Hersbrucker Urbare*, Schriftenreihe der Altnürnberger Landschaft, vol. XV (Nuremberg, 1965), p. 13; Wittmann, *Mon. Wittelsb.*, vol. I, no. 113, p. 270 (1274). On this family see W. Goez, "Über die Rindsmaul von Grünsberg. Studien zur Geschichte einer staufischen Ministerialenfamilie," in Bestmann, et al. (eds.), *Hochfinanz*, vol. III, pp. 1227–49. On the transfers of allegiance, see D. von Gladiss, *Beiträge zur Geschichte der staufischen Reichsministerialität*, Historische Studien, vol. CCXLIX (Berlin, 1934), pp. 111–162, and my *German Knighthood*, pp. 222–24.

81. *Nürnberger Urkundenbuch*, no. 535, p. 324. On the Stauf family, see Wiessner, *Hilpoltstein*, pp. 79–86. For their later history, see R. Dollinger, "Die Stauffer zu Ernfels," *ZBLG* 35 (1972): 436–522. For Ulrich of Stauf, *des keysers kuchenmeister*, see MB, vol. L, no. 334, p. 245 (1333).

82. Wittmann, *Mon. Wittelsb.*, vol. I, no. 113, pp. 269ff.

83. MGH Consts. iii, no. 17, pp. 20f. (1273); Pfeiffer, "Comicia burcgravie"; Dannenbauer, *Entstehung*, pp. 77–95.

84. *Nürnberger Urkundenbuch*, no. 465, p. 289; no. 489, p. 303 (1274); no. 520, p. 317 (1276); no. 953, p. 527 (1298).

85. A. Gerlich, "Reichsgutvindikationen Rudolfs und Albrechts I. von Habsburg," in HBG iii, pp. 161–66. See also E. Schubert, "Das Königsland: zu Konzeptionen des Römischen Königtums nach dem Interregnum," *JFLF* 39 (1979): 23–40.

86. M. Spindler, "Bayern auf Seite König Adolfs von Nassau," in HBG ii, pp. 104–10.

87. Dannenbauer, *Entstehung*, pp. 95–100; H. Niese, *Die Verwaltung des Reichsgutes im 13. Jahrhundert* (Innsbruck, 1905), pp. 312–14. See also F. Schwind, "Reichslandvogt, Reichslandvogtei," in HRG iv, cols. 699–703.

88. MGH Consts. iii, no. 644, pp. 627–31; *Nürnberger Urkundenbuch*, no. 1073, pp. 632–37 (c. 1300).

89. No one knows exactly when this survey, probably conflating more than one record, was drawn up: "Iste sunt curie, que pertinent ad mensam regis Romanorum" in Saxony, Rhenish Franconia, Bavaria, and Lombardy; MGH Consts. i, no. 440, pp. 646–49. See C. Brühl and T. Kölzer, *Das Tafelgüterverzeichnis des*

*römischen Königs (Ms. Bonn S. 1559)* (Cologne and Vienna, 1979); Metz, *Staufische Güterverzeichnisse,* pp. 6–51, and *Das Servitium Regis,* pp. 21–44; J. P. Niederkorn, "Die Datierung des Tafelgüterverzeichnisses. Bemerkungen zu einer Neuerscheinung," *MIöG* 87 (1979): 471–87; H. H. Kaminsky, "Das 'Tafelgüterverzeichnis des römischen Königs': eine Bestandsaufnahme für Lothar III.?" *DA* 29 (1973): 163–96.

90. Stillfried and Maercker, *Monumenta Zollerana,* vol. II, 431, pp. 263f. (1299), shows that yet more of the property had been pledged to the burgraves' sister.

91. Louis was born in 1283, an object of continual detestation to his elder brother. See W. Schlögl, "Beiträge zur Jugendgeschichte Ludwigs des Bayern," *DA* 33 (1977): 182–99.

92. MGH Dipl. Henry IV, no. 418, pp. 556f.

93. MGH Consts. iv–1, no. 210, pp. 180f. (1306).

94. EL ff. 8v, 59r.

95. MB, vol. L, no. 32, p. 31 (1307).

96. *Reg. Eichst.,* nos. 1477f., p. 463 (1311); W. Küster, *Beiträge zur Finanzgeschichte des Deutschen Reiches nach dem Interregnum,* vol. I, *Das Reichsgut in den Jahren 1273–1313* (Leipzig, 1883), pp. 79, 111. The title survived, however; in 1344 the *ministerialis* Henry of Dürrwangen was "Lant vogt ze Nuernberch und ze franken," Bayr. Hsta. München, Ritterorden 1188.

97. In the *officia* of Velden, Hersbruck, and Guntersrieth; MGH Consts. iii, no. 644, pp. 628, 630.

98. This usage, e.g., in MB, vol. XLIX, no. 76, p. 120 (1264); nos. 144 and 147, pp. 236, 240 (1285); *Nürnberger Urkundenbuch,* no. 910–i, p. 542 (1292); MB, vol. XLIX, no. 352, p. 542 (1305).

99. Ibid., no. 86, p. 133 (1269) has "dominus Heinricus de Lapide, quondam in Nvrenberch buttiglerius."

100. The bishops of Eichstätt claimed the town as a fief, EL f7v, "de castro aut dubitatur." But it is unlikely that the castle ever was an episcopal fief. Lordship over it passed, at some point, from the Empire to Bavaria, and so it fell to the dukes when the Hilpoltstein line ended in 1400.

101. Referred to in MB, vol. XLIX, no. 352, p. 542 (1305).

102. E.g., Bayr. Hsta. München, Ritterorden 1294 (1275) for the *milites de Lapide; Nürnberger Urkundenbuch,* no. 506 A, p. 644 (1275).

103. Ibid., no. 387, p. 237 (1260) with Breitenstein mentioned in no. 419, p. 258 (1266). In Walter of Klingenberg's pro-papal phase, she had been intended for Ulrich of Sulzbürg.

104. MGH Consts. iii, no. 644, chap. 20, p. 630. See also W. Schwemmer, *Die ehemalige Herrschaft Breitenstein-Königstein,* Schriftenreihe der Altnürnberger Landschaft, vol. XIII (Nuremberg, 1965).

105. As in *Reg. Eichst.,* no. 807, p. 252 (1262).

106. See *Nürnberger Urkundenbuch,* no. 335, p. 203.

107. *Nürnberger Urkundenbuch,* no. 420, p. 259 (1266): "Heinr. et Hiltboldus filii eiusdem Heinr. de Lapide, qui duas filias Cunr. de Burgelin duxerunt uxores et eidem successerunt." Conrad of Bürglein was Ulrich of Sulzbürg's uncle, his father's younger brother.

108. Ibid., no. 433, p. 677 (1268); MB, vol. XLIX, p. 730, col. 2.

109. MB, vol. XLIX, no. 100, pp. 151f. (1279).

110. Listed by Abbot Hermann of Niederaltaich in *Genealogia Ottonis II. ducis Bavariae,* MGH Scriptores, vol. XVII, pp. 377f. On their acquisition of fisc, see Schlunk, *Königsmacht,* pp. 191–202 and table 16B.

111. Engel, *Weltatlas,* vol. II, p. 113.

112. E.g., MB, vol. XLIX, no. 67, p. 111 (1260) and no. 76, p. 120 (1264).

# 5. The End of the County of Hirschberg, 1280–1305

The regional history of the medieval German Empire was in part made up of competitions over the exercise of jurisdictions; and the princes who possessed them openly relied, in specific places or at opportune moments, upon getting the better of their neighbors' titles. This consideration brings us again to the question of personalities and their influence. In the late thirteenth century there were three powerful men who tried, in the Eichstätt region, to bend circumstances to their advantage: Reinboto of Meilenhart, bishop of Eichstätt (1279–1297), Count Gebhard V of Hirschberg (late 1270s–1305), and Duke Rudolf I of Upper Bavaria (1294–1317). Each prince was possessed of a different type of superior jurisdiction. The bishop enjoyed episcopal immunity and had ecclesiastical courts for the clergy. The count had advocacy over the bishopric and the *Landgericht,* or regional magistracy, of Hirschberg. The duke had oversight of the general peace, the *Landfriede.* All of them possessed manorial jurisdictions in the region, and the allegiance, with its juridical implications, of *ministeriales,* castellans, and townsmen. At first the count was the stronger prince. Then the duke advanced under the aegis of the king, Adolf of Nassau. Finally it was the bishop whose plans came to fruition with the acquisition of the county of Hirschberg by Eichstätt in 1305, although he did not survive to see the outcome. This event outfaced the rising power of Bavaria, reversed the unfavorable compromise of 1245, abolished the onerous cathedral advocacy, and secured Eichstätt's future as a significant territorial authority in southern Germany until the end of ecclesiastical rule in the Holy Roman Empire in 1802. How was all this achieved?

Reinboto of Meilenhart was born a *ministerialis* of the counts of Graisbach, and like so many members of the local knightly families, he secured a place in the cathedral chapter of Eichstätt and eventually became its provost.[1] It is likely that the namesake who was one of the negotiators of the Treaty of Eichstätt in 1245 was his father.[2] Once Reinboto was elected bishop in 1279, the advantage he enjoyed over his predecessors was financial solvency just at a time when the adjacent secular princes were slipping into debt. In Chapter 4 we considered the hard years of closefisted, even dishonorable, episcopal accounting after 1245. But whatever expedients had seemed necessary, the new bishop now possessed a buoyant enough treasury, which he had the skill to use to great advantage in buying up property and jurisdictions from the counts and their *ministeriales* at keen prices. An early sign of the bishop's solidity was a short-term loan of £1,300 to Count Louis of Oettingen, secured upon the persons of twelve of his vassals who would suffer distraint in the event of nonpayment.[3]

After buying valuable advocatial rights over the property and dependents of Solnhofen Abbey from Count Frederick of Hohentrüdingen in 1281 and 1282,[4] the bishop went on to purchase Wernfels Castle from the imperial *ministerialis* Albert Rindsmaul with the permission of his lord for that fief, Burgrave Conrad of Nuremberg, in 1284.[5] In 1295 Burgrave Conrad himself sold to Eichstätt his tenure of the town and environs of Spalt,[6] which were held in fief from the bishops of Regensburg. The latter were compensated by the transfer of Fünfstetten, a fief to Count Gebhard of Hirschberg,[7] but the transaction was worth more to Bishop Reinboto because he was buying out Burgrave Conrad's hereditary tenure, and Eichstätt would therefore receive Spalt unencumbered. A further advantage was the inclusion in the sale of the burgrave's alodial castle of Sandskron on the Massenberg hill overlooking the town.[8] The finest of all these acquisitions were the town, castle, and dominion of Abenberg, sold to Eichstätt by Burgrave Conrad in 1296 and hitherto one of his residences.[9]

Down to the 1290s Abenberg, Wernfels, and Spalt had formed the most southerly portion of the Zollern burgraves' extensive possessions around Nuremberg, but the latter had waned in importance compared with the magnificent inheritance of Andechs-Merania property after 1248 centered upon Bayreuth. To Bishop Reinboto the new purchases were attractive as part of a larger strategy. Evidently he desired to build up a new dominion in the Franconian half of the diocese, to begin to overawe the counts of Oettingen who were unjustly entrenched in the Herrieden lands to the west of Abenberg and Wernfels. The first move appears to have been to promote the significance of the *ministeriales* of Arberg and Muhr, who held strong castles either side of the River Altmühl on the routes toward Herrieden. By the end of the thirteenth century they possessed extensive episcopal fiefs.[10]

After the purchase of Wernfels, the bishop applied to the royal court for forest rights in the extensive woodlands of Steinberg, which stretched from Wernfels to Muhr. This was granted at Augsburg in 1286 after Bishop Reinboto had persuaded the king that no other prince ought to possess such rights in the *Stainberger Vorst*.[11] Its custody was then entrusted to Ulrich of Muhr and his nephew Henry of Neuenmuhr.[12] Wernfels was at once marked out for a key episcopal stronghold, as Mörnsheim and Nassenfels had been in the past. At the beginning of his reign Bishop Reinboto had sought out a capable *ministerialis* from the burgrave's retinue, Rüdiger of Dietenhofen, and promoted him to the vacant household office of marshal.[13] By 1286 he had been appointed castellan at Wernfels,[14] and in a short time Arberg, Wernfels, and Abenberg were to become the centers of newly organized *officia*, districts, for the administration of episcopal manors.

Bishop Reinboto's contemporary as cathedral advocate, Gebhard V of Hirschberg, was also motivated like his forebears to acquire new dominions, but his transactions were not based upon sound finances. For an unknown sum he purchased title to most of the landgraves of Leuchtenberg's extensive fiefs in the diocese,[15] and in 1286 bought the castle of Upper Sulzbürg and its remaining appurtenances from the imperial *ministerialis* Ulrich of Sulzbürg for 2100 silver marks.[16] At the same time he was borrowing money from the townsmen of Regensburg and Nuremberg, and to raise ready money he sold off his last remaining rights in Tirol to Count Meinhard II of Görz and Tirol in 1284.[17] Another expedient had been to levy unwarranted taxes in Eichstätt,[18] thereby flouting the agreements of 1245. Since the count was childless, Bishop Reinboto offered him a daring solution to his financial entanglements in 1291. The bishopric would shoulder his burden of debt in exchange for a will bequeathing the entire alodial possessions of Hirschberg to the church.[19] The arrangement would become void should the count produce legitimate heirs, or the debts be paid off. It was, nevertheless, the best example of Bishop Reinboto's imaginative planning for the temporal future of his see, and after several challenges it did come into effect in 1305. Among the German cathedral and abbatial churches it was not uncommon to receive part or all of dynastic counties by testament, and in Eichstätt's case it would provide an almost ideal settlement in that the episcopal and comital lands were intermingled.

The publication of this agreement caused a sensation in Bavarian politics because the dukes were Count Gebhard's nearest secular heirs, his mother having been Duke Otto II's daughter Sophia. So the dukes had expected to inherit the county by right of blood. Duke Louis II of Upper Bavaria therefore launched a feud against his nephew in protest, but to little avail. The Hirschberg dominion after all was alodial property, and Gebhard

V's freely chosen dispositions had tacitly to be accepted in 1293 when he did concede the eventual right of Bavaria to property not appurtenant to Hirschberg Castle: the town of Hemau, Thongründlein and Painten Forests, and Kösching Castle.[20] Duke Louis II died in the following year but his successor, Duke Rudolf I, reneged on the agreement and there were several bloodstained conflicts and insincere truces in the years following 1294 involving knights and townsmen on both sides.[21] The duke's vassal Henry of Wildenstein, for example, killed one of the count's men, Henry of Attenfeld, a castellan at Hirschberg.[22] In 1300 the duke was required to compensate the latter's offspring.

It is hard to see what the dukes hoped to achieve by these feuds. Incapable of a military conquest of Hirschberg and Eichstätt, it appears that their intention was to intimidate the count and bishop into reconsidering the wisdom of their dispositions since 1291. But the effect was the opposite. In 1296 Count Gebhard issued a revised will in which the question of debt repayments was taken for granted, and the only invalidating clause regarded the possible birth of legitimate heirs.[23] At the same time, a subsidiary testament was drawn up returning the rights of advocacy over the towns of Eichstätt and Berching to the bishops,[24] which would automatically cancel one of the principal jurisdictional and fiscal advantages confirmed to the Hirschbergs in 1245, and markedly enrich the bishop as actual owner of the towns.[25]

As a supporter of Adolf of Nassau, Duke Rudolf I's credibility began to crumble in 1298. The magnates of southern Germany, including the counts of Hirschberg, Oettingen, and Graisbach, had rallied to the new ruler, Albert I (1298–1308), but this did not prevent the duke from launching and losing a final campaign in 1301. He crossed the Danube to try to retake Neumarkt, part of the Staufen inheritance confiscated from him by Albert I, and when this project failed, he ravaged the Hirschberg *cometia,* or county, for eight days. The count and his friends retaliated by wasting the lands of all the ducal vassals north of the Danube whom they could reach.[26] The subsequent collapse of Duke Rudolf's authority therefore confirmed the probability of Gebhard of Hirschberg's legacy to Eichstätt. For the time being, the advance of ducal Bavaria into the Eichstätt region had reached an impasse.

To the dismay of his neighbors, Count Gebhard V continued to exploit and to squander his resources in the manner of childless but profligate aristocrats. He failed to pay back a considerable loan from Marshal Henry of Pappenheim, who was therefore adjudicated some Hirschberg assets in the royal court.[27] The royal agent who drew up the Nuremberg

*Reichssalbüchlein* about 1300 complained that the count had despoiled one of his fiefs, a forest adjacent to Greding, of £1,000's worth of timber.[28] In addition, he had so abused his advocacy over Kastl Abbey, another imperial fief, that Duke Rudolf I had already endeavored to assert his ducal powers in forbidding him any further pledges of the monastic property.[29]

By this time Bishop Reinboto had been succeeded (1297) by the cathedral canon and Bavarian *ministerialis* Conrad of Pfeffenhausen,[30] who also found reason to restrain the count. As cathedral advocate, Gebhard V was still extracting so much from the diocese of Eichstätt, in the style of his rapacious ancestors, that the new bishop felt obliged to impose an interdict and to write letters of complaint to the king and the pope.[31] But in spite of the current encumbrance of his wasteful advocate, Bishop Conrad was able to complete the general line of his predecessor's policy: to purchase property, to reorganize the administration of the episcopal territories, and to finalize the testamentary dispositions of Count Gebhard. In 1301 the bishop bought the castle, town, and manors of Kipfenberg from the imperial *ministerialis* Conrad Kropf of Flüglingen,[32] a small dominion but significant enough to rank thereafter as a separate episcopal *officium* under its own agents.[33] In 1302 Count Gebhard himself sold Sandsee Castle and its lands to the bishop, compelled to this necessity by a new shortage of ready funds.[34] Although he hoped to be able to buy Sandsee back again,[35] he requested the bishop to pay his most pressing creditor in Nuremberg from the purchase money.[36] The count also reserved the fealty of his castellans at Sandsee, who would in the interim serve the bishop as new owner and lord. But the intention of repurchase was never carried out, and upon the count's death this garrison of military vassals, or *homines militaris condicionis,* became the bishop's men.

After the humiliation of Duke Rudolf I in 1301, Gebhard V stood high in royal favor and then joined Albert I for the campaign against Bohemia in 1304. Just before he set out, he confirmed new versions of his principal will in Eichstätt's favor,[37] a precaution probably inspired by Bishop Conrad's prudence. By early March 1305 the count was dead, and the bishop announced that "not only the advocacy over our possessions and those of our chapter, but also the castle of Hirschberg with all its assets has devolved to our church."[38]

\*　\*　\*

Some time before this splendid legacy put Eichstätt in possession of scores of additional manors, villages, castles, vassals, and woodlands, Bishops Reinboto and Conrad II had been aware of the need to create a new administration for their lands. Together with their shrewd purchases from impecunious princes, a revised territorial government based upon the services of *ministeriales* and the reconstruction of castles added up to their most significant achievement. While the crown dabbled with the idea of restoring the fisc all around Nuremberg and the dukes of Bavaria launched unproductive feuds against the count of Hirschberg, the bishops were grounding the territorial autonomy of Eichstätt upon administrative reforms.

To make better use of their patrimony and acquisitions, the bishops relied upon four well-tried methods. The first was to arrange the manors with all their appurtenant woodlands, fisheries, and other profitable rights into *officia,* or "offices," over groups of adjacent manors.[39] Later in the fourteenth century, when the Eichstätt and Hirschberg lands had been united and the Herrieden lands rescued from the counts of Oettingen,[40] there were twelve such *officia* containing at least two hundred manors all told. Each group or *officium* was responsible for paying its annual revenues and other renders at one castle. This leads to the second method, the administration and defense of princely territories from castles garrisoned by *ministeriales.*[41] The bishops expected their household officers, the seneschals, butlers, marshals, and chamberlains, with their especially remunerative fiefs, to take responsibility for this administration. The upper rank of the retinue was therefore concerned with the lands upon which the bishops subsisted directly, the *mensa.*

The third element in such an organization concerned the bestowal upon the *ministeriales* of perhaps a third or even a half of the episcopal possessions as hereditary fiefs to sustain their castles, garrison duties, and field service, which all princes needed to guarantee their status and independence of action in local and imperial politics. These lands and castles were not part of the *mensa,* yet the hereditary services of the *ministeriales,* still called *homines proprii,* or "proprietary vassals," at the beginning of the fourteenth century,[42] were supervised by the same household officers who stood over the *officia.*[43] So it can be discerned that the *ministeriales* of the church usually performed two kinds of function divided upon a family basis between those with household titles and those without. The household officers administered the bishop's immediate property, or *mensa,* from large castles; the rest, with their fiefs and smaller, residential castles, were responsible for the loyal defense of the bishopric. Fourth and lastly, the bishop was also lord of an ecclesiastical establishment in the cathedral town and diocese, but a long history of conflict between German bishops and their chapters had usually resulted in the division of episcopal and chapter lands into independent portions. At Eichstätt this separation of the chapter's possessions and rights was confirmed by papal bull in the twelfth century.[44] The Eichstätt chapter was not rich, and was not often in a position to challenge decisions taken by the bishops.

For more than a century before Bishop Reinboto's accession in 1279, the bishops had been appointing marshals, butlers, seneschals, and chamberlains from among a number of families of *ministeriales,* and their services were in evidence in the era of Eichstätt's economic difficulties after 1245.[45] At the beginning of Bishop Reinboto's reign, the principal surviving members of this administration were Henry, butler of Arberg,[46] and Albert, seneschal of Pfünz.[47] We can then reconstruct from the land register drawn up for Bishop Conrad II in 1300 or 1301 how the new administration had gradually been installed. It is probable that the *officium* of Arberg, made up of old Franconian manors of the bishopric, was already functioning under the butlers, but its contents were much improved in Bishop Reinboto's time, especially by the purchase of extensive woodlands.[48] By 1300 there were about thirty manors in this *officium.*[49] The castle itself, which had been refortified and equipped with eight new machines for casting missiles, had several *ministeriales* for its castellans: the butlers of Arberg and their cousins enfeoffed at Hirschlach, Haag, and Heinersdorf; the Dietenhofen brothers Frederick and Rüdiger; and Henry of Birkenfels, Meinhard of Triesdorf, and Louis of Eyb.[50]

Soon after the purchase of Wernfels, Bishop Reinboto appointed the marshal of his household, Rüdiger of Dietenhofen, as the chief castellan and administrator of the *officium,*[51] and he continued in this post until 1317 at least.[52] Shortly after 1300 there were twenty-five manors in this *officium,* its value being greatly enhanced by the addition of eighteen woodlands, including those appurtenant to Sandskron Castle and to Spalt.[53] Although Eichstätt had bought the title to Spalt in 1295,[54] Burgrave Conrad of Nuremberg retained possession of the town itself until his death in 1314, when it passed to the church outright. Like Arberg, the Wernfels *officium* was being considerably improved in the meantime by purchases and exchanges.[55] The marshal's deputy at Wernfels was the minister Conrad.[56] In 1303 he had married Margaret of Wald whose father had been a *ministerialis* pertaining to Count Ulrich of Hohentrüdingen. Since the princes of the Eichstätt region were reviving their rights *titulo proprietatis,* or "by right of property," to their ministerial retinues, the offspring of this marriage were to be divided between bishop and count.[57]

Like Arberg, Mörnsheim Castle, not far west of Eichstätt, was an ancient stronghold of the see that Bishop Reinboto brought forward as the center of an *officium*. Early in the 1290s the bishop appointed a new chamberlain of the household, Siegfried of Otting, and then enfeoffed him as castellan of Mörnsheim in conjunction with the *ministeriales* of Mörnsheim who held quite extensive fiefs from the church.[58] There were two other posts of castellan there. One went to Siegfried's brother Louis, also called *camerarius,* that is, chamberlain, the other to the bishops' vassals Hermann of Landershofen, Henry of Mündling, and Rüdiger of Gebertshofen, in turn.[59] According to Bishop Conrad's land register, seventeen or eighteen manors paid their revenues at Mörnsheim Castle. Mills, inns, assart tithes, and woodlands are recorded as adding to the value of this *officium*.[60] In 1304 some of the assets were assigned to the chamberlain's office when Siegfried's son Henry was also appointed chamberlain.[61] This charter had envisaged the descent of the office in the Otting family, but a subsequent bishop, Marquard of Hageln (1322–1324), changed his mind and redeemed Mörnsheim from Siegfried of Otting without appointing another chamberlain.[62]

The acquisition of Abenberg in 1296, Kipfenberg in 1301, and Sandsee in 1302[63] added three more *officia* to Eichstätt's administration. For Abenberg Bishop Reinboto again picked out new men, the imperial *ministeriales* Albert and Godfrey of Vestenberg as advocates and castellans. Abenberg, the remnant of a dynastic county, was at £4,000 by far the costliest of Bishop Reinboto's purchases, but was worth it with revenues from twenty-eight manors and five woodlands.[64] Kipfenberg and Sandsee were acquired too late to feature in the oldest land register. The Sandsee *officium* was improved by further purchases.[65] Later it consisted of eighteen manors, and the Kipfenberg *officium* of six.[66]

Although the *officia* of Arberg under a butler, Wernfels under a marshal, and Mörnsheim under a chamberlain provided models for the reorganization of the episcopal *mensa,* it appears that the imminent bankruptcy of the Pfünz family precluded the bishopric's seneschalship from continuing as an active part of the administration. In 1282 Seneschal Albert of Pfünz and his sons gave up their alodial castle as a fief to Eichstätt on the understanding that they would continue as castellans with the title and right of castle guard, "ius castellanie quod vulgariter burchvt dicitur."[67] Even this right they were at once obliged to pledge to the bishop, as well as handing over another fief on the same terms.[68] Albert senior did keep his personal title of seneschal, and his sons had come into his remaining fiefs by the beginning of the fourteenth century.[69] When the land register was drawn up, the manor and forest of Pfünz paid their renders directly to the bishop in Eichstätt.[70]

The marshal's office became vacant at the beginning of Bishop Reinboto's reign, but unlike the seneschalship, it was not permitted to lapse. Hitherto exercised by the castellans of Nassenfels, it was, as we have seen, transferred to Rüdiger of Dietenhofen and combined with his office as castellan of Wernfels.[71] Nassenfels Castle, the strongest in the immediate vicinity of Eichstätt, was transferred first to Count Gebhard V's butler Henry of Hofstetten and Geyern[72] who was also one of the principal vassals of the church,[73] and then to the bishop's brother likewise called Reinboto, *dominus de Milnhart*.[74] Not long after this, Bishop Conrad extensively rebuilt the castle, putting up a new tower and a residence adjacent to it, as well as other buildings. The curtain wall was raised by more than ten feet and the complex surrounded by a moat,[75] giving it much the same appearance that it retains to this day. Under the castellan Reinboto of Meilenhart, other *ministeriales* were enfeoffed with duties of castle guard there: Reinboto of Hütting, Gebhard of Hirnstetten, Hermann and Conrad of Landershofen, and Siegfried Jacko of Jackenberg.[76] Nassenfels Castle was the principal fortification in the *officium* of Eichstätt, where thirty manors paid their renders.[77]

Eichstätt itself was a walled town, and the cathedral complex within it was also a fortified enclosure, but no modern castle was erected until the Willibaldsburg was established as a residence by Bishops Albert I of Hohenfels (1344–1351) and Berthold of Nuremberg (1351–1365), situated upon a spur across the River Altmühl to the west of the town.[78] During the reign of Bishop Philip of Rathsamhausen (1306–1322) a plan was adopted for making Nassenfels the center of the *officium* under a *vicedominus*, or deputy lord, on the Bavarian ducal model. An ecclesiastical officer in origin, the name *vicedominus* was then adopted by secular administrations for functions similar to those of the household officers, and most of the Bavarian ducal lands were run by such *vicedomini*.[79] By 1313 Conrad of Nassenfels was *vicedominus*[80] but his term of office was shortlived because he fell out with the bishop, even taking to arms in a feud, and was dismissed in 1317.[81] The office was allowed to lapse again and in 1318 Nassenfels was enfeoffed to the Bavarian knight Marquard of Seefeld, nephew of the bishop's procurator, Canon Marquard of Hageln.[82] So the possibilities of turning the Eichstätt *officium* into a castle-centered administration under the seneschals of Pfünz or the *vicedominus* of Nassenfels came to nothing.

The remarkable ambitions of Bishop Reinboto of Eichstätt can be set out in ascending order of significance. First, he recovered property alienated under diverse titles "to the right and dominion of his church," as his biographer noted.[83] Second, he spent large sums acquiring new possessions, especially in the Franconian half of the diocese. Third, he organized the administration of the episcopal *mensa*, the lands pertaining directly to the cathedral church, in two ways: by employing capable *ministeriales* and by rebuilding the *castra priora*, the chief castles, as the central points for the *officia*.[84] Fourth, he greatly enlarged his retinue of knights and reactivated their hereditary ties as *ministeriales* to the obedience and service of the church, and so did the adjacent princes, as we shall see. Fifth, he reconciled the restless and extravagant Count Gebhard V of Hirschberg to the disappointment of childlessness, and secured the reversion not only of the onerous cathedral advocacy from him, but also one of the few remaining alodial counties in Bavaria for the benefit of his see. His biographer also remembered the bishop as a diligent and reform-minded churchman,[85] although it was undoubtedly in the secular sphere that he made his mark as one of the most able incumbents of the bishopric, comparable with Bishop Erchanbald who persuaded King Arnulf to hand over Herrieden Abbey in 888, or Bishop Gebhard II of Grögling who had enfeoffed the new secular retinue after 1125.

It was, however, in the northwest of the diocese in the region surrounding Herrieden that the bishop's plans for regenerating Eichstätt's secular status met with least success, the counts of Oettingen being all too powerful and uncooperative as advocates there. In the first place there existed no written instrument like the 1245 Treaty of Eichstätt between the cathedral advocate and the bishop. Second, the towns and *castra priora* from which Bishop Reinboto might realistically have imposed administrative reform as elsewhere in the diocese were themselves in Oettingen hands: Wassertrüdingen and Wahrberg castles, and the towns of Herrieden, Ornbau, and Lehrberg "with all the manors and villages appurtenant to those towns."[86]

Although this is the record in the book of fiefs, Bishop Reinboto had attempted to question it through a survey of Herrieden lands drawn up for him in 1288.[87] It described about forty manors under bailiffs, or *ministri*, in seven places, and this section of episcopal territory is absent from Bishop Conrad II's land register. It records instead the other Eichstätt properties that the church was endeavoring to regain from Oettingen hands; Erlbach and Ehingen with the forest that was admittedly enfeoffed to the counts as advocates;[88] the *officium* of Ornbau;[89] and the revenues of Zell, Lellenfeld and Neunstetten where "the count seized the advocacy by force," "advocatiam comes recepit violenter."[90] The confused status of the Eichstätt and Oettingen titles to possession in these places is reflected in the land register, where the entries on folios 37R to 44V of this much-handled and corrected codex are at their most disordered. The solution to the Oettingen question was left to Bishop Conrad II's successors.[91]

* * *

The temporal concerns of the bishops of Eichstätt toward the end of the thirteenth century showed up the integration of castles and *officia*, manors and the household offices. The recruitment of talented personnel was essential to the workings of such a system, the most significant sources still being the retinues of *ministeriales* enfeoffed in the Eichstätt region since the twelfth century. Not only were the princes actually expanding these retinues down to 1300 and beyond, but they were still insisting upon the hereditary ascription of their knights under the rules relevant to *homines proprii*,[92] the name used for them in Eichstätt's book of fiefs. In many German provinces and territories the servile legal status of *ministeriales* and their very name were tending to disappear by the end of the thirteenth century, but not in the Eichstätt region. Here the princes injected new vigor into the traditional rules,[93] explicitly recruiting, organizing, and disciplining knights under the name of *ministeriales*.

In 1295 for example, Count Berthold of Graisbach generously gave Sophia of Otting, wife of the bishop's knight Ulrich of Muhr, and their children "who . . . belonged to us *ministerialatus iure et titulo*" to Bishop Reinboto.[94] The point of course was that in German law, all the children of servile dependents belonged to their mothers' lords although they inherited their fathers' property.[95] From this marriage the extensive possessions of Ulrich of Muhr, including Altenmuhr Castle,[96] would therefore have passed under the dominion of the counts of Graisbach. Normally lords safeguarded their interests in this respect by insisting upon granting consent before such marriages took place. Ulrich and Sophia of Muhr failed to apply for it when one of the children mentioned above married Elizabeth of Reichenbach, a *ministerialis* belonging to the bishop of Würzburg.[97] Now it would be this younger Ulrich's castle at Neuenmuhr with other Eichstätt fiefs[98] that were in peril of passing, when his children eventually inherited, into the power of the see of Würzburg. With rancor and indignation against this unlicensed union Bishop Conrad II therefore asserted the rules that had applied since 1295 to Ulrich *ministerialatus iure*, "by the law of *ministeriales*," as the 1303 charter puts it. He pressed for an equal division of their children between Eichstätt and Würzburg, the usual solution employed by princes in such cases.

A treaty on the subject had actually been drawn up between these churches in 1243.[99] The bishop also took the opportunity to clarify the military duties that he expected of the knights of Muhr: castle guard, *custodia castri*, at one of the chief castles in their vicinity, Abenberg, Arberg, Wernfels, or Gundelsheim; or service in the field with properly equipped war horses. These rearrangements of the rights over *ministeriales* of Otting, Muhr, and Reichenbach also affected the new chamberlain of the household, Siegfried of Otting. Born as a Graisbach *ministerialis*, like Sophia of Muhr who was possibly his sister,[100] he was transferred to the bishop as one of Eichstätt's *homines proprii*.[101] Siegfried also married a *ministerialis* belonging to the church, since his children are mentioned in 1304 as belonging to Eichstätt *iure ministerialatus*.[102] They were in consequence eligible for the office of chamberlain *iure successionis et feodi*, "by right of succession and enfeoffment," and Siegfried's son Henry was duly appointed. It was envisaged that the most suitable son in each generation would succeed him, as long as they still remained Eichstätt's *ministeriales*.

The continuing emphasis upon the servile status of knights as *ministeriales* was not the result of the diocese of Eichstätt being a social backwater, or of conscious legal archaism by the princes. True, the region was not notably an advanced one in its economic structures. Yet the proximity of three of the most enterprising towns in all Germany, Nuremberg, Regensburg, and Augsburg,[103] and their quite complex connections with the churchmen, secular magnates, knights, and townsmen of the Eichstätt region meant that the latter had not been untouched by social changes either. So the assertion of *ius ministerialatus*, "the law of *ministeriales*," served purposes useful to the organization of retinues, especially where multiple vassalage and the frequency of intermarriage between *familiae*, or households, governed by lords had complicated the question of allegiances. This can nimbly be illustrated from Eichstätt's oldest book of fiefs where, for example, Wolfram of Emmendorf is called *ministerialis ecclesie*, that is, of the church, Albert of Emmendorf is named a Hirschberg vassal, and Ulrich of Emmendorf is one of the Oettingen knights enfeoffed at Wassertrüdingen.[104] A further consideration was that the more pronounced territorial ambitions of Bishop Reinboto and Count Gebhard V after 1280 resulted in a marked expansion of their retinues of enfeoffed knights reminiscent of the similar interest taken by their predecessors in the second quarter of the twelfth century.

The lean years after 1245 had seen an erosion of the bishop's retinue, and many *ministeriales* appear to have been released from their obligations in order to serve other lords.[105] Many families died out, and although some of their fiefs undoubtedly passed to collateral heirs,[106] the bishops could not always afford to enfeoff them formally as Eichstätt *ministeriales* and incorporate them into the retinue. As a result, the cathedral church was reduced to about thirty-five families as the numerical limit under which careers could still be undertaken in Eichstätt's service. This had important consequences for sustaining the regime of the Hirschbergs as cathedral advocates, since the military preponderance that they had gained during the feud of 1225 to 1245 could not be challenged. The bishops cannot have posed much of a threat to the counts of Oettingen for the same reasons, and this may explain the high-handed behavior of these counts toward ecclesiastical property. The relative affluence of Bishop Reinboto's government meant that more knights were recruited to administer and to defend the possessions of the see, old and new. In numerical terms the retinue expanded by nearly thirty names, thus restoring its strength as it stood at the beginning of the thirteenth century.[107]

By this time the complexities of multiple allegiance were much more in evidence, but the possible inconvenience did not in the least deter the princes, who were bent on recruiting the rich and talented knights to the best posts in their service. Before considering these cases, we should note that the bishops had also granted many fiefs to *ministeriales* in other retinues, especially those of the dukes of Bavaria,[108] the counts of Hirschberg,[109] Oettingen,[110] Graisbach,[111] and Hohentrüdingen,[112] and the burgraves of Nuremberg.[113] This indicates that normally the princes expected to cooperate as a regional military force. We hear more about the times when they fell out, since these are what the narrative sources and the charters of treaty tend to record: Eichstätt against Hirschberg before 1245, Hirschberg against Bavaria in the 1290s, the Oettingen-Eichstätt feud over the Herrieden lands after 1310, and so on. But these events were, over the decades, the exceptions. Another fortunate result of the increased complexity of cross enfeoffment and multiple vassalage was the book of fiefs assembled between 1305 and 1320, to record all the possessions of the see given out not only to the bishops' own knights but to those vassals of the neighboring princes. The book recorded all the lands, manors, rights, revenues, woodlands, and castles as held family by family, so that it accompanied the cadastral surveys of 1288 and circa 1300 as an archival record of all Eichstätt's property apart from the chapter's lands just before the accession of the Hirschberg possessions.

One result of the feud between the cathedral church and its advocates, which was terminated in 1245, was that the latter were able in the middle decades of the thirteenth century to retain a larger number of knights in their permanent service,[114] counting roughly fifty family names and top-onymics.[115] In the 1280s and 1290s Count Gebhard V recruited no less than sixty new names into his retinue,[116] many of them with fiefs and castles on the eastern confines of the Hirschberg lands and in the environs of Sulz-bach. Once again these round figures have to be taken as approximations, because the sources do not always afford us the evidence for the affiliations within a single lineage that was actually using more than one toponymic for its family names. The charters for Kastl Abbey, for example, do show that the seneschals of Sulzbach certainly used more than one: Ammerthal, Holnstein, and Sulzbach itself.[117] Some of these vassals arrived in the Hirschberg retinue with the dominion of Sulzbürg purchased in 1286, and others were undoubtedly collected to render the Hirschberg *cometia*, or county, more effective against Duke Rudolf I of Bavaria in the 1290s.

Direct evidence for this can be discerned in the duke's necessary submission to the count in 1300, the latter gaining from him the rights over three of his *ministeriales*: the daughter of Conrad Kropf of Kipfenberg, Arnold Gross of Hilpoltstein and Meckenhausen, and John of Pollanten.[118] The generous scale of enfeoffment was facilitated by Count Gebhard's alliance with the cathedral church, which granted fiefs to so many of his *ministeriales* and also provided assets for the count himself to enfeoff about forty of his knights.[119] These tenures then lapsed upon the count's death in 1305. Gebhard V's motives for expanding his retinue paralleled those of Bishop Reinboto in newly perceived needs for better administration and more effective defense. However, we know very much less about the Hirschberg household and its estate management, although it appears to have relied upon the same method as the bishop's: the combination of household offices, strong castles, and *officia* over manors.

Count Gebhard's butlers were Henry of Hofstetten;[120] Godfrey of Töging;[121] and Godfrey and Liutold of Altenburg and Flügelsberg, who may have derived their title by succession from the butlers of Flügelsberg who had served the ducal household of Bavaria.[122] There were three marshals in evidence: Ulrich of Erlingshofen,[123] Henry of Sulzbach, com-mandant of the town of Beilngries lying at the foot of Hirschberg Castle,[124] and Reinboto of Wellheim.[125] Conrad of Sulzbach was seneschal,[126] and a Godfrey recorded without a toponymic was master of the kitchen, or *magister coquinae*,[127] but there is no evidence for a comital chamberlain. Direct information about the possible authority of these functionaries in the count's *officia* is lacking, but the names of the latter have survived. The one hundred and twenty manors appurtenant to Hirschberg were divided into roughly equal portions,[128] the *officia* of Hirschberg and Eichstätt, where the incomes were respectively paid in. Separate *officia* were the imperial fief of Greding;[129] Sandsee with its manors then sold to the bishop in 1302;[130] the Sulzbach dominion;[131] and the Bamberg fief of Hemau.[132]

In revising their administrations, Bishop Reinboto and Count Gebhard tended to choose from a small group of talented *ministeriales,* not always their own vassals in origin, to promote to the command of the principal castles and to fill the offices at their disposal. When it became likely from 1291 that the two principalities would ultimately merge, there was even less inhibition in enfeoffing the very same persons, or at least their brothers. Another device by which the princes encouraged the esprit de corps of this inner group was through intermarriage. The earliest figure in this circle was the Hirschberg butler Henry of Hofstetten, one of the richest knights in the region.[133] Under Gebhard V's father he had negotiated a significant agreement with Duke Louis II of Bavaria whereby he bought Geyern Castle not far from Weissenburg, a ducal prize taken by force, possibly from the marshals of Pappenheim, and was appointed *castellanus, miles et alius servitor,* "castellan, knight and otherwise retainer," there.[134] The knights of Hofstetten went back to the earliest days of Eichstätt's ministerial retinue,[135] and the bishops made sure of their claim that the butler was still a *ministerialis* of their church.[136]

Henry of Hofstetten's triple allegiance therefore summarized the political changes that had affected the Eichstätt region in the second half of the thirteenth century: the rise of the dukes of Bavaria, and the increased cooperation of bishop and cathedral advocate after 1279. For this reason Henry was Bishop Reinboto's castellan at Nassenfels, a post given up shortly after 1297, and custodian of Pfünz Forest.[137] When the butler's first wife Benedicta died early in the 1280s,[138] the bishop arranged for him to marry Agnes of Muhr, from one of the important Franconian families of *ministeriales* in the bishopric.[139] For the count of Hirschberg, Henry of Hofstetten's chief post was as joint castellan of Hirschberg, and he was entrusted with handing over the Hirschberg possessions to the church in the testaments of 1291 and 1296.[140] Like the bishop's *castra priora,* Hirschberg housed a team of castellans: Henry the butler, Wolfram of Pfalzpaint, Henry of Erlingshofen, Conrad and Albert from the ministerial family called of Hirschberg, and the count's own advocate there, Henry of Attenfeld. By 1304 Henry of Hofstetten was dead,[141] and Henry of Attenfeld had been killed in the feuds with Duke Rudolf of Bavaria.[142] So the castellans were now the three brothers Conrad, Albert, and Godfrey of Hirschberg *milites;* Ulrich of Morsbach; and Hartwig of Simbach as comital advocate.[143] As a stratagem to confound the claims of the Bavarian dukes to the Hirschberg county, Gebhard V had declared at the last moment that Hirschberg Castle was a fief from the bishops after all.[144] This is unlikely to have been the case in tenurial law. But just as the counts commanded the bishops' fortifications at Eichstätt, so the bishops did have the right to appoint one of the castellans for their cathedral advocate's chief residence. It appears that Count Gebhard V made sure the candidates suited him; Henry of Hofstetten, then Henry Tegno of Obereichstätt, then Albert of Hirschberg.[145]

When Henry of Hofstetten died just at the beginning of the fourteenth century,[146] Count Gebhard and Bishop Conrad II saw to it that his widow Agnes of Muhr married another of the principal knights in their service, Godfrey of Wolfstein, and that two of the daughters also married within the circle of most favored *ministeriales*. Agnes of Hofstetten was wedded to the seneschal Conrad of Sulzbach, and her sister Petrissa to Godfrey of Wolfstein's son by his previous marriage, Liutpold. In any case Agnes is likely to have been the sister of Henry of Muhr and Konstein, whose father had come into the latter castle by marriage to Matilda of Konstein before 1273. Henry's own status as *proprius,* or dependent, of the church and vassal of Hirschberg,[147] together with his custody of Neuenmuhr and Konstein castles, made him another important figure during the reign of Gebhard V. In 1291 he stood guarantor for the count in the charter of rights for the town of Eichstätt; for the peace of 1296 with Bavaria; for the sale of Sandsee in 1302; and finally for the transfer of Hirschberg after 1304.[148] The seneschal, Conrad of Sulzbach, who married Agnes of Hofstetten[149] held extensive fiefs from Count Gebhard V, and managed to retain Ammerthal Castle for him against the hostile claim of Duke Louis II of Bavaria.[150] But like his brother-in-law at Geyern Castle, he was also a castellan for the dukes, at Lichtenegg west of Sulzbach.[151]

The other important figure in this constellation of marriages was the imperial *ministerialis* Godfrey of Wolfstein, younger brother of Ulrich of Sulzbürg who donated his estates to the Church and to the Teutonic Order early in the 1280s,[152] and had sold the castle of Upper Sulzbürg with the hill, vineyards, woodlands, and patronage of the parish church to Gebhard of Hirschberg in 1286.[153] These events had several consequences. Godfrey of Wolfstein became the leading knight in Count Gebhard's retinue and was appointed castellan of Upper Sulzbürg[154] with a large income secured upon the taxes from Berching "on grounds of castle guard," *pretexto iuris castellanie*.[155] He and the count acted as guardians for Ulrich of Sulzbürg's only child Adelheid, who was left with a handsome sum in cash.[156] Later she was married to Henry of Hofstetten's only son by his first marriage, the butler of Geyern. When present, Godfrey of Wolfstein was involved in the count's principal affairs as his guarantor: the agreement with the town of Eichstätt drawn up in 1291; peace with the dukes of Bavaria in 1293 and 1296; the count's will in the latter year; and the sale of Sandsee in 1302.[157]

Another result was that the count acquired vassals from the Sulzbürg retinue as his *ministeriales:* the knights of Buchfeld, Ellenbrunn, Geiersreuth, Hofen, Trosberg, and Wappersdorf.[158] Godfrey of Wolfstein was an imperial *ministerialis* as well as Count Gebhard V's vassal, and so were the knights of Vestenberg, whom he had recruited into his retinue by the 1290s.[159] Four of them are recorded as his men in the bishop of Eichstätt's oldest book of fiefs,[160] and one of them was chosen to supervise the bishop's *officium* of Abenberg, purchased in 1296, as *castellaneus in Abenberch*. This was Albert of Vestenberg who called himself *des Riches dienstman,* or "*ministerialis* of the Empire," in 1295.[161] These knights had apparently relinquished control of Vestenberg Castle to cousins,[162] but they still possessed Dettelsau Castle not far from Abenberg.[163]

The other family of imperial *ministeriales* with a significant bearing upon the retinue politics of Eichstätt and Hirschberg were the knights of Emetzheim, Flüglingen, and Kipfenberg surnamed Kropf. Like the marshals of Pappenheim and the butlers of Reicheneck, they were too prominent to seek careers under the bishops or the counts, but they did more or less align their interest and their marriages to suit the wishes of the episcopal and comital households. In 1250 Conrad Kropf was cited as *fidelis,* or liegeman, of Emperor Frederick II,[164] and acted as Conradin's marshal during the Italian campaign of 1268.[165] After the catastrophe of Tagliacozzo, he is said to have been one of the German noblemen executed alongside Conradin at Naples in October 1268.[166] His castle was Flüglingen, inherited from one of the bishop of Eichstätt's *ministeriales*.[167] The other branch had resided at Emetzheim Castle since the twelfth century,[168] and much later the castle was recorded as a fief from Eichstätt.[169] In 1270 the marshal's widow Bertha bequeathed property to the Teutonic

Order,[170] and went on to arrange profitable marriages for her children. By 1277 Conrad had wedded the heiress of the dominion of Kipfenberg[171] and Irmengard married Ulrich of Sulzbürg. Of her younger sons, Godfrey was castellan of Flüglingen and Henry was a canon of Eichstätt,[172] while her nephews Conrad and Ulrich entered Count Gebhard V's retinue.[173] Conrad Kropf of Kipfenberg's second wife was Petrissa of Sulzbürg, widow of Hilpolt of Hilpoltstein. Since Conrad's son by his first marriage had not survived and there were no children by the second, he and Petrissa sold Kipfenberg to Eichstätt in 1301,[174] as we have seen, and retired to the town house provided for them at Nuremberg.[175] Petrissa's offspring by her first marriage were installed in the meantime over the dominion of Hilpoltstein. The Kropf cousins at Emetzheim had, like other imperial *ministeriales,* sought out a new lord in the region, and were vassals of the burgraves of Nuremberg.[176]

It was also from the burgraves' retinue of *ministeriales* that Bishop Reinboto and Count Gebhard V sought out the last of the new families to be taken on as administrators, the knights of Dietenhofen.[177] In the 1280s Otto of Dietenhofen was Burgrave Frederick's magistrate in the Nuremberg *Landgericht;*[178] Rüdiger of Dietenhofen was Count Gebhard's castellan at Sandsee;[179] another Rüdiger was appointed marshal of the see of Eichstätt and castellan at Wernfels,[180] as we have seen; and Marshal Rüdiger's brother Frederick was appointed castellan at Arberg.[181] The marshal also had a younger brother with the same forename,[182] and he too was a castellan of Arberg by about 1300.[183] The oldest book of fiefs shows that the three brothers had been transferred to Eichstätt as *homines proprii,*[184] that is, in dependent legal status.

*    *    *

The concatenation of two truly princely characters, the farsighted churchman and the ambitious aristocrat, just at a time when the borderland of Franconia, Bavaria, and Swabia offered an unprecedented opportunity for territorial consolidation, has preserved for us a unique insight into the regional politics of the Empire at the end of the thirteenth century. Why was this region different? Usually we discern that the territorial plans of the bishoprics and their secular neighbors in Germany were impossible to reconcile, and this resulted in dangerous hereditary feuds: notably the counts of Tecklenburg at war with Osnabrück; the dukes of Brunswick-Lüneburg with Halberstadt and Hildesheim; the margraves of Brandenburg with Magdeburg; the counts of Habsburg with Basel; the dukes of Bavaria with Salzburg and Regensburg; the counts of Tirol with Brixen and Trent; the dukes of Brabant and their allies with Cologne; the counts-palatine of the Rhine with Trier, Worms, and Speyer; the landgraves of Hesse with Mainz; and the counts of Henneberg with Würzburg, struggles of which the chronicles are full just at this time. On past form one would have expected the same of the counts of Hirschberg against Eichstätt, yet Bishop Reinboto and Count Gebhard V emerge from the sources as kindred spirits with a parallel commitment to their region, county, and diocese, albeit with somewhat divergent aims and hopes, so that the bishop's appellation for the count, *amicus noster karissimus,* "our dearest friend,"[185] counts for more than scribal rhetoric.

Possibly this political relationship would not have run so smoothly had the count and countess not been childless, because it would have been much more difficult to reconcile the hopes and ambitions of the cathedral church as a territorial authority with the advocatial rights of the powerful Hirschberg line, which Gebhard V undoubtedly hoped to propagate. One inference that can be drawn from the texts of the wills of 1291 and 1296 is that the count and his wife were not so old in the 1290s as to rule out the possibility of their producing an heir, because provision was duly made for this. It would automatically have cut out the church of Eichstätt's claim, as we saw above.[186] So we can perceive that the dignified relationship existing between bishop and advocate was established before the moment when the ultimate demise of the dynasty had to be recognized. No doubt this arose not only from the wisdom and restraint of Bishops Reinboto and Conrad II and from the residual good sense of the fiery Count Gebhard V, but also from the tradition of cooperation, however irksome, forced upon the cathedral church since the Treaty of Eichstätt in 1245. Now came the time to pluck the reward of avoiding confrontation: the wills of 1291, 1296, and 1304.

The sources that Bishop Reinboto prudently had preserved[187] are rich enough to reveal to us what count and bishop could plan and carry out in detail: through the bishop's command of his ecclesiastical institutions; the count's command of his *Landgericht,* or regional jurisdiction;[188] the manorial landscape over which they reigned through their castellans and *officia;* the expanded retinues of *ministeriales* who carried out their tasks; and the annual round of local politics in which, for example, the burgraves of Nuremberg could be trusted and the dukes of Bavaria could not. The most important decision of all was taken at the bishop's house in Eichstätt on

15 December 1291 when the canons, knights, and townsmen watched the count of Hirschberg bequeath his possessions to the bishopric upon the sacred oath of his castellans, for whom Butler Henry of Hofstetten-Geyern stepped forward to append his seal to the document.[189] As undying corporations the bishoprics of Germany did enjoy a certain advantage over their lay competitors for territorial power, and in this case it paid off; Hirschberg did pass to Eichstätt in 1305. In addition, Bishops Reinboto and Conrad II had made shrewd purchases of property, reformed their territorial administration, and recruited new personnel. Now the see had three further secular objectives in view early in the fourteenth century: to secure the Hirschberg inheritance from disappointed competitors; to wrest the Herrieden lands from the counts of Oettingen; and to bid for the county of Graisbach as its ruling dynasty also declined toward failure.

## Notes

1. *Reg. Eichst.*, no. 917, pp. 281f.

2. MB, vol. XLIX, no. 46, p. 85.

3. Ibid., no. 109, pp. 163–65 (1280). On the system, see F. Beyerle, "Der Ursprung der Bürgschaft. Ein Deutungsversuch vom germanischen Rechte her," *ZRGGA* 47 (1927): 567–645; W. Ogris, "Die persönlichen Sicherheiten im Spätmittelalter. Versuch eines Überblicks," ibid. 82 (1965): 140–89; E. Kaufmann, "Bürgschaft und Einlager im spätmittelalterlichen fränkischen Recht," in *Les Sûretés personelles,* part 2, Recueils de la Société Jean Bodin pour l'Histoire comparative des institutions, vol. XXIX (Brussels, 1971), pp. 653–72, and "Bürgschaft," in HRG i, cols. 565–69; H. Kellenbenz, "Einlager," ibid., cols. 901–4.

4. MB, vol. XLIX, nos. 113–17, pp. 171–80, no. 120, pp. 184–86.

5. Stillfried and Maercker, *Monumenta Zollerana*, vol. II, no. 291, pp. 156–60, and *Reg. Eichst.*, no. 983, pp. 304f. (1284); MB, vol. XLIX, no. 144, pp. 236f. (1285), no. 150, pp. 244f. (1286), no. 178, pp. 281f. (1291).

6. Stillfried and Maercker, *Monumenta Zollerana,* vol. II, no. 403, pp. 232f. (1295), and no. 414, pp. 245ff. (1297).

7. MB, vol. XLIX, no. 373, pp. 573–76 (1294), and EL ff. 61r–v; *Reg. Eichst.*, no. 1112, pp. 336f. for the count's rear tenants there.

8. O. Puchner and H. Kunstmann, "Sandskron und Nagelhof," *Jahresbericht des Historischen Vereins für Mittelfranken* 74 (1954): 13–38.

9. Stillfried and Maercker, *Monumenta Zollerana,* vol. II, no. 411, pp. 241f., and MB, vol. XLIX, no. 222, pp. 339–42 for both exemplars: *Prima litera super castro et opido Abenberch, prima et secunda litera concordant.* For Abenberg used as the burgrave's toponymic, Stillfried and Maercker, *Monumenta Zollerana,* vol. II, no. 279, p. 149 (1283) and Bayr. Hsta. München, Ritterorden 1320 (1303).

10. EL ff. 15v, 17r–v, 52r–53v.

11. MB, vol. XLIX, no. 149, pp. 242f: "ius forestarum, quod vulgo wilpant dicitur."

12. Ibid., no. 206, pp. 320f. (1295), where their tenure was rearranged.

13. *Reg. Eichst.*, no. 937, p. 290 (1282); MB, vol. XLIX, no. 141, p. 233 (1284).

14. Ibid., no. 150, p. 244.

15. See ibid., no. 130, p. 199, and no. 134, pp. 206f. (1283); EL f. 2v.

16. *Nürnberger Urkundenbuch*, no. 742, p. 433.

17. Wiesflecker, *Meinhard der Zweite*, pp. 99f.

18. MB, vol. XLIX, no. 176, pp. 276–79 (1291).

19. Ibid., no. 181, pp. 286–88 and *Reg. Eichst.*, no. 1090, pp. 330f.

20. Wittmann, *Mon. Wittelsb.*, vol. II, no. 189, pp. 7–12.

21. Ibid., no. 203, pp. 70f. (1295), and no. 214, pp. 101–04 (1300); MB, vol. XLIX, no. 232, pp. 359f., and no. 235, pp. 365f. (1296).

22. On the ducal *ministeriales* of Wildenstein, see G. Voit, *Die Wildensteiner*, Sonderheft der Mitteilungen der Altnürnberger Landschaft (Nuremberg, 1964).

23. MB, vol. XLIX, no. 223, pp. 342–44; *Reg. Eichst.*, no. 1145, p. 350.

24. MB, vol. XLIX, nos. 224f., pp. 345–48.

25. The oldest land register, ES ff.15r–17v, records significant revenues or *Redditus in Peyrchingen* and its adjacent manors, especially Sulzkirchen and Rudertshofen.

26. *Hermanni Altahensis continuatio tertia*, p. 57.

27. MGH Consts. iv–2, nos. 1056f., pp. 1095f. (1299).

28. *Nürnberger Urkundenbuch*, no. 1073, chap. 14, pp. 635f.

29. Bayr. Hsta. München, Kl. Kastl 27 (1299).

30. *Reg. Eichst.*, nos. 1183–1315, pp. 360–404 (1297–1305).

31. MB, vol. XLIX, nos. 266–70, pp. 412–19 (1299–1302).

32. Ibid., nos. 295–98, pp. 454–61; nos. 300f., pp. 463–66.

33. See Bayerisches Staatsarchiv Nürnberg, Hochstift Eichstätt Literalien 9, ff. 124r–126v (1407).

34. MB, vol. XLIX, no. 312, pp. 481–85; *Reg. Eichst.*, no. 1251, pp. 387f.

35. MB, vol. XLIX, no. 313, pp. 485–87 (1302–1305).

36. Ibid., nos. 314 and 316, pp. 488–91 (1302); see also no. 320, p. 495 (1303).

37. Ibid., nos. 344f., pp. 527–32.

38. Ibid., no. 350, pp. 538–40.

39. See Niermeyer, *Mediae latinitatis lexicon minus*, p. 738 for *officium* as "group of estates run by a manorial agent."

40. See Chapter 7.

41. On the general significance of castles in southern Germany, see H.-M. Maurer, "Rechtsverhältnisse der hochmittelalterlichen Adelsburg vornehmlich in Südwestdeutschland," in H. Patze (ed.), *Die Burgen im deutschen Sprachraum. Ihre rechts- und verfassungsgeschichtliche Bedeutung*, VF, vol. XIX, part 2 (Sigmaringen, 1976), pp. 77–190; R. Endres, "Zur Burgenverfassung in Franken," ibid., pp. 293–329; P. Fried, "Hochadelige und landesherrlich-wittelsbachische Burgenpolitik im hoch- und spätmittelalterlichen Bayern," ibid. pp. 331–52; A. Antonow, *Planung und Bau von Burgen im süddeutschen Raum* (Frankfurt am Main, 1983); F. Uhlhorn, "Die territorialgeschichtliche Funktion der Burg. Versuch einer kartographischen Darstellung," *BDLG* 103 (1967): 9–31.

42. EL ff. 15v–23v.

43. See MB, vol. XLIX, no. 55, p. 97 (1250).

44. Ibid., no. 12, pp. 30–33 (1179); no. 20, pp. 44–47 (1186).

45. See Chapter 4, ns. 3–6.

46. MB, vol. XLIX, no. 109, p. 165 (1280); no. 113, p. 172 (1281).

47. Ibid., nos. 118f., pp. 181–84 (1282).

48. ES f. 1r.

49. Ibid., ff. 34r–36v, 37v.

50. Ibid. f. 2r; EL ff. 17v, 52r–53v; *Reg. Eichst.*, no. 1123, p. 342 (1294), and no. 1135, p. 346 (1295).

51. MB, vol. XLIX, no. 150, p. 244 (1286); EL f. 18v; ES ff. 29r–33v.

52. *Reg. Eichst.*, no. 1621, p. 502.

53. ES ff. 1r–v.

54. Stillfried and Maercker, *Monumenta Zollerana,* vol. II, no. 403, pp. 232f.

55. E.g., *Reg. Eichst.*, no. 1031, p. 315 (1287); no. 1245, p. 385 (1302); no. 1266, p. 391 (1303).

56. EL ff. 18v, 23r; ES f. 29r.

57. MB, vol. XLIX, no. 327, p. 503; see also no. 326, pp. 501f.

58. *Reg. Eichst.*, no. 1144, p. 349 (1296); *Gesta episc.*, p. 594; EL ff. 19r–v, 29r, 71r.

59. ES ff. 2r, 10r.

60. Ibid. ff. 10r–13v; see MB, vol. XLIX, no. 121, pp. 186f. (1282), for property transferred into the *officium.*

61. Ibid., no. 343, pp. 524–26.

62. *Gesta episc.*, p. 594.

63. MB, vol. XLIX, no. 222, pp. 339–42 (1296); no. 295, pp. 454–56 (1301), no. 312, pp. 481–85 (1302).

64. ES ff. 1v, 24r–28v.

65. *Gesta episc.*, p. 591; MB, vol. XLIX, no. 356, p. 543 (1305); *Reg. Eichst.*, no. 1665, p. 518 (1321).

66. Nürnberg, Eichstätt Literalien 9 (1407), ff. 97v–103r, 124r–126v.

67. MB, vol. XLIX, nos. 118f., pp. 181–84.

68. Ibid., no. 125, pp. 192f. (1282).

69. EL ff. 20r–v.

70. ES f. 9v.

71. See ns. 51f. above.

72. See MB, vol. XLIX, no. 255, pp. 392–94 (1297).

73. EL ff. 27v–28v, 71r.

74. ES f. 2r.

75. *Gesta episc.*, p. 592.

76. ES f. 2r. On these knights' fiefs see EL ff. 20v, 22v, 31r–v. Siegfried Jacko sold most of his fiefs, including "locum sive aream castelli quondam dicti Jackenberch," to Kaisheim in 1299; Bayr. Hsta. München, Kl. Kaishem 366.

77. ES ff. 5r–9v. There were nine woodlands; f. 1v.

78. Bresslau, *Chronik Heinrichs Taube,* p. 56; *Gesta episc.*, p. 597; C. Tillmann, *Lexikon der deutschen Burgen und Schlösser,* 4 vols. (Stuttgart, 1957–1961), p. 1224.

79. Niermeyer, *Mediae latinitatis lexicon minus,* pp. 1093–95; Spindler, *Anfänge,* pp. 128–30, 156–58; W. Volkert, "Ämte und Gerichte," in HBG ii, pp. 547f. In French the equivalent was *vidame,* in German *Viztum.*

80. *Reg. Eichst.*, no. 1521, pp. 475f.

81. Ibid., no. 1622, p. 502.

82. Ibid., no. 1635, p. 506. On this family, see W. Volkert, "Zur Geschichte der Herren von Seefeld (Das Urbar von 1393)," in D. Albrecht, A. Kraus, K. Reindel (eds.), *Festschrift für Max Spindler zum 75. Geburtstag* (Munich, 1969), pp. 215–37.

83. *Gesta episc.*, p. 591.

84. Ibid. has "castra etiam priora, que apud ipsam invenit ecclesiam, muris aliisque sollempnibus edificiis restauravit."

85. See his legislation in MB, vol. XLIX, no. 122, pp. 187–89 (1282); no. 139, pp. 212–31 (1283); no. 151, pp. 245f. (1286); no. 234, pp. 363f. (1296).

86. EL f. 4r.

87. F.-X. Buchner, "Das älteste Salbuch von Herrieden," *Sammelblatt des historischen Vereins Eichstätt* 29 (1914): 25–46.

88. ES ff. 37r, 38v; EL f. 4r.

89. ES ff. 39r–42r.

90. Ibid. ff. 42v–44r.

91. See Chapter 7.

92. On continuity and change in this sphere, see the variety of discussion in H. Lieberich, *Landherren und Landleute. Zur politischen Führungsschicht Baierns im Spätmittelalter,* Schriftenreihe zur bayerischen Landesgeschichte, vol. LXIII (Munich, 1964); E. Reidenauer, "Kontinuität und Fluktuation im Mitgliederstand der fränkischen Reichsritterschaft. Eine Grundlegung zum Problem der Adelsstruktur in Franken," in *Gesellschaft und Herrschaft. Eine Festgabe für Karl Bosl zum 60. Geburtstag* (Munich, 1969), pp. 87–152; Fleckenstein (ed.), *Herrschaft und Stand;* J. B. Freed, "Nobles, Ministeriales, and Knights in the Archdiocese of Salzburg," *Speculum* 62 (1987): 575–611; D. Rübsamen, *Kleine Herrschaftsträger im Pleissenland. Studien zur Geschichte des mitteldeutschen Adels im 13. Jahrhundert,* MDF, vol. XCV (Cologne and Vienna, 1987); and my "German Bishops and Their Military Retinues," pp. 174–79.

93. On them, see my *German Knighthood*, pp. 53–75.

94. MB, vol. XLIX, no. 218, pp. 334f.

95. See my *German Knighthood*, pp. 163–78.

96. EL f. 15v.

97. MB, vol. XLIX, no. 326, pp. 501f. (1303).

98. EL f. 17r.

99. MB, vol. XLIX, no. 45, p. 84.

100. Both had offspring mentioned in 1303 and 1304, the inference being that they had recently reached adulthood.

101. EL f. 22r; f. 31r records his origin as a Graisbach *ministerialis.*

102. MB, vol. XLIX, no. 343, p. 526.

103. See E. Schremmer, "Die Wirtschaftsmetropole Nürnberg" and "Die Wirtschaftsmetropole Augsburg," in HBG iii, pp. 478–97, 1080–96 and the literature cited there; see also P. Schmid, *Regensburg. Stadt der Könige und Herzöge im Mittelalter,* Regensburger Historische Forschungen, vol. VI (Kallmünz/Opf., 1977) and "Die Anfänge der regensburger Bürgerschaft und ihr Weg zur Stadtherrschaft," *ZBLG* 45 (1982): 483–539; K. Bosl, *Die Sozialstruktur der mittelalterlichen Residenz- und Fernhandelsstadt Regensburg. Die Entwicklung ihres Bürgertums vom 9.–14. Jahr-*

*hundert,* Bayerische Akademie der Wissenschaften. Abhandlungen der phil.-hist. Klasse, new ser., vol. LXIII (Munich, 1966); J. Jahn, "Topographie, Verfassung und Gesellschaft der mittelalterlichen Stadt—das Beispiel Augsburg," in P. Fried (ed.), *Miscellanea Suevica Augustana. Der Stadt Augsburg dargebracht zur 2000-Jahrfeier 1985,* Augsburger Beiträge zur Landesgeschichte Bayerische-Schwabens, vol. III (Sigmaringen, 1985), pp. 9–41; K. Bosl, *Die wirtschaftliche und gesellschaftliche Entwicklung des Augsburger Bürgertums vom 10. bis zum 14. Jahrhundert,* Bayerische Akademie der Wissenschaften, phil.-hist. Klasse, Sitzungsberichte, vol. III (Munich, 1969); D. Schröder, *Stadt Augsburg,* Historischer Atlas von Bayern, Teil Schwaben, vol. X (Munich, 1975); W. Baer, "Das Stadtrecht vom Jahre 1156," "Der Weg zur königlichen Bürgerstadt (1156–1276)," and "Die Entwicklung der Stadtverfassung 1276–1368," in G. Gottlieb et al. (eds.), *Geschichte der Stadt Augsburg. 2000 Jahre von der Römerzeit bis zur Gegenwart,* 2d ed. (Stuttgart, 1985), pp. 132–34, 135–40, 146–50. See also F. Opll, *Stadt und Reich im 12. Jahrhundert (1125–1190),* Forschungen zur Kaiser- und Papstgeschichte des Mittelalters. Beihefte zu J. F. Böhmer, Regesta Imperii, vol. VI (Vienna, Cologne, and Graz, 1986), pp. 33–39, 125–28, 135–42. See EL ff. 67r–69r for *cives* of Nuremberg, Regensburg, and Rothenburg with Eichstätt fiefs.

104. EL ff. 19r, 36r, 46r. These *ministeriales* go back at least to 1119; MB, vol. XLIX, no. 5 B, p. 22.

105. See my *"Ministeriales,"* pp. 219–21, 375–77.

106. Konstein Castle had, for example, passed by marriage to the knights of Muhr by 1273: see the sequence of names from Cuno and his son Cuno of Stein (MB, vol. XLIX, no. 29, p. 63 [1210]), Cuno the younger (*Reg. Eichst.,* no. 724, p. 221 [1243]), Cunegunde "vidua de Chuonenstein" and her daughter Matilda (MB, vol. XLIX, no. 64, p. 107 [1256]), Ulrich the younger of Muhr, the latter's husband, called Ulrich of Konstein (Bayr. Hsta. München, Ritterorden 3018 in 1273), to their descendants at Konstein with shares of the Muhr fiefs (EL ff. 17r, 33v–34v).

107. My *"Ministeriales,"* pp. 222, 378f.; EL ff. 15v–23v, 27v–29r, 52r–53v.

108. EL ff. 10r–14v.

109. Ibid. ff. 32r–41v.

110. Ibid. ff. 43v–49v.

111. Ibid. ff. 31r–v.

112. Ibid. ff. 54r–55r.

113. Ibid. ff. 41v–43r.

114. See Chapter 3, ns. 59–62.

115. See my *"Ministeriales,"* pp. 223f., 380; EL ff. 32r–41v, 62r–64v.

116. See my *"Ministeriales,"* pp. 224f., 381f.; EL ff. 32r–41v.

117. Bayr. Hsta. München, Kl. Kastl 19 (1253), 37 (1308), 109 (1343).

118. Wittmann, *Mon. Wittelsb.,* vol. II, no. 214, pp. 101f.

119. EL ff. 62r–64v.

120. E.g., MB, vol. XLIX, no. 107, pp. 160f. (1280).

121. EL ff. 32r, 62r.

122. Bayr. Hsta. München, Kl. Rebdorf 27 (1278); MB, vol. XLIX, no. 232, p. 360, and no. 235, p. 366 (1296); EL f. 32r for both toponymics, and MB, vol. XLIX, no. 312, pp. 481–85 (1302), where Godfrey *pincerna* of Altenburg seals as Godfrey of Flügelsberg.

123. EL f. 35r.

124. Ibid. f. 41r.

125. Bayr. Hsta. München, Kl. Rebdorf, fasc. 4 (1300).

126. E.g., MB, vol. XLIX, no. 190, p. 299 (1293); nos. 223f., pp. 342–46 (1296).

127. EL f. 39v.

128. Wittmann, *Mon. Wittelsb.*, vol. II, no. 222, pp. 134–41 and *Reg. Eichst.*, no. 1346, pp. 418ff. (1305). See MB, vol. XLIX, no. 312, p. 482 (1302) for the phrase "in officio nostro Eystetense."

129. MGH Consts. iii, no. 644, p. 630 (c. 1300).

130. MB, vol. XLIX, nos. 312f., pp. 481–87; p. 487 for the possessions "ad castrum et officium in Sandeser spectantibus."

131. See Wittmann, *Mon. Wittelsb.*, vol. II, no. 227, pp. 147f. (1307); MB, vol. XXXVI/A, pp. 630f., 641–48 (1326).

132. See Wittmann, *Mon. Wittelsb.*, vol. II, no. 189, p. 8 (1293); MB, vol. XXXVI/A, pp. 648f. (1326).

133. His tenures form a separate entry in the bishops' book of fiefs, EL ff. 27v–28v. His parents Henry and Elizabeth of Hofstetten were still alive in 1255; *Reg. Eichst.*, no. 782, p. 243.

134. Wittmann, *Mon. Wittelsb.*, vol. I, no. 124, pp. 305f. (1276).

135. *Reg. Eichst.*, no. 311, p. 101 (1122).

136. Ibid., no. 950, p. 294 (1282); EL f. 18v under the Eichstätt *homines proprii*.

137. MB, vol. XLIX, no. 255, pp. 392–94 (1297).

138. She is in evidence from Bayr. Hsta. München, Kl. Rebdorf 23 (1261) to *Reg. Eichst.*, no. 970, pp. 299f. (1282), and deceased in MB, vol. XLIX, no. 135, pp. 207f. (1283).

139. In MB, vol. XLIX, no. 189, p. 297 (1293) she is "nunc uxor mea," "now my wife."

140. Ibid., no. 181, p. 287, no. 223, p. 343.

141. See Bayr. Hsta. München, Kl. Rebdorf, fasc. 4 (1304) for a dispute about his property.

142. Wittmann, *Mon. Wittelsb.*, vol. II, no. 214, pp. 102f. (1300).

143. MB, vol. XLIX, no. 344, p. 529 (1304).

144. See Chapter 2, n. 38; MB, vol. XLIX, no. 344, p. 527 (1304) and recorded as a fief in EL f. 3v.

145. MB, vol. XLIX, no. 255, p. 393 (1297) (*pincerna*); EL f. 15v for "jus hereditarium in castellania in Hirzberg" (*Tegno*); EL f. 62v, 1305 (for Albert's *purchuta*, right of castle guard).

146. He was alive in October 1300; Bayr. Hsta. München, Kl. Eichstätt/St. Walburg, fasc. 6.

147. EL ff. 17r, 33v, 34v.

148. MB, vol. XLIX, no. 176, p. 279 (1291); nos. 232 and 235, pp. 360 and 366 (1296); nos. 312 and 314, pp. 483 and 488 (1302); nos. 344f., pp. 529 and 531 (1304).

149. Both still alive in 1334: Bayr. Hsta. München, Kl. Kastl 86.

150. Wittmann, *Mon. Wittelsb.*, vol. II, no. 189, pp. 7–12 (1293).

151. *Nürnberger Urkundenbuch*, no. 1073, p. 636 (c. 1300).

152. Ibid., no. 739, pp. 430ff. (1286) is Ulrich's main testament, executed in no. 747, p. 437 (1287) and confirmed by Godfrey in no. 749, pp. 437f. and by Ulrich's

widow Irmengard in no. 757, p. 442 (1287). See also the legacies to Eichstätt (MB, vol. XLIX, no. 148, pp. 241f. [1285]), Seligenporten (Bayr. Hsta. München, Kl. Seligenporten 34 in 1286 and *Nürnberger Urkundenbuch,* no. 737, pp. 429f. [1286]), Rebdorf (Bayr. Hsta. München, Kl. Rebdorf 31f. [1286–1287]), and Heilsbronn (Schuhmann and Hirschmann, *Urkundenregesten . . . Heilsbronn,* no. 179, p. 94 [1286]).

153. *Nürnberger Urkundenbuch,* no. 742, pp. 432f.

154. See MB, vol. XLIX, no. 223, pp. 342–44 (1296): he headed the list of Hirschberg vassals in EL f. 32r.

155. See *Reg. Eichst.,* no. 1380, p. 440 (1307); on the Wolfsteins and their future, Heinloth, *Neumarkt,* pp. 73–111; Wiessner, *Hilpoltstein,* pp. 52–55.

156. *Nürnberger Urkundenbuch,* no. 759, pp. 443f. (1288).

157. MB, vol. XLIX, no. 176, p. 279; no. 190, p. 299; no. 223, pp. 342–44; no. 232, p. 359; no. 235, pp. 365f.; no. 312, p. 483.

158. EL ff. 38r, 39r, 40r, 41r.

159. E.g., MB, vol. XLIX, no. 176, p. 279 (1291).

160. EL f. 33v.

161. *Nürnberger Urkundenbuch,* no. 894 A, p. 646.

162. Ibid., no. 731, p. 424 (1285); Schuhmann and Hirschmann, *Urkunden-regesten . . . Heilsbronn,* no. 261, pp. 134f. (1302).

163. Stillfried and Maercker, *Monumenta Zollerana,* vol. II, no. 399, p. 230 (1295); Bayr. Hsta. München, Brandenburg-Ansbach/Ansbach 899 (1307).

164. Dertsch and Wulz, *Urkunden . . . Oettingen,* no. 19, pp. 7f.

165. See Wittmann, *Mon. Wittelsb.,* vol. I, no. 90, p. 221, no. 92, p. 224, no. 93, p. 226 (1266–1268) at Augsburg and Verona.

166. Discussed in P. Herde, "Die Schlacht bei Tagliacozzo. Eine historisch-topographische Studie," *ZBLG* 25 (1962): 679–744.

167. *Reg. Eichst.,* 690, p. 209 (1235); also a brother or son "Heinricus iuvenis Cropf de novo castro Flugelingin" in Bayr. Hsta. München, Brandenburg-Ansbach/Wülzburg 1885 (1255).

168. *Reg. Eichst.,* no. 480, p. 153 (1187).

169. EL f. 43r.

170. Bayr. Hsta. München, Ritterorden 1284.

171. Hoffmann, *Urkunden . . . Kaisheim,* no. 295, p. 169.

172. For Henry *Struma* as canon, ibid. no. 296, pp. 169f. (1277), and Bayr. Hsta. München, Kl. Rebdorf, fasc. 4 (1300).

173. See *Nürnberger Urkundenbuch,* no. 618, p. 366 (1281) and EL f. 32r.

174. MB, vol. XLIX, no. 295, pp. 454–56.

175. Ibid. no. 296, p. 457; no. 300, pp. 463f. (1301). They also received an income from Eichstätt; EL f. 70v.

176. EL f. 43r.

177. As burgravial vassals in Stillfried and Maercker, *Monumenta Zollerana,* vol. II, no. 5, p. 3 (1235).

178. E.g., *Nürnberger Urkundenbuch,* no. 674, p. 396 (1282).

179. *Reg. Eichst.,* no. 983, p. 304 (1284).

180. Ibid., no. 937, p. 290 (1282); MB, vol. XLIX, no. 150, p. 244 (1286). He received fresh fiefs in 1295; ibid., nos. 214f., pp. 329–31.

181. *Reg. Eichst.*, no. 1062, p. 322 (1289) and no. 1135, p. 346 (1295).

182. MB, vol. XLIX, no. 141, p. 233 (1284).

183. ES f. 2r.

184. EL ff. 18r–v.

185. MB, vol. XLIX, no. 228, p. 353, and no. 234, p. 363 (1296).

186. See ns. 19 and 23 above.

187. His archive as represented in ibid., nos. 103–244, pp. 156–378 (1279–1297) outstrips the entire previous deposit of surviving material going back to the see's foundation in the eighth century.

188. The best sources are the reports compiled for King Louis IV, so the *Landgericht* will be treated in Chapter 6.

189. *Donacio castri Hirzperch* at MB, vol. XLIX, no. 181, pp. 286–88, states that the other castellans "propria non haberent sigilla."

# 6. Eichstätt and the Hirschberg Inheritance

The death of so powerful and well-endowed a nobleman as the last count of Hirschberg caused another stir in Bavarian politics. The dukes of Bavaria had never explicitly committed themselves to accepting the count's wills, and their predecessors had been quite up to occupying comital inheritances by force. Hardly had Gebhard V been interred at Rebdorf Abbey when Bishop Conrad II, just at the wrong moment, also found himself upon his deathbed.[1] In some haste the chapter therefore elected as their next bishop King Albert I's chancellor, Provost John of Zürich, as their best safeguard against the challenge awaited from the dukes of Bavaria.[2] Meanwhile one of Bishop Conrad's notaries, the canon Thomas of Herrieden,[3] prepared a joint memorial to the bishop and count for the continuations to the Eichstätt *Liber Pontificalis*, and he may have been responsible for the verse commemorating the bequest of Hirschberg to the church:

> Montem Cervorum clarum castrumque decorum
> Et res Chuonrado Gebhardus ego tibi trado,
> Que Willibaldi vice suscipias patris almi,
> Eternam requiem michi quod petat atque salutem.[4]

This can be rendered into English approximately as "I, Gebhard, transfer to you, Conrad, splendid Hirschberg with its castle and possessions, which you accept for Willibald our bountiful patron, claiming for me eternal rest and salvation." This echoed the salvatory intention expressed in the count's testaments, which quoted Matt. 6:20: "Lay up for yourselves treasure in heaven, where neither moth nor rust doth corrupt."[5]

The election of Bishop John, the measures taken to repeat Count Gebhard's wills and to publicize them, the previous alignment of Eichstätt and Hirschberg with the court of Albert I, and Duke Rudolf I's political eclipse since 1298 meant that the Bavarian threat was by no means so serious as feared at first. Nevertheless, Duke Rudolf and his younger brother Louis IV, usually on bad terms with each other, did cooperate to the extent of insisting upon an inquiry before they would accept the validity of a testamentary execution by the seven Hirschberg castellans and knights specified in 1304. This was conceded by the Church of Eichstätt in September 1305. Marshal Henry of Pappenheim was appointed to chair a committee on which the knights Henry of Seefeld, Hadmar of Laaber, and Berthold of Rehling were to appear for the dukes; and for the bishop, his marshal Rüdiger of Dietenhofen, his chamberlain Siegfried of Mörnsheim, and Louis of Eyb.[6] In October they delivered judgment at the ducal castle of Gaimersheim,[7] deviating very little from Count Gebhard V's intentions. What the dukes gained was the criminal jurisdiction of the county, the right to send judges for the three cases that carried the death penalty according to Bavarian custom and *Landfrieden:* homicide, robbery, and rape. The dukes claimed that the jurisdiction was a lapsed fief held from them by the count: "unser grafschaft di uns ledich ist wurden mit dem lantgericht," in short, the *Landgericht* of Hirschberg. In 1304 Gebhard V had himself conceded that the *Landgericht* was a fief, which would, upon his decease, revert to its overlord.[8] But he did not specify whether he thought this meant the dukes or the king.

By the end of the thirteenth century it was accepted that the neighboring *Landgerichte* of Nuremberg and Graisbach were imperial fiefs, but the ducal Bavarian claim to the Hirschberg *Landgericht* in 1305 was not disputed by the royal court. Apart from this valuable and prestigious jurisdiction, to the details of which we will return below, the substance was conceded, as Count Gebhard had planned, to the bishop of Eichstätt; Hirschberg Castle, over a hundred and twenty manors with their people, villages, and seignorial jurisdictions, and the woodlands. The best part of the comital retinue of knights, with their fiefs and castles, passed to the allegiance and service of Bishop John. And for the reasons that were outlined toward the end of the Introduction, the advocacies over the cathedral church and its lands, and indeed over the chapter and the episcopal towns, were permitted to lapse altogether.

Apart from the Hirschberg *Landgericht,* the dukes laid claim to further assets that were not considered to be appurtenant to Hirschberg Castle. The most important was the dominion of Sulzbach, in Hirschberg hands since the dissolution of the Sulzbach dynasty in 1188. King Albert I claimed it as a lapsed imperial fief, but the dukes rightly showed that it had always been an alodial inheritance. In 1307 the king accepted a compromise that left the dukes in possession.[9] Sulzbach, Werdenstein, and Ammerthal castles and the towns of Hirschau and Pfaffenhofen were converted into imperial fiefs conferred upon the dukes, who also succeeded the count as feoffee at Rosenberg Castle, purchased by Gebhard V's father before 1253.[10] Another perquisite of the Sulzbach domain was the advocacy of Kastl Abbey. In a separate will drawn up in 1301, Gebhard V had intended that the advocacy would lapse upon his death,[11] but the dukes set this aside and took the office for themselves. At Rebdorf and Plankstetten abbeys it proved possible to abolish the Hirschberg advocacies because they were Eichstätt fiefs,[12] and no new advocate was appointed. Count Gebhard left minor legacies to these houses,[13] to the cathedral chapter, to the nunnery of St. Walpurgis at Eichstätt, and to the distant priory of Berchtesgaden,[14] founded two centuries earlier by his collateral ancestors, the counts of Sulzbach. Other valuable Hirschberg possessions falling to the dukes had reluctantly been specified by Count Gebhard in 1293: Kösching Castle, Painten and Thongründlein forests, and the town of Hemau.[15]

In 1305 or 1306 the Eichstätt chapter complained that the dukes had overstepped this agreement by occupying manors in the Thongründlein district that belonged "by title of property," *titulo proprietatis,* to Hirschberg Castle, and should therefore have passed to their church.[16] The exact outcome of this dispute is not known, but it appears to have turned upon a generous concession by the bishop of Bamberg, who was overlord of Hemau and the Thongründlein *districtum,* or area.[17] The whole of the latter remained in ducal hands as a hereditary fief from the bishops of Eichstätt.[18] Three other strongholds not dependent upon Hirschberg Castle also had to be disposed of: Dollnstein and Wellheim, which were successfully claimed by the counts of Oettingen,[19] and Konstein Castle, which was delivered to Bavaria by its castellan, Henry of Muhr. Like the butlers of Hofstetten-Geyern, this knight owed allegiance to Eichstätt, Hirschberg, and Bavaria.[20] When his heirs failed in 1376,[21] the castle and dominion were thereafter directly administered by ducal officials.

The treaty of Gaimersheim in October 1305 averted the principal threat to Eichstätt's justifiable claims, but confusions still abounded over the intentions of the royal court. The king's *Landvogt* at Nuremberg, Dietegen of Kastel, thought that Sulzbach, Kastl, and Greding ought to revert to the Empire. As we saw in Chapter 4,[22] the valuable town and *officium* of Greding, with other more minor properties, were finally conceded to Eichstätt in 1311.[23] In the king's estimation the see of Eichstätt now ranked in political significance above the *Landvogtei* of Nuremberg. Bishop John was the royal chancellor, and when he was transferred to Strasbourg in 1306,[24] the new bishop of Eichstätt provided by the papacy was the king's confessor, Philip of Rathsamhausen, abbot of Pairis in Alsace.[25] The rightful territorial claims of the bishopric were too well established to leave the crown with much room for maneuver. In any case Pope Clement V wrote to the king to assist the new bishop in establishing and maintaining Eichstätt's property,[26] presumably against the dukes of Bavaria, the counts of Oettingen, and the *Landvogt* of Nuremberg. Bishop Philip (1306–1322) proved himself a most able successor to bishops Reinboto and Conrad II in that he solved the problem of the Oettingen stranglehold over the western properties of the see.[27] But he was hamstrung by the onerous Hirschberg debts, by the failure to establish Nassenfels Castle under its *vicedominus* as the center of an administrative *officium*,[28] and by the debilities of old age. In 1316 he therefore resigned the see to Canon Marquard of Hageln as procurator.[29] His other achievement was to establish firm episcopal rule over groups of people closely affected by the end of Hirschberg rule: the townsmen of Eichstätt and Berching and the *ministeriales* in Count Gebhard's retinue.

Turning first to the problems of finance, the bishopric was potentially enriched by the renders from more than a hundred and twenty Hirschberg manors. The see must also have been relieved by the abolition of comital taxes in town and country, which affected episcopal property, and had been in force since 1245 and earlier.[30] But as so often in the history of medieval administration, what the bishops noticed was a dire shortage of ready cash, and this turned into a drawn out crisis as they were pressed to repay the Hirschberg debts. Within two weeks of Count Gebhard's death, Bishop Conrad sold property to the provost of Spalt to raise sums against "the grave burden of debt which that lord count had contracted during his lifetime."[31] The last few weeks of the bishop's life were overshadowed by such sales, and his notary Thomas claimed that he had had to pay out more than £3,000.[32] Bishop Philip was then obliged to sell off property at irregular intervals[33] as well as raising major loans that totaled more than £4,000.[34] We are informed that he still had difficulty in finding the cash for the Hirschberg creditors,[35] and at one point his advocate at Hirschberg, Hilpolt of Hilpoltstein, was required to pay one of the Nuremberg moneylenders with a claim falling due.[36]

Writing in the mid-fourteenth century, Henry Taube of Selbach claimed that Marquard of Hageln as Bishop Philip's vicar and then as his successor in the bishopric (1322–1324) paid out an enormous total in excess of £18,000, clearing the debt burden contracted "in the time of his predecessors."[37] But the canon's account of the see's debts is rather unclear since he also states that under subsequent bishops the church continued to suffer from debts contracted before Bishop Marquard's time.[38] Possibly he confused the Hirschberg debts still outstanding with new debts contracted to pay for the war with Count Conrad of Oettingen, and other undertakings. During the 1340s Canon Henry stated that the see's finances had been in a poor state for forty years,[39] that is, ever since Eichstätt had shouldered the encumbrance of Count Gebhard's debts. So it appears likely that the debt burdens, both on the Hirschberg estate and the bishopric's own, ran concurrently until they were paid off by bishops Albert of Hohenfels (1344–1351) and Berthold of Nuremberg (1351–1365).[40]

Another expedient tried by Bishop Philip was to appeal to the royal court against the Jews to whom Count Gebhard had become indebted. Henry VII exempted Eichstätt from increases in the interest upon such debts,[41] and by 1313 the bishop appears to have been exempted from interest altogether, as well as achieving a temporary suspension of repayment of the principal sums.[42] In 1315 King Louis IV ratified these concessions, which foresaw that only the original loan sums need be repaid.[43] By this time Eichstätt's forces were fighting the king's enemies as part of his wider struggle to secure the German throne, and further relief was therefore forthcoming. The town of Weissenburg and its revenues were pledged for nothing to Bishop Philip;[44] the sum of £1,000 was promised from the king's *officia* of Landshut and Straubing;[45] and all the bishopric's debts to Jews were then canceled.[46] Since more than £18,000 still had to be found for debts between 1316 and 1322, the latter two measures may not have been put into effect. But it does appear that the see did gain some sort of fiscal relief at the expense of the Jews, without averting a continual emergency in the episcopal treasury.

The acquisition of Weissenburg, the advocacy of which the Bavarian dukes had wrested from the marshals of Pappenheim by the end of the thirteenth century, was significant in that this town would have become the urban center of the episcopal principality, ahead of Eichstätt, Greding, Berching, and Herrieden, which were not so favorably situated within Germany's commercial road network. In 1325, however, the king decided to redeem it for the agreed sum of £1,250 because he could pledge it again, with the town of Windsheim thrown in, to Burgrave Frederick of Nuremberg for £6,000.[47] Later, Weissenburg regained its independence as an imperial town.

The end of the Hirschberg advocacy again placed the bishops in full command of their cathedral town. The treaty of 1245 had confirmed the military defense of Eichstätt and Berching, and some of the taxes raised there, to the counts of Hirschberg.[48] The bishop appointed a secular magistrate, the *iudex civitatis Eystetensis,*[49] but during the 1280s Count Gebhard V had evidently overstepped his acceptable rights in Eichstätt. In 1291 Bishop Reinboto had therefore obliged him to grant a charter to the townsmen[50] guaranteeing privileges that fell far short of a self-governing communal form. Twelve townsmen were sworn in to supervise the watch, to oversee the markets, and to settle commercial cases arising with other towns. They were warned not to interfere with the prerogatives of the bishop, chapter, or advocate. The inhabitants were divided into *cives,* or townsfolk, who were granted complete freedom in contracting marriages, and persons of servile condition belonging to the bishop or count, who still required specific license unless they married among themselves. The citizen body was also granted unrestricted right of passage to and from the town, and its members might settle elsewhere as they chose. The count also promised not to levy any unjust exactions, and guaranteed that justice would be administered according to ancient custom. Significantly, this agreement was drawn up, not with the bishop as owner of Eichstätt, but with the *cives Eystetenses* as Count Gebhard's *fideles.* In 1296 he bequeathed his *ius advocaticium,* or advocacy, over them and over Berching to the bishopric,[51] and this duly took effect in 1305.

Clearly comital rights in Eichstätt were burdensome in spite of the 1291 charter, because Bishop Philip decided it was necessary to make concessions in 1307 to permit the town to recover from the Hirschberg regime.[52] The terms about the watch committee, marriage, and freedom of movement were confirmed. The bishop's control of the courts, and his right to appoint the magistrates, were restated. Within the cathedral precinct, the canons and their households enjoyed certain exemptions of their own. The relief offered to the town was financial. For thirty years the bishops would not be levying any taxes which the count had forced into custom. The church would receive £250 a year in taxes, the incomes from the tolls, and tribute from the Jews of Eichstätt.[53] The town appears not to have been significant enough to promote a discernible movement toward urban liberty, as the neighboring cathedral cities of Regensburg and Augsburg had achieved. Perhaps the bishops of Eichstätt did owe it to the counts of Hirschberg as advocates that such a tendency was not permitted to manifest itself. In any case, the citizen body seems to have done well out of its relationship with the bishops, nearly thirty of them being vassals of the see for income-bearing fiefs.[54]

&ast;   &ast;   &ast;

Although the accession of the Hirschberg lands and the assumption of full control over Eichstätt at first proved a financial disappointment to the bishops, the transfer of most of Count Gebhard V's retinue of knights to episcopal allegiance did turn Eichstätt into quite a formidable military power. We have already perceived that both the episcopal and comital retinues were considerably expanded at the end of the thirteenth century,[55] and the notary Thomas followed the wording of the count's wills when he reported in the *Liber Pontificalis* that rights over the *homines militaris condicionis,* or "vassals of military status," were acquired by Eichstätt.[56] The count's *ministeriales* had owed allegiance at the castles of Hirschberg, Sandsee, or Sulzbach. Those attached to Sulzbach passed automatically into Bavarian service.[57] The small group of Sandsee knights who had doubled as episcopal castellans there since 1302 became the bishop's vassals outright. Sulzbürg Castle was handed over by Godfrey of Wolfstein, as Count Gebhard had outlined in 1296.[58] As castellan he continued to serve Bishop Philip,[59] and accompanied him to Frankfurt in 1314 for Louis the Bavarian's election to the Empire.[60]

Although the direct evidence for transfers of allegiance is lacking,[61] the greater number of Count Gebhard's knights, as *ministeriales* attached to Hirschberg Castle, submitted to Eichstätt. There were some hundred and seventy knights in both episcopal and comital service about 1300. At the next count, after the accession of Bishop Rabno, seneschal of Wilburgstetten in 1365,[62] there were about ninety episcopal knights, but this list is incomplete. The next list, for Bishop Frederick of Oettingen's accession in 1384, is over two hundred strong, and includes the best part of the surviving Hirschberg military vassals according to the reckoning about 1300.[63] The transfer of the Hirschberg allegiances underlines the evidence, discussed in Chapter 5,[64] for the princes' reinforcement of the status of their knights as *ministeriales* and *homines proprii,* or vassals of servile status, in the Eichstätt region at the end of the thirteenth century. One Hirschberg knight who refused to submit to this was Rüdiger of Erlingshofen. By 1312 he had been broken by force, and committed himself and his heirs to accept no other lord than the bishop of Eichstätt, "des eigen ich bin," or "whose property I am," according to the traditional rules on status for *ministeriales*.[65] To rub in the lesson, his castle was knocked down.[66]

The administrative reform introduced into the see at the close of the thirteenth century provided the bishops with a system to apply to their much extended territory after 1305. This allowed for subdivision into a dozen *officia;* their defense by large central castles; and the employment of groups of castellans at Hirschberg, where Hilpolt of Hilpoltstein succeeded Hartwig of Simbach as Bishop Philip's advocate;[67] at Nassenfels under its *vicedominus* until 1315 or 1316,[68] followed by new "castellani nostri in Nazzenvels," "our castellans in Nassenfels";[69] at Sandsee and Abenberg under new advocates;[70] at Mörnsheim where the chamberlain Siegfried of Otting remained in command until Bishop Marquard's time;[71] and the consortium that ran Arberg and its *officium*.[72] For the other *officia*, Berching, Greding, and Spalt, little is known about their castellans and administrators in the decades after 1305. At Wernfels the bishop's marshal Rüdiger of Dietenhofen was still in office in 1317.[73] At that time the Herrieden *officium* had just been devastated during the feud to regain control of it.[74] Kipfenberg was temporarily pledged to raise yet more cash, and was redeemed again by Bishop Marquard.[75]

The war in the northwest of the diocese, the concessions to Eichstätt town, the wrangle at the royal court over possession of Greding, and the apparent threat of bankruptcy were far from exhausting the bishops' problems as heirs of the Hirschberg possessions. One of them concerned the regional magistracy or *Landgericht* of Hirschberg, inherited by the dukes of Bavaria in 1305. Very little is known about this *Landgericht* as actually exercised under Count Gebhard V, it being called the *iudicium provinciale*, or regional jurisdiction, in 1302.[76] In 1304, when the count temporarily held the *Landgericht* of Graisbach as well, the crown confirmed the privilege of exclusive jurisdiction in the two counties[77] against possible claims made by adjacent *Landgerichte*. In the years after 1305, the dukes apparently appointed judges who overstepped the rights and duties of the *Landgericht* at the expense of the bishop's manorial jurisdictions in the Bavarian half of the diocese, of the juridical autonomy of the clergy, and of the urban immunities there.[78] Then in 1316 Canon Marquard of Hageln came to a temporary agreement with the current *Landrichter*, or judge, Conrad of Haslach, that his courts would concern themselves solely with the "three cases" in Bavarian criminal jurisdiction that carried capital sentences: "umb diube, notnunft und umb totshlege," that is, theft, rape, and homicide.[79]

In 1319 the church requested King Louis IV to arrive at a permanent solution to the problem of this *Landgericht*'s competence. This was important for our purpose because a committee was set up to establish what the procedures were thought to have been under Count Gebhard V,[80] and the subsequent edict was based for the main part upon its findings.[81] The king agreed that normally a freeborn lord aged more than twenty-four would sit as *Landrichter*. Juries of seven or more men, preferably knights, would attend the court, and the felonies to be tried were outlined slightly more widely than in 1316: arson, rape, secret murder and open homicide, and the similar distinction between theft and robbery. The accused were to be brought to trial within fourteen days, being taken under constraint to the next meeting of the peripatetic courts.[82] Conviction on these counts resulted in the death penalty, and the *Landrichter* was entitled to requisition timber for gallows. Assault, causing bodily harm, and grievous damage could still be compounded by heavy fines. Other profitable rights exercised by the *Landrichter* included supervision of safe conducts for traffic on the highways and waterways, and licenses for building new castles, mills, and inns.[83] Sources for the cases heard in this *Landgericht* are not numerous for the earlier fourteenth century either. There are, however, records for civil disputes heard on fiefs, tithes, head taxes, and other rights and jurisdictions.[84] The reasonably comprehensive Hirschberg edict of 1320 is valuable for its general picture of the functions of the south German *Landgerichte*, as well as preserving some idea of juridical practice at the end of the thirteenth century, under Count Gebhard V.

Bishop Philip of Rathsamhausen had been a strong supporter of Louis the Bavarian during his contest with Frederick of Austria for the title to the Empire.[85] For this reason the emperor may have been inclined to deal leniently with the see when a new bishop, Henry V of Reicheneck (1329–1344), and a section of his clergy upheld the cause of the Avignon papacy against him.[86] But one consequence was to eclipse the bishopric's political importance, since it was divided internally over the issue. Bishop Gebhard III, count of Graisbach (1324–1327), was the last of the pro-Bavarian bishops for the time being. He accompanied Louis IV to Italy, and died of a pestilence at Pisa.[87] Pope John XXII then provided the abbot of Ebrach to the see, but the chapter refused to accept him and elected as procurator one of their canons, Burgrave Frederick of Nuremberg. The pope tried again, and in 1329 provided Henry, butler of Reicheneck.

The emperor prevaricated about these events. In 1330 he offered his special protection to the bishopric, obviously against its pro-papal pastor,[88] and then decided to recognize the new bishop after all.[89] No doubt the reason was to prevent a further series of hostile enactments from Avignon, since the emperor could rely upon the cathedral chapter and town of Eichstätt to support him against the bishop. Under the provost, Albert of Hohenfels, the chapter exempted itself from any share in the responsibility for the see's debts, a measure that the emperor endorsed.[90] The provost then bought two of the *castra priora,* Nassenfels and Mörnsheim, from the impoverished bishop.[91] In 1337 Henry of Reicheneck recognized the extreme weakness of his position. He resigned all the temporalities to the canons and the last of his secular supporters, Hilpolt of Hilpoltstein, was removed from the advocacy of Hirschberg.[92]

When the bishop died in 1344, the chapter was able to install Albert of Hohenfels as his successor, but before long the wider political realities again began to turn against Eichstätt's pastor. The election of Charles IV in 1346 was a victory for Avignon; Louis the Bavarian died in 1347; and Pope Clement VI refused to recognize Albert as bishop. In 1351 these conflicts of interest were settled amicably. Albert of Hohenfels resigned in favor of Burgrave Berthold of Nuremberg who reigned as bishop until 1365. Albert retained the government of the see in spiritual and temporal affairs, resigning them on grounds of age in 1353. He died in 1355.[93] For Eichstätt one advantage of Albert of Hohenfels' long predominance as provost, bishop, and procurator was his great personal wealth. In any case, his understanding of financial affairs meant that at least the Hirschberg debts appear to have been paid off by about 1350, although his successor still found other encumbrances upon the see. On the other hand, the uncertainties about the episcopal office since the death of Bishop Gebhard III in 1327 had also weakened the bishopric, and activated a number of feuds among the knights that inevitably cast the diocese into further disorder. Henry Taube conventionally described these men as *tyranni,* or tyrants, and says that Louis the Bavarian connived at their attacks upon Bishop Henry V in the 1330s.[94] These disorders continued into the time of Bishops Albert and Berthold,[95] which is why they decided to build a new fortified residence, the Willibaldsburg, on a well-defended site but within view of Eichstätt.[96]

As our best source for the events of the first half of the fourteenth century concerning the episcopal court of Eichstätt, Henry Taube certainly delivers a gloomy report, substantiated by what we know of major and minor feuds as well as the Hirschberg debts. But for Louis the Bavarian's decision to compromise with the pro-papal Bishop Henry V in 1331, the case might have been as bad as the continual Bavarian attacks upon the diocese between 1292 and 1301.[97] Actually, Emperor Louis had little to fear from the bishop because the castles of Mörnsheim, Nassenfels, Hirschberg, and Sandsee came into the hands of his own party in the Eichstätt region under the direction of Albert of Hohenfels. However, not until the reign of Bishop Frederick IV (1383–1415) did Eichstätt's potential as a territorial principality remade by the Hirschberg inheritance again begin to make a splash in imperial and ecclesiastical politics. As his biographer pointed out, he proved well able to hold his own in the frequent feuds and wars that were engulfing the provinces of Bavaria, Swabia, and Franconia.[98] His successes were remembered for a long time. In the sixteenth century Count William Werner of Zimmern related in his chronicle of the bishops of Eichstätt that "for many years Bishop Frederick had ruled the bishopric very wisely, cleverly, and soundly, for God and nature had bestowed upon him particularly good fortune."[99]

## Notes

1. On their deaths, *Reg. Eichst.*, no. 1297, p. 400, and no. 1315, p. 404.

2. Ibid., no. 1316, pp. 408f., and MB, vol. XLIX, nos. 359f., pp. 552–56 (1305) where he is "sacre imperialis aule cancellarius."

3. Attested in ibid. no. 311, p. 481 (1302), and no. 350, p. 540 (1305). In the *Liber Pontificalis* continuation, he claimed that upon Bishop Conrad II's business, "quasi his omnibus personaliter interfuit eaque ut plurima vidit, percepit et audivit"; *Gesta episc.*, p. 592.

4. *Gesta episc.*, p. 592.

5. MB, vol. XLIX, no. 181, p. 286 (1291); no. 223, p. 343 (1296); no. 344, p. 527 (1304).

6. Ibid., no. 362, pp. 558–60; *Reg. Eichst.*, no. 1345, pp. 417f.

7. Wittmann, *Mon. Wittelsb.*, vol. II, no. 222, pp. 134–41; *Reg. Eichst.*, no. 1346, pp. 418ff.

8. MB, vol. XLIX, no. 344, p. 528: "excepto dumtaxat provinciali iudicio, quod domino feodi, ad quem do iure pertinet."

9. Wittmann, *Mon. Wittelsb.*, vol. II, nos. 225 and 227, pp. 144–48 (1306–1307).

10. MB, vol. XLIX, no. 58, pp. 100f. (1253).

11. Bayr. Hsta. München, Kl. Kastl 30 A.

12. EL f. 3v as fiefs; MB, vol. XLIX, no. 345, p. 532 (1304) on their reversion to Eichstätt, confirmed by the royal court in *Reg. Eichst.*, no. 1430, p. 452 (1309).

13. See ibid., no. 1297, p. 400 (1296); Bayr. Hsta. München, Kl. Plankstetten Literalien 1, *Grund- und Salbuch, 1461*, ff. 5r–6r (1301).

14. See *Nürnberger Urkundenbuch*, no. 841, p. 500 (1293); MB, vol. XLIX, nos. 226–28, pp. 348–54 (1296); *Reg. Eichst.*, no. 1542, p. 481 (1314). On the nunnery, see Holzbauer, *Mittelalterliche Heiligenverehrung*, pp. 146–53.

15. See Wittmann, *Mon. Wittelsb.*, vol. II, no. 189, pp. 7–12.

16. MB, vol. XLIX, no. 363, pp. 561f. (1305–1306).

17. Wittmann, *Mon. Wittelsb.*, vol. II, no. 223, p. 142 (1305).

18. EL f. 2r.

19. See Chapter 7.

20. EL ff. 17r, 33v–34v, and Wittmann, *Mon. Wittelsb.*, vol. II, no. 228, pp. 149–51 (1308).

21. See Kuno of Laiming and Konstein in Lieberich, *Landherren*, p. 116, note 486.

22. Chapter 4, note 96.

23. *Reg. Eichst.*, nos. 1477f., p. 463; no. 1494, p. 468. See also the archbishop of Mainz's letter on the subject; L. Steinberger, "Ein unbekanntes Schreiben Erzbischof Peters von Mainz an König Heinrich VII.," *Neues Archiv* 40 (1915–1916): 427–31.

24. *Reg. Eichst.*, no. 1351, pp. 421f.

25. Ibid., no. 1354, pp. 423–33.

26. Ibid., no. 1356, p. 433 (1306).

27. See Chapter 7.

28. See Chapter 5, notes 79–82.

29. *Reg. Eichst.*, no. 1611, p. 499.

30. See Chapter 3, note 101.

31. MB, vol. XLIX, no. 350, pp. 538–40 (1305).

32. *Gesta episc.*, p. 592.

33. *Reg. Eichst.*, no. 1363, p. 435 (1306); no. 1509, p. 472 (1312); nos. 1547f., pp. 483f. (1314); no. 1567, p. 488 (1315); no. 1619, p. 501 (1317); no. 1647, p. 509 (before 1319).

34. Ibid., no. 1629, p. 504 (1317) and no. 1635, p. 506 (1318).

35. E.g., MB, vol. L, no. 33, p. 32 (1307–1316).

36. *Reg. Eichst.*, no. 1569, p. 488 (1315).

37. Bresslau, *Chronik Heinrichs Taube*, p. 125 and *Gesta episc.*, p. 594.

38. Bresslau, *Chronik Heinrichs Taube*, p. 127.

39. Ibid., p. 128.

40. Ibid., pp. 129, 131.

41. MGH Consts. iv–1, nos. 357f., pp. 305f. (1310) and nos. 680f., pp. 648f. (1311).

42. Ibid., iv–2, no. 1136, p. 1135.

43. Ibid., v, no. 202, pp. 182f.

44. Ibid., nos. 297f., pp. 258f. (1315).

45. *Reg. Eichst.*, no. 1584, p. 492 (1315).

46. MGH Consts. v, no. 318, p. 272 (1315).

47. G. Landwehr, *Die Verpfändung der deutschen Reichsstädte im Mittelalter*, Forschungen zur deutschen Rechtsgeschichte, vol. V (Cologne and Graz, 1967), p. 446.

48. MB, vol. XLIX, no. 46, pp. 85–87; *Reg. Eichst.*, no. 738, pp. 226f.

49. See MB, vol. XLIX, no. 172, p. 270 (1289).

50. Ibid. no. 176, pp. 276–79; *Reg. Eichst.*, no. 1081, pp. 327f.

51. MB, vol. XLIX, no. 224, pp. 345f.; *Reg. Eichst.*, no. 1146, pp. 350f.

52. MB, vol. L, no. 35, pp. 33–38; *Reg. Eichst.*, no. 1400, pp. 445f.

53. On Eichstätt's own coinage, see E. B. Cahn, *Die Münzen des Hochstifts Eichstätt*, Bayerische Münzkataloge, vol. III (Grünwald bei München, 1962).

54. EL ff. 29v–31r. Compare with the findings of R. Brandl-Ziegert, "Die Sozialstruktur der bayerischen Bischofs- und Residenzstädte Passau, Freising, Landshut und Ingolstadt. Die Entwicklung des Bürgertums vom 9. bis zum 13. Jahrhundert," in K. Bosl (ed.), *Die mittelalterliche Stadt in Bayern*, Beiträge zur Geschichte von Stadt und Bürgertum in Bayern, vol. II (Munich, 1974), pp. 18–127.

55. See Chapter 5, notes 107, 116.

56. *Gesta episc.*, p. 592.

57. E.g., Bayr. Hsta. München, Kl. Kastl 37 (1308), 48 (1313), 63 (1323).

58. MB, vol. XLIX, no. 223, p. 343; see Godfrey as castellan there in 1307; *Reg. Eichst.*, no. 1380, p. 440.

59. E.g., ibid., no. 1392, p. 443 (1307).

60. Ibid., no. 1555, p. 485.

61. The oldest episcopal book of fiefs, assembled for the most part between 1305 and 1320, still preserves the categories of allegiance prior to Count Gebhard V's death in 1305.

62. EL ff. 74r–85r.

63. Ibid. ff. 90r–122r.

64. Chapter 5, notes 94–102.

65. *Reg. Eichst.*, no. 1514, pp. 473f. (1312); see my *German Knighthood*, pp. 53–75 on the rules.

66. Bresslau, *Chronik Heinrichs Taube*, p. 124: "Huius tempore castrum Erlieshoven est destructum." The site was sold to Eichstätt in 1332; MB, vol. L, no. 326, p. 237.

67. See *Reg. Eichst.*, no. 1392, p. 443 (1307), and no. 1415, p. 449 (1308).

68. Ibid., no. 1581, p. 491 (1315).

69. E.g., MB, vol. L, no. 336, p. 247 (1333).

70. Ibid., no. 77, p. 71 (1311); *Reg. Eichst.*, no. 1509, p. 472 (1312); no. 1632, p. 505 (1318).

71. *Gesta episc.*, p. 594.

72. EL ff. 52r–53v.

73. MB, vol. L, no. 170, pp. 127f.

74. See Chapter 7.

75. See *Reg. Eichst.*, no. 1649, p. 510 (1319), and *Gesta episc.*, p. 595.

76. MB, vol. XLIX, no. 312, p. 483; see H. O. Müller, *Das kaiserliche Landgericht der ehemaligen Grafschaft Hirschberg. Geschichte, Verfassung und Verfahren*, Deutschrechtliche Beiträge. Forschungen und Quellen zur Geschichte des deutschen Rechts, vol. VII, part 3 (Heidelberg, 1911); H. Kalisch, "Die Grafschaft und das Landgericht Hirschberg," *ZRGGA* 34 (1913): 141–94; H. E. Feine, "Die kaiserlichen Landgerichte in Schwaben im Spätmittelalter," ibid. 66 (1948): 228ff.; Hirschmann, *Eichstätt*, pp. 24–28; Heinloth, *Neumarkt*, pp. 23–30; W. Volkert, "Die spätmittelalterliche Gerichtsbarkeit," in HBG ii, pp. 543f.

77. MGH Consts. iv–1, no. 187, p. 161.

78. See *Reg. Eichst.*, no. 1608, p. 498 (1316). On the distinctions between higher

and lower courts in Bavarian jurisdiction, see E. Wohlhaupter, *Hoch- und Nieder-gericht in der mittelalterlichen Gerichtsverfassung Bayerns,* Deutschrechtliche Beiträge, vol. XII, part 2 (Heidelberg, 1929), pp. 141–335; P. Fried, "Grundherrschaft und Dorfgericht im spätmittelalterlichen Herzogtum Bayern," in H. Patze (ed.), *Die Grundherrschaft im späten Mittelalter,* VF, vol. XXVII, part 2 (Sigmaringen, 1983), pp. 277–312; Volkert (as in n. 76), pp. 535–38; Wittmann, *Mon. Wittelsb.,* vol. II, no. 193, pp. 22–33 (1293) and no. 217, pp. 110–26 (1300).

79. MGH Consts. v, no. 381, pp. 320f., and *Reg. Eichst.,* no. 1612, pp. 499f.

80. MB, vol. L, no. 198, p. 147, and *Reg. Eichst.,* no. 1642, pp. 507f.

81. MGH Consts. v, no. 597, pp. 475–77, and *Reg. Eichst.,* no. 1660, pp. 514ff. (1320). On the king's own initiatives as a law giver see H. Lieberich, "Kaiser Ludwig der Baier als Gesetzgeber," *ZRGGA* 76 (1959): 173–245, and "Oberbayerisches Landrecht," in HRG iii, cols. 1129–33; H. Angermeier, *Königtum und Landfriede im deutschen Spätmittelalter* (Munich, 1966), pp. 123–74; W. Jaroschka, "Das ober-bayerische Landrecht Ludwigs des Bayern," in Glaser (ed.), *Zeit,* pp. 379–87; G. Pfeiffer, "Die bayerisch-fränkische Landfriedenseinung Kaiser Ludwigs vom 1 Juli 1340," in *Festschrift für Hermann Heimpel zum 70. Geburtstag,* Veröffentlich-ungen des Max-Planck-Instituts für Geschichte, vol. XXXVI, part 2 (Göttingen, 1972), pp. 801–14; and C. Rotthoff, "Die politische Rolle der Landfrieden zwischen Maas und Rhein von der Mitte des 13. Jahrhunderts bis zum Auslaufen des Bacha-racher Landfriedens Ludwigs des Bayern," *RVB* 45 (1981): 75–111.

82. There were a number of meeting places in the county; see the cases recorded in *Reg. Eichst.,* no. 1612, pp. 499f. (1316); MB, vol. L, no. 198, p. 147 (1319); Ordinariatsarchiv Eichstätt 44f. (1338); Bayr. Hsta. München, Kl. Plankstetten 16 (1339).

83. H. C. Peyer, *Von der Gastfreundschaft zum Gasthaus. Studien zur Gastlichkeit im Mittelalter,* MGH Schriften, vol. XXXI (Hanover, 1987), p. 104.

84. E.g., MB, vol. L, no. 379, p. 269 (1338); no. 387 A, p. 275 (1339); no. 416, pp. 291f. (1342); no. 605, p. 393 (1351); Bayr. Hsta. München, Kl. Plankstetten 16 (1339), Kl. Seligenporten fasc. 23 (1343), Ritterorden 1379 (1345); Ordinariatsarchiv Eichstätt 44f. (1338).

85. On this period, see H. Angermeier, "Bayern in der Regierungszeit Kaiser Ludwigs IV. (1314–1347)," in HBG ii, pp. 141–81, and "Kaiser Ludwig der Bayer und das deutsche 14. Jahrhundert," in Glaser (ed.), *Zeit,* pp. 369–78.

86. On these problems, see A. Schütz, "Der Kampf Ludwigs des Bayern gegen Papst Johannes XXII. und die Rolle der Gelehrten am Münchner Hof," in Glaser (ed.), *Zeit,* pp. 388–97; H. Angermeier in HBG iii, pp. 158f; H. S. Offler, "Empire and Papacy: the Last Struggle," *Transactions of the Royal Historical Society,* series 5, 6 (1956): 21–47.

87. Bresslau, *Chronik Heinrichs Taube,* p. 125.

88. MB, vol. L, no. 306, pp. 223f.

89. Ibid., no. 312, pp. 228f. (1331).

90. Ibid., no. 329, pp. 240f. (1332).

91. Ibid., no. 322, pp. 234f. (1332), and no. 357, p. 257 (1336).

92. On these events, Bresslau, *Chronik Heinrichs Taube,* pp. 127f.; MB, vol. L, no. 379, p. 269 (1338). See Hilpolt as "pfleger ze hirsperg" in Bayr. Hsta. München,

Kl. Plankstetten Literalien I, f. 70v (1334) and the Bavarian knights of Wildenstein at Sandsee in MB, vol. L, no. 383 A, p. 271.

93. All this explained in Bresslau, *Chronik Heinrichs Taube,* pp. 128–31.

94. Ibid., pp. 127f.

95. MB, vol. L, nos. 458 and 462, pp. 314ff. (1345); no. 479, p. 325 (1345); no. 544, pp. 354f. (1348); nos. 603f., pp. 391f. (1351); Bayr. Hsta. München, Brandenburg-Ansbach 2075 (1345) and Kl. Eichstätt/St. Walburg for 15 Nov. 1344 and 8 Mar. 1345.

96. Bresslau, *Chronik Heinrichs Taube,* p. 56; *Gesta episc.,* p. 597; F. Merzbacher, *Die Bischofsstadt,* Arbeitsgemeinschaft für Forschung des Landes Nordrhein-Westfalen. Geisteswissenschaften, vol. XCIII (Cologne and Opladen, 1961), p. 30.

97. See Chapter 5, notes 20–26.

98. *Gesta episc.,* pp. 602–06.

99. W. Kraft, *Die Eichstätter Bischofschronik des Grafen Wilhelm Werner von Zimmern,* Veröffentlichungen der Gesellschaft für fränkische Geschichte, series 1, vol. III (Würzburg, 1956), p. 73: "Darnach regiert er dàs bischthumb lange jar gantz weyslich, geschicktlich und wol, dan got und die natur in mit aynem besonderen glück darzu begabet."

# 7. Bishop and Count in the West of Eichstätt's Region

To the west of Eichstätt, where the see divided ecclesiastical jurisdiction with the bishops of Augsburg, important political connections were built up with three dynasties as the principal episcopal feoffees there: the counts of Oettingen, Graisbach, and Hohentrüdingen. The relationship with the Oettingen resembled Eichstätt's position with regard to the counts of Hirschberg in that the Oettingen counts were advocates of the most substantial episcopal properties in the west of the region. The bishops had also conferred direct fiefs upon a large number of Oettingen castellans and *ministeriales,* more than seventy of them.[1] The arrangements with the other two dynasties were slightly more favorable to the bishops because the castles of Graisbach and Hohentrüdingen were fiefs held from Eichstätt,[2] giving the bishops the legal possibility of claiming part or all of their dominions as lapsed fiefs appurtenant to those castles, should the dynasties eventually fail. In a charter issued in 1265, Count Berthold II of Graisbach had confirmed what fiefs he held of Bishop Hildebrand,[3] including "mediam partem castri in Greifspach," or "half of the castle of Graisbach," his chief residence. In the oldest Eichstätt book of fiefs a generation later, this was improved to "superum castrum in Graispach" or "the upper castle at Graisbach." These counts' vassals enjoyed direct fiefs from the church of Eichstätt too; seventeen Graisbach men and nineteen Hohentrüdingen.[4]

Although Eichstätt itself was situated in Bavaria, these relationships were the modernized version of the bishopric's long-standing connections with Franconia and Swabia. As we have seen,[5] the crown gave an extensive forest to Eichstätt in the eleventh century,[6] the boundary passing at one point "where two provinces are divided, namely Swabia and Franconia." Early in the twelfth century Duke Frederick of Swabia's *Landfriede* for his duchy was approved by the bishops of Augsburg and Eichstätt[7] because the latter had interests there. But little is known about Eichstätt's dealings with the aristocracy of the western half of the region in the twelfth century.

Indeed, there is not a great deal of reliable evidence about the Oettingen and Hohentrüdingen dynasties before the thirteenth,[8] and attempts to show derivations from the local counts of the tenth and eleventh centuries by means of comparing forenames have not proved convincing. The origins of the Graisbachs are better known, and show both the mobility between castle residences and the significance of scattered inheritances among the south German nobility at the time when dynasties or lineages with new toponymics derived from large castles were emerging from the wider kin-groups of the tenth and eleventh centuries.[9]

The dynastic name of Graisbach was adopted in the thirteenth century. Before this the counts had resided in Lechsend Castle, called Lechsgemünd in medieval times, and used the latter as their toponymic.[10] In his *Book of the Saxon War,* Bruno of Merseburg reported that a nobleman, or *princeps,* called Henry of Lechsgemünd fell at the Battle of Mellrichstadt in 1078, fighting on the side of Henry IV.[11] Then a Cuno of Lechsgemünd married into the powerful Swabian family of the counts of Achalm,[12] and his descendants included a Liutgard who married into the Bavarian dynasty of Frontenhausen, Matrei, and Mittersill. By the 1130s she and her husband, Count Henry of Frontenhausen, had apparently dispossessed their cousins of Lechsgemünd. They established a new dynasty also called after Lechsgemünd and gave it local solidity by founding a Cistercian monastery at Kaisheim nearby.[13]

As so often in German regional history, the ecclesiastical establishments preserved information about the use and abuse of their property by the secular nobility, and this yields information about the Oettingen dynasty. By the thirteenth century they had become advocates of Neresheim Abbey, which duly suffered from their depredations.[14] To make amends to the Church, not only had they given Oettingen Castle to the Teutonic Order by about 1240 but they also founded a nunnery at Kirchheim in 1270.[15] In the meantime, Wallerstein Castle had become their chief residence; but unlike the counts of Grögling and Dollnstein removing to Hirschberg and the counts of Lechsgemünd to Graisbach, they did not adopt the toponymic as their family name.[16] Although they possessed a considerable retinue of *ministeriales* and castellans in the thirteenth century, there is not much information about such families in Oettingen service in the twelfth.[17] The fact that their retinue was about a hundred strong by the end of the thirteenth century indicates the considerable power and wealth of the dynasty at this time.[18] And like the counts of Hirschberg and Graisbach, and the burgraves of Nuremberg, the Oettingen had also established their authority as *Landrichter* over a wide area in the thirteenth century.[19]

Just at the time when the see of Eichstätt was recuperating its secular authority under Bishop Reinboto of Meilenhart, his program began to face a serious challenge from the younger branch of the Oettingen dynasty. As we have seen,[20] the Oettingen were in possession of major advocacies over episcopal territory on the Franconian and Swabian side of the Eichstätt region. Before 1279 they appear to have agreed upon a division of dynastic property and resources to the detriment of the younger branch of the family. But the share of the latter did include some of these advocacies in the name of Count Louis the younger of Oettingen and of his brother Conrad, who seems actually to have exercised them. Even by German aristocratic standards, which tolerated quite violent individual behavior, this Count Conrad was a troublemaker, the bane of the Church, hated by his own family and neighbors; and eventually he was declared an outlaw. He fled into sanctuary at Kaisheim Abbey where he died in 1313. So far as we can tell, he planned to usurp the Eichstätt fiefs, principally the towns of Herrieden and Ornbau and the castles of Wahrberg and Wassertrüdingen, into an appanage of his own. As the bishops of Eichstätt discovered, there was not at first very much they could do about this, in spite of holding strong castles under loyal *ministeriales* in these districts. Fortunately for the see, it then proved possible to play upon the family quarrels of the Oettingen. The church in consequence received consistent support from Count Louis the elder, uncle of Count Conrad and his chief enemy. This aspect of the affair became apparent as early as the 1280s.

In 1286 Bishop Reinboto came in person to Arberg Castle because the younger counts of Oettingen had built a new castle upon the see's land at Ornbau, the town adjacent to Arberg. The bishop complained to his metropolitan, Archbishop Henry of Mainz, that this infringed the bishopric's rights, and that the counts' officials were already drawing from that district certain incomes to which they were not entitled.[21] The bishop also asked for the king's protection until the case he intended to bring in the royal court could be heard. This took a long time, until 1289.[22] The younger counts of Oettingen were required to dismantle the fortifications, their uncle Count Louis of Oettingen being one of the judges responsible for the decision. He was also awarded the task of mediator between his nephews and the bishop in any subsequent dispute, and his *ministeriales* guaranteed that the royal court's judgment would be carried out. The bishop had in the meantime carried out the cadastral survey of the Herrieden lands, which we examined in Chapter 5.[23] On the basis of three sources, the 1288 register, the oldest Eichstätt book of fiefs, and the general survey of the bishop's *mensa* about 1300, it can be shown that the titles to the episcopal lands in the west of the region were in disarray, due chiefly to these counterclaims of the counts of Oettingen as advocates. In the Ornbau case, it is worth noting the earlier injunctions of the royal court on this point against secular advocates, because the construction of castles or towns upon ecclesiastical land usually forecast its eventual loss from the Church. In 1220 Frederick II had established "that no buildings, whether castles or towns, shall be constructed upon the landed property of churches, on occasion of advocatial right or upon any other pretext. And if it happens that they are so constructed against the will of those to whom the land belongs, they shall be destroyed by royal authority."[24] This is what happened at Ornbau in 1289.

Another clue to these disorders in the northwest of the bishopric was provided in 1294 by the provost of Roggenburg in the diocese of Augsburg. He transferred control of his convent's property at Kalbensteinberg to Eichstätt, mentioning the episcopal fortifications in the neighborhood that would provide security "from the incursions of the malign," as opposed to the secular protection forthcoming from advocates who were little better than robbers: "considering that when the remedy of protection is sought from lay persons for ecclesiastical possessions, this often borders upon the peril of oppression and damage," and so on.[25]

One reason why Count Gebhard V of Hirschberg as principal advocate of the see gave no discernible assistance to Eichstätt in its Franconian affairs was his close relationship with the Oettingen dynasty. Countess Udelhild of Oettingen, cofounder of Kirchheim,[26] is thought to have been a Hirschberg by birth; and her granddaughter Sophia of Oettingen was Count Gebhard's wife. She was therefore entitled to her widow's jointure out of the Hirschberg possessions in 1305, and Bishop John of Eichstätt had conferred Wellheim Castle upon her by 1306.[27] More was claimed for her by Count Louis the elder of Oettingen, and in 1309 he agreed upon a committee of clerics and knights who would adjudicate the possessions in question.[28] Evidently the Oettingen had already occupied Dollnstein Castle and had even attacked the bishop's own property, to force forward a conclusion, the main outstanding question being whether Dollnstein ought to be a fief from Eichstätt or owned by the Oettingen as an alodial patrimony.[29] Certain other villages, castles, and assets were also in dispute, but the church was confirmed in the better part of them. Another acquisition for the Oettingen was Gebhard of Hirschberg's fief from the bishop of Regensburg, the town of Wemding, for which Count Louis paid an entry fine in 1306.[30]

Soon after the settlement of 1309, a new crisis in imperial politics provided Bishop Philip of Rathsamhausen with the opportunity for breaking with Count Conrad of Oettingen altogether. The central figure to emerge in this story was Conrad's maternal uncle, Count Eberhard the Illustrious of Württemberg, a powerful prince with a wide circle of alliances as well as a rooted enmity to the imperial towns of Swabia. By 1309 both these aspects of his policy had brought the count into disfavor with the new German king, Henry of Luxemburg, and he was declared beyond royal grace, *sine regis gracia*.[31] Eberhard the Illustrious maintained close ties with Duke Henry of Carinthia,[32] who had succeeded in 1307 to the Bohemian throne in right of his wife Anna, the elder Przemyslid heiress. Although the Czechs had acquiesced in this arrangement, King Henry VII hoped to expel him and to replace him as king with his own son John, who was to be married for the purpose to the younger heiress, Elizabeth.[33]

In the preparations of 1309 and 1310 for the necessary campaign to Prague as well as the projected Roman expedition for his imperial coronation, Henry VII gradually persuaded the German princes to support his plans, but Count Eberhard of Württemberg refused to give up his commitments to the Carinthian candidate in Bohemia. In February 1310 Henry VII himself came to Eichstätt and learned of the see's difficulties.[34] Two decisions were apparently made at this time. First, Bishop Philip was to leave for Italy to prepare the ground among the Italian communes for the king's passage through to Rome. Second, Conrad of Oettingen, as a confederate of Württemberg, was to be accused of treason to the Empire. In May he was outlawed by the royal court, and was automatically deprived of all his fiefs.[35] This gave Bishop Philip the legal pretext for reclaiming all the usurped lands and advocacies, thus solving the entangled question of Conrad's rights, and in the summer of 1310 the king specifically confirmed that his fiefs had lapsed.[36]

For the king, these arrangements worked relatively smoothly. He was able to install his son as king of Bohemia without real resistance from Henry of Carinthia or the Czech nobles and church, and was able to leave for Italy late in 1310. At the heart of imperial affairs, Bishop Philip had duly visited northern Italy in the summer of 1310;[37] attended John of Luxemburg's coronation in Prague in February 1311;[38] and joined Henry VII in Italy in the summer of that year.[39] The count of Württemberg provided much more trouble than the duke of Carinthia, and a large-scale war broke out in Swabia as its imperial *Landvogt,* the Swabian towns, and the king's other allies attempted to deal with him.[40] The count's successes encouraged Conrad of Oettingen, who refused to submit to the ban of May 1310 and prepared for war with the church of Eichstätt. Bishop Philip's response for the time being was to leave its prosecution to the elder branch of the Oettingen as a continuation of their internal dynastic wrangles, which had degenerated into a full-scale feud.

The Ellwangen Annals recorded for 1308 that Count Louis of Oettingen had fallen upon his cousin Conrad's possessions, and had devastated his entire district by arson.[41] One incentive for the Oettingen was a projected division of the spoils with Eichstätt.[42] Herrieden and Ornbau would revert to the church. Wassertrüdingen Castle was to be taken, handed over to the Oettingen, and its fortifications destroyed. Wahrberg Castle, which Conrad had called his own, *castrum nostrum,* in 1299,[43] was to be taken and handed over to the bishop, then to be destroyed or left standing as he chose. All the rest of Conrad's possessions, his alods as well as his fiefs from Eichstätt, were to be seized and divided equally between the bishop and the counts, with the exception of Reichenbach Forest (now the Öttinger Forst), which would be held in its entirety by the Oettingen as a fief from Eichstätt. The parties also agreed to consult about the construction of fortifications in the future, since the control of castles had provided Conrad of Oettingen with the opportunity for his usurpations in the first place.

At first the war made a little progress for the episcopal alliance, although it did prove a grievous expense. Somehow Count Conrad was caught in the open away from his castles, and had to flee into sanctuary with the Cistercians at Kaisheim where, as we have already noted, he died in 1313. But his widow Adelheid and her brother, the younger Craft of Hohenlohe,[44] remained in control of the castles, and apparently intended to hold on to them for Conrad's daughter Margaret. Craft was in any case married into the Württemberg family, and was aligned with Eberhard the Illustrious' plans. At this stage King John of Bohemia as imperial vicar tried to negotiate a compromise. Wahrberg Castle, which Countess Adelheid claimed as her widow's jointure, *iure dotalicio,* would be given up; Bishop Philip would pay her £400; and another place refortified by Conrad of Oettingen to secure Herrieden, Burgoberbach Castle, was to be destroyed.[45] The title to Burgoberbach typified the dilemma of the church in that its castellans were originally Eichstätt's *ministeriales*[46] but the castle had passed, apparently by inheritance or a subsequent enfeoffment, to the

Oettingen's *ministeriales* of Thann,[47] and then to other castellans who were holding it for Craft of Hohenlohe.

The scheme for establishing peace was never carried out. News of Henry VII's sudden death in Italy gave encouragement to all the disaffected parties in Germany, and by 1314 there was the prospect of another civil war as Louis IV of Bavaria and Frederick III of Austria emerged as rival candidates for the throne. John of Bohemia and Philip of Eichstätt were among those princes who saw Louis IV as Henry VII's most worthy successor. Not surprisingly, Count Eberhard the Illustrious and his allies, including Craft of Hohenlohe, decided after prevarication to back Frederick the Handsome of Austria.[48] This had important consequences for the wrangle over the Eichstätt lands, because the Württemberg and Hohenlohe interest kept open another theater of war much to the detriment of Louis of Bavaria's main concern, to deal with the Austrian threat. In fact, Craft of Hohenlohe almost succeeded in doing Frederick of Austria's work for him. We hear that early in 1315, when Louis IV was returning to Bavaria from his election at Frankfurt, Craft attacked him under cover of darkness and nearly managed to burn him to death in the house where he was passing the night.[49]

Just as Conrad of Oettingen's feud with Bishop Philip had intensified as a result of wider imperial policies planned by Henry VII, so its termination was part of Louis of Bavaria's strategy of bringing to an end the opposition to his rule in southern Germany.[50] Early in 1316 armed contingents provided by the Bavarian duchy, the see of Eichstätt, the counts of Oettingen, and the imperial towns laid siege to Herrieden, still the main stronghold of Craft of Hohenlohe and Adelheid of Oettingen. The siege lasted several weeks until the walls could be breached, the town being sacked and burned to the ground. Within a few days Wahrberg Castle was also besieged and taken, and the campaign came to a successful conclusion with the fall of Craft of Hohenlohe's own base at Schillingsfürst. It then remained to divide the acquisitions, as envisaged in 1311.

Although substantial fiefs were still in the hands of the counts of Oettingen, the arrangements of 1316–1317 resembled Eichstätt's success in 1305 in bringing the advocacy of the Hirschbergs to an end. What Eichstätt gained in the west of the region was taken over outright; in future the church was to appoint its own officials; and the only proviso was the king's prohibition of Herrieden's refortification by wall or moat.[51] After some further hesitations the agreement of 1311 with the counts of Oettingen was fulfilled in 1317.[52] Bishop Philip kept Herrieden, Ornbau, Wahrberg, and all their appurtenances in their entirety; the counts received Wassertrüdingen with all its assets and a grant of £600 from the bishop; and they were confirmed in the other Eichstätt fiefs, particularly Ehingen Forest, which they had rightfully held since the twelfth century. The title to Burgober-bach Castle was also regained by the church.[53] In 1322 or 1323 Bishop Marquard of Eichstätt prudently arranged a final settlement with Adelheid of Oettingen, who had in the meantime married Count Louis of Rieneck in lower Franconia.[54] In return for £2,100, which was paid over by the end of 1324, Adelheid, her daughter Margaret of Oettingen, and Craft of Hohen-lohe renounced any further claim to Wahrberg, Herrieden, and Burgober-bach.[55] The last embers of the feud were successfully extinguished.

One reason for the failure of Conrad and Adelheid of Oettingen to acquire a viable territory of their own was that Eichstätt had better titles to the lands, towns, castles, and advocacies in question, and enforced them by arms between 1310 and 1316. Another was that the greater resources of the house of Oettingen in fortifications, *ministeriales,* manors, and forests were possessed by the rival senior branch, which was therefore in a strong position to hound Conrad of Oettingen out of his holdings in 1312 and 1313. At the end of the thirteenth century there were about a hundred names of knightly families in the Oettingen retinue[56] of whom about three quarters also held Eichstätt fiefs.[57] There is only fragmentary evidence for those *ministeriales* whose services Conrad of Oettingen sought against his cousins and the church of Eichstätt. The oldest episcopal book of fiefs records the fiefs that had been subenfeoffed by Conrad to some of his supporters, the titles therefore falling in to the church in 1313.[58] There are a few other references to the *ministeriales* in Conrad's entourage and to the castellans and fortifications upon which he relied.[59] One of these castles was nick-named Pfaffenangst, roughly translatable as "priests' bane," an indication of its role in the feud.[60]

One of Conrad's enemies was Seneschal Henry of Limburg and Re-chenberg, who received custody of Wahrberg as his reward in 1322.[61] But one of the seneschal's own men, Tegelein *famulus,* or "servant," was also a vassal of Conrad of Oettingen.[62] The other Oettingen seneschals, the Maihingen brothers, were in camp with the bishop in 1313,[63] their brother Frederick holding the unenviable ecclesiastical post of provost of Her-rieden throughout the troubles.[64] In abolishing the Oettingen advocacies, regaining command of their own fortifications, and installing their own officials, the bishop of Eichstätt and his vicar Marquard of Hageln had gained a considerable victory, completing the work outlined by Bishops Reinboto and Conrad II at the end of the thirteenth century. The land register of 1407 records the renders of over forty manors in the *officium* of Herrieden,[65] the town itself having been refortified, against the wishes of the royal court, by Bishop Henry of Reicheneck after 1329.[66]

\*   \*   \*

The relationship of Eichstätt and Oettingen resembled the connection with the Hirschbergs in the sense that advocacies were liable to be misused. The relationship of Eichstätt and Graisbach also resembled the Hirschberg connection in that the bishops made a bid to inherit the county of Graisbach, a venture that ended this time in failure. Toward the end of the thirteenth century the counts of Graisbach faced severe economic difficulties. Unlike Count Gebhard V of Hirschberg, they did not quite have the status to attract investment by greedy creditors with loans to spare, and were constrained to sell extensively from their much more meager property.[67] Their most notable sale was to Count Gebhard V, the greater part of the *Landgericht* of Graisbach and its forest rights, just at the beginning of the fourteenth century.[68] The sale price of £1,000 was relatively modest for three reasons. First, the *Landgericht* would pass back to Count Berthold III should Gebhard of Hirschberg die childless, which had seemed the likely eventuality ever since the first Hirschberg testament of 1291. Second, the count of Graisbach might buy back the magistracy at any time, upon restoration of the sale price. Third, a strip of territory along the north bank of the Danube containing the principal castles, estates, and *ministeriales* of the Graisbachs was exempted from the sale. Upon Count Gebhard's death in 1305 the *Landgericht* duly reverted to Berthold of Graisbach.

That the Graisbachs were far less well endowed than the Hirschberg and Oettingen dynasties is also shown by the size of the retinue that they could maintain, a mere twenty families of knights at the end of the thirteenth century.[69] Household offices were held by the *ministeriales* of Graisbach and Schweinspoint, as seneschals and butlers respectively.[70] Much earlier, the Lechsgemünd *ministerialis* Diepold of Schweinspoint had achieved transitory fame under Otto IV in Italy, serving as count of Acerra and duke of Spoleto by royal appointment.[71] Like their masters, the Graisbach *ministeriales* and castellans were poor, and their best expedient was gradually to sell off their property to Kaisheim Abbey.[72] Bishop Reinboto of Meilenhart was himself a Graisbach *ministerialis* by birth, and in the

1290s chose Siegfried of Otting from the Graisbach retinue as his chamberlain and castellan of Mörnsheim, as we have seen.[73] The bishop also did something for his brother, another poverty-stricken knight,[74] by portioning his daughters out of the substance of the church of Eichstätt. The girls' mother, Gertude of Strass, belonged *iure ministerialatus,* by ministerial status, to Duke Louis II of Bavaria, and so therefore did they. In 1291 the duke compensated the church by relinquishing in advance half the grandchildren with their inheritances, *iure ministerialatus,* to Eichstätt.[75] This arrangement affecting three retinues of *ministeriales* again demonstrates the care with which the princes were still inclined, at the end of the thirteenth century, to apply their rights of ownership over unfree knights.[76]

When Count Berthold III of Graisbach died without issue in 1324, Eichstätt made a serious attempt to acquire his county, which was adjacent to its *officia* of Mörnsheim, Eichstätt, and Nassenfels. However, there was no will of the kind that Gebhard V of Hirschberg had left in Eichstätt's favor. Berthold III's nearest heir was his brother Gebhard, the cathedral provost of Eichstätt. Since Bishop Marquard of Hageln died in the same year, the chapter hopefully installed Gebhard as their next bishop some months before his brother's decease. Henry Taube reports that the new bishop did intend to bequeath Graisbach Castle with all its rights and assets to the church.[77] But the king successfully put forward a claim of his own, on the grounds that the Graisbach *Landgericht* was a vacant imperial fief. As new count and *Landrichter* he appointed a relation of the Graisbachs, Count Berthold of Neuffen and Marstetten, in 1326.[78] The church of Eichstätt decided to lodge no complaint. Bishop Gebhard was appointed counsellor of the royal court, and accompanied Louis the Bavarian to Italy. Excommunicated for his pains by Pope John XXII, the bishop died at the siege of Pisa in 1327, and was buried in Lucca.[79]

What Eichstätt did gain was the Graisbach dominion of Gundelsheim from the bishop *racione hereditatis sue,* through inheritance, and this became a new *officium* of the church.[80] So the arrangements of 1305 whereby the *Landgericht* of Hirschberg was separated from the castle, *ministeriales,* and landed patrimony was not repeated by Louis IV in 1326. Instead he stated that "we have enfeoffed, and enfeoff as a direct fief, the county of Graisbach which has fallen vacant to us and the Empire from the late Berthold, count of Graisbach" to the count of Marstetten, the assets being listed as "forest rights, *ministeriales,* dependents and estates, regional magistracies, and everything which belongs to it."[81] The new count was one of Louis the Bavarian's closest advisers, and enjoyed a variety of offices in addition to *Landrichter* of Graisbach; imperial vicar in Lombardy, advocate of Ottobeuren Abbey, and captain of Upper Bavaria.[82] One of the emperor's later plans was to acquire Graisbach and Marstetten as an appanage for a grandson, Frederick of Bavaria, who was married for the purpose to Count Berthold's daughter and heiress Anna. In the end, their only child Elizabeth went to Italy as bride of Marco Visconti and died young. The arrangement about the appanage had not been put into effect when Berthold of Marstetten died in 1342. The county of Graisbach was taken over by the emperor's officials, and became a *Landgericht* of Upper Bavaria.[83]

The see's attempt to succeed to Graisbach was an obvious extension of the policy of purchase and acquisition pursued by the bishops since the 1280s. In possession of Weissenburg, albeit temporarily, from 1315 and of Herrieden again from 1316, it appeared that the bishop might become the most formidable authority in the Franconian half of the diocese. But the dispositions made by Emperor Louis IV presaged the see's being out-flanked in this area by stronger secular neighbors, the dukes of Bavaria and the burgraves of Nuremberg,[84] in the course of the fourteenth century.

As we have seen, the Franconian *nobiles,* or lords, of Hohentrüdingen were also substantial vassals of Eichstätt in the west of the region,[85] notably as advocates of Heidenheim Abbey since the twelfth century at least.[86] In the course of the thirteenth century they became much more substantial a dynasty through Frederick of Trüdingen's marriage to Margaret of Andechs, one of the three heiresses of Duke Otto VIII of Merania, who died in 1248. Although the bishops of Bamberg claimed most of the duke's remaining lands in Franconia, Frederick and his brothers-in-law, the count of Orlamünde and the burgrave of Nuremberg, were able to make good their own claims by the early 1260s.[87] This accession of wealth and authority enabled the Hohentrüdingen dynasty to adopt the more prestigious status of counts.[88] About 1290 Margaret of Andechs' grandsons divided their territories, Frederick taking the new dominions near Bamberg and Ulrich keeping the original patrimony around Hohentrüdingen. Count Ulrich possessed no *Landgericht,* but in other respects his county matched that of his neighbor, Count Berthold III of Graisbach.

At the end of the thirteenth century there were some twenty families of knights in Count Ulrich's retinue,[89] of whom the most significant were the seneschals of Spielberg,[90] the strongest of the comital castles after Hohentrüdingen and Alerheim. Although the church of Eichstätt might have claimed ultimate rights over the county through the overlordship of Hohentrüdingen Castle and hence its appurtenant assets, the main beneficiaries of the collapse of this dynasty were the counts of Oettingen and the burgraves of Nuremberg. When Count Ulrich died in 1310 he left two daughters under the guardianship of his elder brother, Count Frederick. Upon the latter's death in 1332 his nieces' husbands, counts Henry of Schauenburg and Berthold of Marstetten and Graisbach, carried out another division of the lands. Hohentrüdingen was awarded to Count Berthold, and Spielberg to Count Henry. The former therefore passed to Bavaria in 1342, while the latter was conferred upon Henry of Schauenburg's daughter Imagina and her future husband, one of the young counts of Oettingen.[91] Thus it became a permanent possession of the Oettingen principality. Hohentrüdingen itself was pledged by Bavaria to the burgraves of Nuremberg.[92] Although this was envisaged as a temporary arrangement, the castle was never redeemed and the burgraves kept it for good.

For the temporal standing of the bishopric of Eichstätt, the net result of fourteenth-century politics in the western half of the diocese was a mixed blessing. The main point was the reacquisition of Herrieden and its *officium*, and this was achieved by 1316. But the attendant feuds had also entrenched more firmly the authority of the counts of Oettingen, who made significant gains from the houses of Hirschberg and Hohentrüdingen as well as having their legitimate Eichstätt fiefs confirmed for good.[93] In 1362 Bishop Berthold still thought it worthwhile to acquire overlordship of both castles at Wallerstein as the chief residences of the Oettingen counts, thus giving Eichstätt ultimate claims upon Oettingen territory should the dynasty fail.[94] Yet as overlords of Graisbach and Hohentrüdingen, the bishops had done badly in the 1320s and 1330s, when the main beneficiary was Louis the Bavarian's vassal, Count Berthold of Neuffen-Marstetten. Upon the latter's death in 1342 these assets had passed, as we have seen, to Bavaria. Nevertheless, the richest of the princes with an interest in the Eichstätt region were now the burgraves of Nuremberg. In the fourteenth and fifteenth centuries they were able to accept so much pledged property and to make so many shrewd purchases that their *Landgericht* of Cadolzburg[95] was gradually transformed into the more substantial territory known eventually as the margravate of Ansbach.[96]

We can perceive that in dealing with the counts in the western half of the region, bishops Philip and Marquard (1306–1322) had not been nearly so successful in planning and execution as bishops Reinboto and Conrad II (1279–1305) had been vis-à-vis the last count of Hirschberg, although there is little to choose between all four churchmen in their skill and capacity as competent politicians in the secular sphere. One reason is that the tenurial and military circumstances were much more complicated in the west, there being several dynasties to outface. Another is that watertight testamentary instruments such as Count Gebhard V's wills of 1291, 1296, and 1304 provided much more impressive title to lands and rights than Eichstätt's claims of ultimate lordship over Hohentrüdingen, Graisbach, and Wassertrüdingen Castles[97] and by inference, over their appurtenances.

A third reason can simply be found in personalities. Gebhard V of Hirschberg had been a violent, greedy, and ambitious nobleman who liked to have his own way. But once he had made up his mind to the legacy of his principality to Eichstätt, it was entirely in character that he refused to be browbeaten by the dukes of Bavaria. His tenacity was vindicated by the defeat of Duke Rudolf I of Bavaria and his own subsequent rise in importance as a figure in the Empire during the reign of Albert I. But in the west of the region, Count Conrad of Oettingen was little better than an aristocratic brigand with whom no bargain would hold, and his relatives, although they backed the church of Eichstätt, were opportunists seeking confirmation for their titles in fief to Eichstätt property.

But the man whose obvious talent as a statesman overrode every other consideration was Louis IV of Bavaria. He was a prudent, even-tempered prince with considerable powers of leadership and management, whose concern for orderly governance in lands adjacent to Upper Bavaria was not unreasonable. Having regained Herrieden for Eichstätt in 1316, he did not consider it unjust to continue a secular dynasty in the county of Graisbach from 1326, in spite of the see's hopes of gaining it for the church. Apart from Count Berthold of Neuffen's right as an heir of the Graisbachs, the main consideration must have been the efficient administration of justice through the *Landgericht*. The Hirschberg *Landgericht* had already proved awkward to administer since 1305 because the bishops owned the territory while Bavaria owned the jurisdiction, and this unusual experiment was not to be continued for the Graisbach *Landgericht*. For Bavaria this decision also paid off in political terms, for when Bishop Henry of Reicheneck (1329–1344) backed the Avignon papacy, the pro-Bavarian regime in Graisbach was of some value in outflanking Eichstätt's territory.

*Notes*

1. EL ff. 43v–49r.
2. Ibid. ff. 2v, 5r.
3. MB, vol. XLIX, no. 78, pp. 122f., and *Reg. Eichst.*, no. 831, p. 259.

4. EL ff. 31r–v, 54r–55r.

5. See Chapter 2, n. 46.

6. MGH Dipl. Henry III, no. 303, pp. 411–13 (1053). For the episcopal property along the River Wörnitz, see Kudorfer, *Nördlingen,* pp. 322–33.

7. MGH Consts. i, no. 430, pp. 613–15 (1104). See K. S. Bader, "Probleme des Landfriedensschutzes im mittelalterlichen Schwaben," *Zeitschrift für württembergische Landesgeschichte* 3 (1939): 1–56.

8. Members are attested at the royal court, e.g., MGH Dipl. Conrad III, no. 79, p. 141 (1142); no. 192, p. 351 (1147); no. 260, p. 452 (1151). See also Grupp, *Regesten,* pp. 1–3, and *Reg. Eichst.,* no. 358, p. 113 (c. 1141). The leading account is by Dieter Kudorfer, *Die Grafschaft Oettingen* (1985). See also his *Nördlingen,* pp. 64–123, and A. Layer, "Die Territorien der Grafen und Fürsten von Oettingen," in HBG iii, pp. 991–93.

9. For fresh summaries of this process, see K. Schmid, "Zur Entstehung und Erforschung von Geschlechterbewusstsein," *ZGOR* 134 (1986): 21–33, and my forthcoming *Princes and Territories,* pp. 135–51.

10. Graisbach used in MB vol. XLIX, no. 46, p. 86 (1245), but Lechsgemünd still in Hoffmann, *Urkunden . . . Kaisheim,* no. 141, p. 91 (1256).

11. Lohmann, *Brunos Buch vom Sachsenkrieg,* p. 92.

12. For the ramifications of this family, see Leyser, "German Aristocracy," pp. 48–51. For Cuno, see MGH Dipl. Henry IV, no. 426, p. 572 (1091); and his marriage is reported in *Bertholdi Zwifaltensis Chronicon,* MGH Scriptores, vol. X, pp. 106f.

13. For the details see Kraft and Guttenberg, "Gau Sualafeld und Grafschaft Graisbach." See Henry of Frontenhausen and Lechsgemünd in MGH Dipl. Conrad III, no. 31, p. 52 (1139).

14. *Annales Elwangenses; Neresheimenses et Chronicon Elwangense,* MGH Scriptores, vol. X, pp. 24f.

15. Bayr. Hsta. München, Ritterorden 7694 A (1242); Dertsch and Wulz, *Urkunden . . . Oettingen,* no. 48, p. 20 (1270); Kudorfer, *Nördlingen,* pp. 281–88.

16. For its frequency as the place for issuing comital charters, Dertsch and Wulz, *Urkunden . . . Oettingen,* no. 42, pp. 17f. (1266) to no. 414, p. 152 (1336). See also Hoffmann, *Urkunden . . . Kaisheim,* no. 161, p. 101 (1261).

17. The most reliable sources are Muffat, *Schenkungsbuch . . . Berchtesgaden,* no. 89, p. 287 (c. 1140); no. 97, p. 292 (1140–1150); no. 180, p. 344 (1188); *Wirtembergisches Urkundenbuch,* vol. IV (Stuttgart, 1883), no. 61, pp. 359f. (1153); *Reg. Eichst.,* no. 506, p. 164 (1197); Bayr. Hsta. München, Brandenburg-Ansbach/Anhausen 1255 (1160–1220); Hoffmann, *Urkunden . . . Kaisheim,* no. 16, pp. 14f. (c. 1193).

18. See my *"Ministeriales,"* pp. 386–97. Some of these served in an administrative capacity as seneschals, butlers, and chamberlains; MB, vol. XLIX, no. 50, p. 92 (1248); Hoffmann, *Urkunden . . . Kaisheim,* no. 162, p. 101 (1261); no. 169, p. 106 (1262); Bayr. Hsta. München, Brandenburg-Ansbach/Anhausen 1275 (1250) and 1279 (1252); *Reg. Eichst.,* no. 983, p. 305 (1284); *Wirtembergisches Urkundenbuch,* vol. IX, no. 3747, p. 209 (1288).

19. E.g., Dertsch and Wulz, *Urkunden . . . Oettingen,* no. 179, p. 70 (1299).

20. See Chapter 5, notes 86–90, and EL f. 4r. For earlier disputes between

Eichstätt and the counts, MB, vol. XLIX, no. 50, pp. 91f. (1248); no. 102, pp. 154f. (1279).

21. *Reg. Eichst.*, no. 1005, p. 311; for what follows, see the good new account by Robert Schuh, "Territorienbildung im oberen Altmühlraum. Grundlagen und Entwicklung der eichstättischen Herrschaft im 13. und 14. Jahrhundert," *ZBLG* 50 (1987): 463–91.

22. MGH Consts. iii, no. 669, pp. 655f., and *Reg. Eichst.*, no. 1055, pp. 320f.

23. See Chapter 5, note 87.

24. MGH Consts. ii, no. 73, p. 90 (1220), repeated in no. 171, p. 212 (1232).

25. MB, vol. XLIX, no. 202, pp. 315–17; see also Dertsch and Wulz, *Urkunden . . . Oettingen*, no. 107, p. 42 (1282) for the *defensio*, or advocacy, of Burgrave Conrad of Nuremberg here.

26. Ibid., no. 42, pp. 17f. (1266) and no. 48, p. 20 (1270).

27. Mentioned in *Reg. Eichst.*, no. 1434, p. 453 (1309); see also no. 1347 A, p. 420 (1305).

28. MB, vol. L, no. 47, pp. 48ff. and *Reg. Eichst.*, no. 1421, pp. 450f.

29. MB, vol. L, no. 54, pp. 53f; *Reg. Eichst.*, no. 1434, pp. 453f. (1309). EL f. 3v claims it as an Eichstätt fief to the Hirschbergs, but MB, vol. L, no. 760, p. 502 (1360) shows, probably correctly, that it was alodial property.

30. Dertsch and Wulz, *Urkunden . . . Oettingen*, no. 206, pp. 79f.

31. H. Haering, *Der Reichskrieg gegen Graf Eberhard den Erlauchten von Württemberg und seine Stellung in der allgemeinen deutschen Geschichte* (Stuttgart, 1910), p. 13.

32. Ibid., pp. 10f.; MGH Consts. iv–2, no. 1207, pp. 1261f. (1308).

33. E. Hillenbrand (ed.), *Vita Caroli Quarti. Die Autobiographie Karls IV.* (Stuttgart, 1979), p. 80.

34. *Reg. Eichst.*, no. 1354, pp. 427f., and nos. 1443–45, p. 456 (1310).

35. The date is known from a later source; MGH Consts. iv–2, no. 1097, pp. 1111f. (1313); see *Reg. Eichst.*, no. 1463, p. 459.

36. Ibid., no. 1472, pp. 461f.

37. Ibid., nos. 1464–71, pp. 460f.

38. Ibid., no. 1479, pp. 463f.

39. Ibid., nos. 1490f., p. 467.

40. MGH Consts. iv–1, no. 450, pp. 392f. (1310); no. 663, pp. 634f., and nos. 670f., pp. 642f. (1311); ibid., iv–2, nos. 758–60, pp. 748–51 and nos. 762f., pp. 752f. (1312).

41. *Annales Elwangenses*, p. 25.

42. See *Reg. Eichst.*, no. 1472, pp. 461f. (1310), then MB, vol. L, no. 70, pp. 65f.; *Reg. Eichst.*, no. 1481, p. 464; and Dertsch and Wulz, *Urkunden . . . Oettingen*, no. 232, p. 89 (1311).

43. Schuhmann and Hirschmann, *Urkundenregesten . . . Heilsbronn*, no. 234, p. 122. It had passed as an Eichstätt fief from the *liberi* of Wahrberg to the Oettingen; see EL ff. 4r, 6v; Dertsch and Wulz, *Urkunden . . . Oettingen*, no. 32, pp. 12f. (1257); *Reg. Eichst.*, no. 885, pp. 272f. (1275).

44. On this family see A. Gerlich in HBG iii, pp. 308–10, and sources in K. Weller, *Hohenlohisches Urkundenbuch*, 3 vols. (Stuttgart, 1899–1912). They were

*domini*, e.g., EL f. 4v, sometimes called counts after a post held in Italy in the earlier thirteenth century; see Zinsmaier, "Ungedruckter Stauferurkunden," p. 202 for the Hohenlohe brothers as *comites Romaniole*. The comital title was regularly used from the fifteenth century.

45. *Reg. Eichst.*, nos. 1535f., p. 479 (1313).

46. *Reg. Eichst.*, no. 392, p. 123 (1150), and no. 539, p. 173 (1208); MB, vol. XXX/1, no. 724, p. 220 (1234) and vol. XXXVII, no. 260, pp. 286f. (1240).

47. Bayr. Hsta. München, Ritterorden 3019 (1275); *Nürnberger Urkundenbuch*, no. 801, pp. 473f. (1290); EL ff. 45v, 46v.

48. Haering, *Reichskrieg*, pp. 29f.

49. *Reg. Eichst.*, no. 1593, pp. 394f.

50. See A. Gerlich, "Franken in der Zeit Kaiser Heinrichs VII. und während des Thronstreites (1314–1322)," in HBG iii, pp. 166–69.

51. MGH Consts. v, no. 361, p. 302 (1316) and *Reg. Eichst.*, no. 1597, p. 496 (1316).

52. MB, vol. L, no. 174, p. 130, and *Reg. Eichst.*, no. 1626, p. 503.

53. MB, vol. L, no. 190, p. 141; *Reg. Eichst.*, no. 1633, p. 505 (1318).

54. On this dynasty see A. Gerlich in HBG iii, pp. 306f.

55. *Reg. Eichst.*, no. 1714, p. 534; Stillfried and Maercker, *Monumenta Zollerana*, vol. II, no. 590, p. 385 (1324).

56. See my *"Ministeriales,"* pp. 386–97, and for this retinue later in the fourteenth century, E. Grünenwald, *Das älteste Lehenbuch der Grafschaft Oettingen (14. Jahrhundert bis 1477)*, Schwäbische Forschungsgemeinschaft bei der Kommission für bayerische Landesgeschichte, series 5, vol. II (Augsburg, 1976).

57. EL ff. 43v–49v.

58. Ibid. ff. 66r–v; *Haec feuda coeperunt vacare ex morte D. Ch. Comitis de Oetingen, quae modo ad collationem Ecclesiae Eystetensis pertinent.*

59. Dertsch and Wulz, *Urkunden . . . Oettingen*, no. 168, p. 65 (1298); *Reg. Eichst.*, no. 1196, p. 371 (1298) and no. 1295, p. 399 (1297–1305); Schuhmann and Hirschmann, *Urkundenregesten . . . Heilsbronn*, nos. 275 and 278, pp. 141–43 (1304); Bayr. Hsta. München, Ritterorden 7747 (1307).

60. EL ff. 66v, and Tillmann, *Lexikon*, p. 797.

61. MB, vol. L, no. 235, p. 180. The office of castellan was sold back to Bishop Berthold in 1355; ibid., no. 671, pp. 449f.

62. EL f. 66v.

63. *Reg. Eichst.*, no. 1535, p. 479.

64. Ibid., no. 1117, p. 338 (1294); Dertsch and Wulz, *Urkunden . . . Oettingen*, no. 229, p. 88 (1311), MB, vol. L, no. 320, pp. 232f. (1331).

65. Staatsarchiv Nürnberg, Hochstift Eichstätt Literalien 9, f. 1r: *Et primo die zins und guelt in dem Ampt Herrieden.*

66. Bresslau, *Chronik Heinrichs Taube*, p. 128: "et opidum Herridense procuravit muro muniri."

67. *Reg. Eichst.*, no. 1006, p. 311 (1286); no. 1242, p. 384 (c. 1300); no. 1359, p. 434 (1306); Bayr. Hsta. München, Kl. Kaisheim 315, 329 (1291–1292); MB, vol. XLIX, no. 353, pp. 543f. (1305); ES ff. 13r. 46r.

68. MB, vol. XLIX, no. 309, pp. 475–78 (1302–1304).

69. Hoffmann, *Urkunden . . . Kaisheim,* no. 385, pp. 222f. (1283) and no. 389, p. 225 (1284); Bayr. Hsta. München, Kl. Kaisheim 303 (1290), 354 and 356 (1296), 366 (1299); EL ff. 31 r–v; *Reg. Eichst.,* nos. 949, p. 294 and 961, p. 297 (1282); no. 968, p. 299 (1283).

70. Seneschals from Hoffmann, *Urkunden . . . Kaisheim,* no. 197, p. 120 (1266) to *Reg. Eichst.,* no. 1578, p. 490 (1315); butlers from Hoffmann, *Urkunden . . . Kaisheim,* no. 370, p. 214 (1283), to Bayr. Hsta. München, Kl. Kaisheim 505 (1329). See also the office of *venator,* reminiscent of the see of Bamberg; ibid. 263 (1284) to 631 (1347).

71. E. Winkelmann, "Über die Herkunft Dipolds des Grafen von Acerra und Herzogs von Spoleto," *Forschungen zur deutschen Geschichte* 16 (1876): 159–63; D. P. Waley, *The Papal State in the Thirteenth Century* (London, 1961), pp. 59–65.

72. Hoffmann, *Urkunden . . . Kaisheim,* nos. 369f., pp. 213f. (1283); no. 385, pp. 222f. (1283); Bayr. Hsta. München, Kl. Kaisheim 288 (1289), 303 (1290), 313f., 316 (1291), 351 (1295), 366 (1299), 379 (1300), 382 (1301), 392 (1304), 405 (1307), 412 (1308), 415 (1309).

73. See Chapter 5, note 58.

74. Sales of his property in Bayr. Hsta. München, Kl. Kaisheim, 330 (1292), and *Reg. Eichst.,* no. 1115, pp. 337f. (1294).

75. MB, vol. XLIX, no. 370, pp. 570f. (1291): *Dux Bawarie dividit pueros Meilen-hartarii cum ecclesia Eystetensi.*

76. Compare with Schlunk, *Königsmacht,* pp. 69–82, who emphasizes the integrity of the imperial retinue of *ministeriales* into the later thirteenth century.

77. Bresslau, *Chronik Heinrichs Taube,* p. 125.

78. H.-M. Maurer, "Die hochadeligen Herren von Neuffen und von Sperber-seck im 12. Jahrhundert," *Zeitschrift für württembergische Landesgeschichte* 25 (1966): 59–130.

79. Bresslau, *Chronik Heinrichs Taube,* pp. 125f.

80. As n. 65 above, ff. 94r–97v. Gundelsheim Castle had previously been in the hands of Eichstätt (c. 1301–1305; see *Reg. Eichst.,* no. 1242, p. 384, and no. 1359, p. 434), then the Teutonic Order (1321–1324; Bayr. Hsta. München, Ritterorden 1956) by temporary purchases.

81. MGH Consts. vi–1, nos. 200 and 204, pp. 135–37.

82. H. Angermeier in HBG ii, pp. 156, 167f., and A. Layer in iii, p. 969.

83. See the new *Landrichter* in Bayr. Hsta. München, Brandenburg-Ansbach/ Heidenheim 1497 (1342) and Solnhofen 1597 (1343), 1600f. (1344–1345).

84. Their principal purchase was Ansbach; Stillfried and Maercker, *Monumenta Zollerana,* vol. II, no. 671, pp. 441f. (1331). See also Hofmann, *Gunzenhausen-Weissenburg,* pp. 27–30.

85. EL ff. 5r–v, 54r–55r.

86. *Reg. Eichst.,* nos. 394f. and 397f., pp. 125–27 (1150–1152) and no. 435, p. 138 (1163).

87. A. Gerlich, "Adel und Ritterschaft," in HBG iii, pp. 313f.

88. Frederick *nobilis* in *Reg. Eichst.,* no. 815, p. 55 (1263); as count in Wittmann, *Mon. Wittelsb.,* vol. I, no. 99, p. 234 and Schuhmann and Hirschmann, *Urkunden-regesten . . . Heilsbronn,* no. 127, p. 68 (1269).

89. See my "*Ministeriales*," pp. 399–401.

90. Bayr. Hsta. München, Brandenburg-Ansbach/Anhausen 1293 (1278); EL f. 54r; MB, vol. XLIX, no. 324, pp. 499f. (1303).

91. See Stillfried and Maercker, *Monumenta Zollerana*, vol. III, no. 44, p. 38 (1337).

92. Ibid., no. 269, pp. 235f. (1351) and no. 292, pp. 253f. (1353).

93. Then in 1347 the Ehingen forest was given outright to Oettingen in exchange for property nearer to Eichstätt; MB, vol. L, nos. 515f., p. 340.

94. Ibid., no. 792, pp. 525ff. (1362). In exchange, the Oettingen title to Wasser-trüdingen was converted from fief to alod.

95. Stillfried and Maercker, *Monumenta Zollerana*, vol. III, no. 221, p. 194 (1349) for its transfer from Nuremberg.

96. On its development see A. Schwammberger, *Die Erwerbspolitik der Burg-grafen von Nürnberg in Franken bis 1361,* Erlanger Abhandlungen zur mittleren und neueren Geschichte, vol. XVI (Erlangen, 1932); A. Gerlich, "Die Burggrafschaft Nürnberg (Markgraftümer Ansbach-Bayreuth)," in HBG iii, pp. 295–304. See also Hofmann, "Territorienbildung in Franken," in Patze (ed.), *Territorialstaat,* vol. II, pp. 255–300.

97. EL ff. 2v, 4r, 5r.

# Conclusion: Eichstätt in Bavarian and German History

In order to interpret regional power and its diversity in the Eichstätt region between 1100 and 1350, it has been necessary to examine several related phenomena. In the first place, there were the rights and jurisdictions over material resources possessed and exercised by counts and bishops, and we have seen how they were acquired, defended, and exchanged. Second, bishops and counts necessarily relied upon military and administrative manpower to maintain their rights, and we could discern shifts within the social structure of the region, both through the rise and decline of families enfeoffed as vassals, and through the uses made of the terms indicating status, that is, *miles, liber,* and *ministerialis,* within the retinues. In general the term *miles,* meaning knight or vassal, could be applied to the free men, the *liberi* who held fiefs and performed military service, although their numbers were in decline by the twelfth century. The same word, *miles,* was applied to *ministeriales* in the thirteenth century as well as the twelfth[1] since it suited their military function and their tenure of fiefs, but as we saw in Chapters 4 and 5, there were reasons for asserting the prestige and status of *ministerialis* into the fourteenth century as well. The agrarian structure with its manorial forms and the ecclesiastical structure as reformed after 1050 or 1100 persisted almost unchanged, but the effectiveness of the Church as an organized ruling force was continually vitiated by advocatial pressures and excesses between 1225 and 1305.

The third problem has been to try to understand the political process. Bishops were installed or elected, counts succeeded their fathers or uncles, and with the titles came clusters of rights that the men in question exercised or defended or exceeded in accordance with their inherited expectations, or according to the emergencies of the day. Political decisions thus depended to a great degree upon the force of individual personality, and during my investigations, this force came forward distinctly out of the detritus of archives and the compositions of the chroniclers. It has even proved possible to delineate the personal powers of judgment exhibited by some of the counts and bishops, dukes and *ministeriales,* as they impinged upon the local political process. In medieval Germany, where law and order under the crown, the *Landfrieden,* and the local jurisdictions were hard to maintain, the political decisions taken by such personalities were often of a military nature, because the feud was a normal annual event. As Ekkehard Kaufmann has put it: "Over centuries the state was hardly in a position itself to guarantee peace effectively, so that until the end of the fifteenth century the feud would be recognized legally as a means of self-help, within known limits and forms."[2]

Counts, bishops, and their retinues eventually stamped a political character upon the borderland of Franconia, Bavaria, and Swabia, which I have called "the Eichstätt region." In fact the frontier established in the seventh and eighth centuries between the Franconian *gens,* or people, in the Sualafeld and the Bavarian *gens* in the Nordgau remained unchanged throughout the Middle Ages, but this line was deliberately spanned by the diocese of Eichstätt ever since its inception by the Carolingians.[3] But in German political geography the dioceses were by no means the same thing as the territorial dominions that the prince-bishops were assembling in the thirteenth and fourteenth centuries. To some extent the principalities were born out of competition for jurisdictions, landownership, and the control of resources in a given region. In the Eichstätt region, it appeared that the bishops would be outstripped by the counts who were their feoffees and advocates, but such threats to their temporal independence were put down during the reigns of bishops Reinboto, Conrad II, and Philip (1279–1322). Eichstätt was not therefore condemned to follow the examples of Brixen at the hands of the counts of Tirol, Havelberg at the hands of the margraves of Brandenburg, or Merseburg at the hands of the margraves of Meissen. Nevertheless, it is probable that had the dukes of Upper Bavaria inherited the Hirschberg lands and advocacies, as seemed likely until Gebhard V of Hirschberg's will of 1291, then the see of Eichstätt would have been engulfed in material terms by the power of Bavaria. For different reasons this had already happened to an ecclesiastical establishment of comparable economic stature, the landed estate of the abbey of St. Emmeram at Regensburg,[4] and was to happen to the monastery of Waldsassen by the end of the Middle Ages.[5]

Apart from Salzburg, the Bavarian bishops had, by the end of the thirteenth century, worked out a modus vivendi with the Bavarian dukes, to whom they posed no real threat.[6] In territorial terms, Eichstätt and Passau[7] were more successful than Freising and Regensburg, although the elements of their power were similar: an ancient endowment of landed property guarded by reconstructed castles such as Donaustauf and Wörth for Regensburg, Burgrain and Ismaning for Freising, and Obernzell and Viechtenstein for Passau.[8] Like Eichstätt in 1305, Regensburg and Freising also came into entire comital inheritances, Hohenburg in 1248 and Werdenfels in 1294 respectively. But unlike the Hirschberg lands, which were intermingled with those of the cathedral church, Hohenburg and Werdenfels were remote enclaves useless for the purpose of territorial consolidation. What Eichstätt had in common with Passau was a notable enrichment through the gift of an important monastery and its lands. In Passau's case this was Niedernburg Abbey and its lands in 1161,[9] a transaction far less complicated for that bishopric than the drawn-out history of the Herrieden resources between 888 and 1316. Another way in which the sees of Passau and Eichstätt were shown to have been more successful temporal enterprises than Regensburg or Freising is in geographical nomenclature. *Bistum*, or bishopric, was, in its Middle High German version, applied to all the sees of Germany but was not normally the description for their temporal endowment, that is, land, castles, and towns, for which *Hochstift* was the term.[10] For Passau and Eichstätt, however, their new subventions in land encouraged the application of *Bistum* as an actual regional name, and this still survives for what had been the temporal cores of those bishoprics' territories as secured since 1161 and 1305, through the Niedernburg and Hirschberg grants.[11]

Instead of explaining the emergence of Eichstätt's secular domination in terms of a theory, "the rise of territorial lordship,"[12] I prefer to see it in terms of creative political personalities, their traditions, their inherited resources, and their expectations. These personages were the counts and bishops of the Eichstätt region whose careers were closely linked by the institutions of vassalage and ecclesiastical advocacy.[13] This type of political and legal relationship appears with some clarity under Count Hartwig of Grögling and his brother Bishop Gebhard II of Eichstätt (1125–1149), which then, after many vicissitudes including the assassination of Count Gebhard II of Hirschberg in 1245, culminated in the agreements made between Bishops Reinboto and Conrad II and the last count of Hirschberg. The elements of their collective power had by that time been made plain: the ecclesiastical jurisdiction of a bishop matched by the secular *Landgericht* of Hirschberg; the command of castles and their garrisons of *ministeriales;* the domination of towns and the communications between them; and the ownership of other resources that conferred income in cash and kind, that is, the manorial landscape, the woodlands, and the monastic advocacies. After the dukes of Bavaria decided to honor Count Gebhard V's dispositions at Gaimersheim Castle in 1305, they too made a truly constructive contribution to the regional structure through Louis the Bavarian's confirmation of the Hirschberg *Landgericht* in 1320,[14] although this was not directly conceived as a part of Bavaria's juridical reform in the fourteenth century.[15]

Given the relatively greater strength of the dukes of Bavaria, the burgraves of Nuremberg, and the counts of Oettingen as the adjacent territorial powers, the bishops of Eichstätt had, in political terms, reached their optimum dimension by the middle of the fourteenth century. The contours of this temporal jurisdiction lasted until the end of ecclesiastical rule in the Holy Roman Empire in 1802 and 1803.[16] Compared with some of the bishops in southern Germany, the incumbents at Eichstätt possessed a handsome principality, not on the scale of Bamberg or Würzburg but richer than Regensburg or Freising. Some idea of the relative standing of the south German ecclesiastical princes can be gleaned from the military assessments worked out in the fifteenth-century imperial parliaments, or *Reichstage*. The figures are not easy to compare because the demand upon individual principalities varied at each assessment. Nevertheless, the contributions expected from Eichstätt were lower than from the bishoprics of Würzburg and Bamberg, generally higher than Augsburg, Brixen, Freising, and Regensburg, and comparable to Passau and Trent.[17] The figures must be treated with caution. After all, the Turkish crusade planned for 1467 never took place, and Eichstätt appears to have exceeded its quotas for the Hussite Wars.[18] However, the assessments reveal something about Eichstätt's status among the princes in general and the German sees in particular. They show what the parliaments considered Eichstätt's military potential to be, in an era when armed contingents were a significant guide to territorial power. Würzburg and Bamberg were rich, Brixen and Regensburg were poor, and Eichstätt stood roughly equal to Passau and Trent.

The military capacity of the bishops of Eichstätt also struck the biographers who continued Henry Taube of Selbach's tradition in the *Liber pontificalis* down to 1445, mentioning their diligence in the field and their careful maintenance of fortifications.[19] This aspect of episcopal rule did not appeal to the reformers of the fifteenth century. Apart from the well-known strictures of the anonymous author of the *Reformatio Sigismundi* against warlike bishops,[20] the local wars of the mid-fifteenth century aroused unfavorable comment in verse from Ulrich Wiest of Augsburg:[21]

The Prince-Bishop of Mainz loves sword and fire;
He ought to stay at home, sing in his choir,
And pray he may be spared from rack and pyre.

The Bishop of Eichstätt joins him in the ranks,
While Babenberg delights in martial pranks;
Thus we who proffer alms are rendered thanks!

In successfully avoiding undue Wittelsbach influence over the ensuing centuries, Eichstätt shared with Augsburg, Bamberg, and Passau the geographical advantage of lying upon the borders of the Bavarian duchy.[22] After the problems of the Avignon period,[23] Eichstätt and Bavaria were nearly always in accord on ecclesiastical and religious policy until the electors' attack upon episcopal independence in the eighteenth century.[24] During the Great Schism, Bavaria and its bishops were Urbanist,[25] and as an outpost of Catholicism against evangelical Ansbach, Upper Palatinate, and Pfalz-Neuburg in the sixteenth and seventeenth centuries,[26] Eichstätt enjoyed the sympathy and support of ducal Bavaria. In the secular sphere, the inheritance of the Hirschberg lands in 1305 was a success. But it contained the paradox of ducal criminal jurisdiction over the greater part of Eichstätt's much expanded territory. This divided supremacy was a potential source of conflict until the later eighteenth century,[27] and was more serious than the border disputes with other powerful neighbors such as the margraves of Ansbach, which, again, were not finally solved until the treaties of the eighteenth century.[28] At Paris in May 1802 the secular reign of the German bishops was declared to be at an end. Enlightened thought and Napoleonic diplomacy confined St. Willibald's successor to his spiritual cure once more.[29]

Modern ideas of political progress tend to be unfair to medieval institutions that have not left easily recognizable descendants. But the territorial fragmentation of Germany, however chaotic, did represent the painful construction of small-scale political and juridical structures with which the regionalized societies of medieval Germany had to make do.[30] For such reasons, provincial history uncovered through the sources for the Eichstätt region provides an instructive example of what had happened in medieval politics to the German countryside. It is possible to perceive here "the rise of territorial lordship" as a possible description, *Land und Herrschaft* held together in the uncertain clutches of the bishops of Eichstätt, with the *Landrichter* of the dukes of Bavaria, the manorial rights of the *ministeriales,* the political ambition of the counts of Oettingen, and the purchasing power of the burgraves of Nuremberg as the potential rivals for long-lasting and realistic jurisdiction. The rather rough-hewn and archaic character of a borderland society persisted right through the three-cornered history of medieval Eichstätt, Hirschberg, and Bavaria. The latter was able to develop more modern characteristics of a statelike political form even quite early in the fourteenth century.[31] The bishoprics tended not to possess the resources, the personnel, or the techniques to follow into such structures until early modern times.[32]

In attempting to explain the Eichstätt region in its political, social, and legal realities as it emerged into the aristocratic, ecclesiastical, and knight-dominated world of the castle-building twelfth and thirteenth centuries, I believe that I have shown it to be most convincing to rely upon discourse about the personalities and careers of dominant counts and bishops. This, of course, is what the earliest sources, from St. Willibald's biography to the account assembled by the *Anonymus Haserensis* had done. What is remarkable is that, in spite of a "modernizing" archive containing the new land register, cartulary, and book of fiefs in constant use from the early fourteenth century, the narrative sources continued in the same biographical vein for providing political explanation. These were Henry Taube of Selbach's trenchant compositions on the lives of the bishops who were his contemporaries,[33] as well as the continuations containing so much down-to-earth military, fiscal, and legal detail composed by his followers. The episcopal biographies were framed by laudatory verse,[34] and although these exercises in encapsulating character were given up by the end of the fourteenth century, similar rhetoric still informed the applause accorded to the bishops' personalities. Bishop Albert of Hohenrechberg (1429–1445) is described as follows:[35]

Hic itaque reverendus pater affabilis, mitis, humilis, hospitalis, compatiens adversitatibus proximorum suorum, totus amator pacis fuit, pluries et plus condolens de adversitatibus principum et ceterorum vicinorum suorum quam de adversitatibus aut dampnis sibi illatis, ita ut quandoque propriam substanciam exponeret pro concordia vicinorum. Expensas magnas fecit in dietis, lites ut extingweret et discordias sedaret. Quare ardenter ab omnibus principibus, comitibus, baronibus, militibus, communi vulgo et toto clero suo amabatur, vocantes eum ad consilia et tractatus eorum ut amicum et patrem fidelem. Nam licet esset mediocris literature, fuit tamen vir mire prudencie tam ex naturali industria quam prudencia acquisita. Que omnia conscribere, longum processum requirerent.

All this can be rendered not too inaccurately as follows:

Accordingly this reverend father, so affable, kindly, religious, hospitable, and sympathetic to his neighbors' misfortunes, was a great lover of peace, more often feeling for the adversities of the princes and others of his neighbors than causing hardship by insisting on debts due to him, so that he sometimes put out his own substance for the sake of concord among neighbors. He incurred great expenses in meetings in order to extinguish quarrels and to settle discords. Therefore he was warmly regarded by all princes, counts, barons, knights, the common people, and all his clergy, who invited him to their assemblies and synods like a friend and true father. For although he was of mediocre learning, he was a man of uncommon prudence, as much from natural diligence as through wisdom acquired. To write up all about this would take a long time.

This idealized aristocratic world of honorable princes cultivating personalized methods of political relationship and rule, which we have been able to observe for the Eichstätt region since the twelfth century, reached its final literary expression in Count William Werner of Zimmern's humanist exercise in regional historiography, his *Chronicle* of the bishops of Eichstätt, composed early in the sixteenth century.[36] The most effective political mechanism within this relatively slow moving, rural, aristocracy-dominated border society was the personality, luck, and career of successive prince-bishops who were without the resources to copy the more sophisticated governing systems of neighboring ducal Bavaria.[37]

## Notes

1. See Chapter 3, ns. 42 to 54.

2. *Deutsches Recht*, p. 20: "Über Jahrhunderte war der Staat so wenig in der Lage, selbst den Frieden wirkungsvoll zu garantieren, dass bis zum Ausgang des 15. Jahrhunderts die Fehde in gewissen Grenzen und Formen als Mittel der Selbsthilfe auch rechtlich anerkannt wurde."

3. M. Spindler and G. Diepolder, *Bayerischer Geschichtsatlas* (Munich, 1969), pp. 16f.

4. See R. Budde, "Die rechtliche Stellung des Klosters St. Emmeram in Regensburg zu den öffentlichen und kirchlichen Gewalten (vom 9. bis zum 14. Jahrhundert)," *Archiv für Urkundenforschung* 5 (1913): 153–238; E. Klebel, "Landeshoheit in und um Regensburg," in Bosl (ed.), *Zur Geschichte der Bayern*, pp. 565–

643; A. Schmid, "Die Territorialpolitik der frühen Wittelsbacher im Raume Regensburg," *ZBLG* 50 (1987): 367–410.

5. K. Ackermann, "Die Grundherrschaft des Stiftes Waldsassen 1133–1570," in A. Kraus (ed.), *Land und Reich. Stamm und Nation. Festgabe für Max Spindler,* vol. I, *Forschungsberichte Antike und Mittelalter,* Schriftenreihe zur bayerische Landesgeschichte, vol. 78 (Munich, 1984), pp. 385–94.

6. In HBG ii, see M. Spindler, pp. 66–68, W. Volkert, pp. 478f., H. Glaser, pp. 594–601.

7. See L. Veit, *Passau. Das Hochstift,* Historischer Atlas von Bayern, Teil Altbayern, vol. XXXV (Munich, 1978), pp. 6–85.

8. Spindler and Diepolder, *Geschichtsatlas,* pp. 18–21.

9. MGH Dipl. Frederick I, no. 322, pp. 146f.

10. Lexer, *Mittelhochdeutsches Handwörterbuch,* vol. I, *bistuom* at col. 283, *hôchstift* at col. 1317. See also F. Merzbacher, "Hochstift (*ecclesia cathedralis*)," HRG ii, cols. 178–79.

11. On such regions see T. Gebhard, "Landschaft und Region in der volkskundlichen Forschung Bayerns," in Kraus (ed.), *Land und Reich,* pp. 135–46.

12. On this problem see chap. 3 of my forthcoming *Princes and Territories,* pp. 61–73.

13. See Chapter 2, n. 36. Since HRG has not yet reached "Vogt, Vogtei," see the summary by R. Laprat, "Avoué, Avouerie ecclésiastique," in A. Baudrilart, A. de Meyer, E. van Cauwenbergh (eds.), *Dictionnaire d'histoire et de géographie ecclésiastiques,* vol. V (Paris, 1931), cols. 1220–41.

14. See Chapter 6, ns. 76–84.

15. On this see Lieberich, "Oberbayerisches Landrecht," HRG iii, cols. 1129–33.

16. Spindler and Diepolder, *Geschichtsatlas,* pp. 25, 30–32, 35; A. Wendehorst, "Eichstätt," in *Lexikon des Mittelalters,* R.-H. Bautier et al. (eds.), vol. III (Munich and Zürich), 1986, cols. 1671–73.

17. *Deutsche Reichstagsakten,* vol. VIII (Göttingen, 1956), no. 145, pp. 156–65 (1422); vol. IX, no. 408, pp. 524–34 (1431); and E. von Frauenholz, *Das Heerwesen der germanischen Frühzeit, des Frankenreiches und des ritterlichen Zeitalters,* Entwicklungsgeschichte des deutschen Heerwesens, vol. I (Munich, 1935), app. lxxviii, pp. 294–301 (1467). For discussion of the methods, see S. Rowan, "Imperial Taxes and German Politics in the Fifteenth Century: An Outline," *Central European History* 13 (1980): 203–17. In his description of Germany, Aeneas Sylvius gives a slightly different impression of the comparative worth of some of the German bishoprics, including Eichstätt; see A. Schmidt, *Enea Silvio Piccolomini, Deutschland. Der Brieftraktat an Martin Mayer,* Die Geschichtschreiber der deutschen Vorzeit, vol. CIV, 3d ed. (Cologne and Graz, 1962), pp. 106–107.

18. *Gesta episc.,* p. 608.

19. Ibid., pp. 597–609. I have not been able to consult the later biographies.

20. H. Koller, *Reformation Kaiser Siegmunds,* MGH Staatsschriften des späteren Mittelalters, vol. VI (Stuttgart, 1964), e.g., pp. 230ff.

21. "Der geistlichen Fürsten Hoffahrt," trans. G. Strauss, *Manifestations of Discontent in Germany on the Eve of the Reformation* (Bloomington and London, 1971), pp. 100f.

22. Spindler and Diepolder, *Geschichtsatlas,* pp. 26f., 30–32.

23. See Chapter 6, ns. 86–94.

24. L. Hammermayer, "Staatskirchliche Reformen und Salzburger Kongress," in HBG ii, pp. 1091–96.

25. Most of the German bishops yielded to Pisan obedience in 1409, but Bishop Frederick of Eichstätt (1383–1415), like his colleague at Freising, stuck to Gregory XII for another year; Engel, *Weltatlas,* vol. II, p. 119.

26. Spindler and Diepolder, *Geschichtsatlas,* p. 28.

27. H. Rall, *Kurbayern in der letzten Epoche der alten Reichsverfassung 1745–1801,* Schriftenreihe zur bayerischen Landesgeschichte, vol. XLV (Munich, 1952), pp. 132ff.

28. Hirschmann, *Eichstätt,* pp. 36–39.

29. E Bauernfeind, *Die Säkularisationsperiode im Hochstift Eichstätt bis zum endgültigen Übergang an Bayern 1790–1806,* Historische Forschungen und Quellen, vol. IX (Munich and Freising, 1927); E. Reiter, "Stubenberg, Joseph Graf von (1740–1824)," in E. Gatz (ed.), *Die Bischöfe der deutschsprachigen Länder 1785/1803 bis 1945. Ein biographisches Lexikon* (Berlin, 1983), pp. 747–49.

30. Originally I wrote "It would be more prudent to observe in the territorial fragmentation of Germany not the triumph of chaos but the outcome of reasonably orderly social and legal processes that did provide alternative institutions to those of a centralized or national monarchy." But a perceptive critic found the phrasing "the outcome of reasonably orderly social and legal processes" to be "excessively optimistic, especially since it seems to pass over in audible silence all the violence recorded in the previous seven chapters." Let the reader judge for him- or herself.

31. From a large literature see W. Volkert, "Staat und Gesellschaft. Erster Teil: Bis 1500," in HBG ii, pp. 475–558; S. Hofmann, "Die zentrale Verwaltung des bayerischen Herzogtums unter den ersten Wittelsbachern," in Glaser (ed.), *Zeit,* vol. I, pp. 223–39; P. A. Sprinkart, *Kanzlei, Rat und Urkundenwesen der Pfalzgrafen bei Rhein und Herzöge von Bayern 1294 bis 1314 (1317),* Forschungen zur Kaiser- und Papstgeschichte des Mittelalters. Beihefte zu J. F. Böhmer, Regesta Imperii, vol. IV (Cologne and Vienna, 1986); K. Bosl, "Stände und Territorialstaat in Bayern im 14. Jahrhundert," in Patze (ed.), *Territorialstaat,* vol. II, pp. 343–68; P. Fried, "Zur 'staatsbildenden' Funktion der Landfriede im frühen bayerischen Territorialstaat," in D. Albrecht, A. Kraus, K. Reindel (eds.), *Festschrift für Max Spindler zum 75. Geburtstag* (Munich, 1969), pp. 283–306.

32. As more heavily populated *Siedlungslandschaften,* the sees of Würzburg and Bamberg were, however, ahead of Eichstätt in terms of organisation and institutions: see e.g., E. Schubert, *Die Landstände des Hochstifts Würzburg,* Veröffentlichungen der Gesellschaft für fränkische Geschichte, 9th series, vol. XXIII (Würzburg, 1967), and S. Bachmann, *Die Landstände des Hochstifts Bamberg. Ein Beitrag zur territorialen Verfassungsgeschichte* (Bamberg, 1962). For comparative discussion on bishoprics, see A. Gerlich, "Staat und Gesellschaft. Erster Teil: Bis 1500," in HBG iii, pp. 274–92 on "Die Hochstifte," and A. Wendehorst, "Die geistliche Grundherrschaften im mittelalterlichen Franken. Beobachtungen und Probleme," in Patze (ed.), *Grundherrschaft im späten Mittelalter,* vol. II, pp. 9–24. For their subjects, see the remarks of H. H. Hofmann, "Bauer und Herrschaft in Franken," *Zeitschrift für Agrargeschichte und Agrarsoziologie* 14 (1966): 1–29, and "Der Adel in

Franken," in H. Rössler (ed.), *Deutscher Adel 1430–1555. Büdinger Vorträge 1963,* Schriften zur Problematik der deutschen Führungsschichten in der Neuzeit, vol. I (Darmstadt, 1965), pp. 95–126. For general problems of comparison between secular and ecclesiastical rule, see G. Gudian, "Die grundlegenden Institutionen der Länder," and A. Wolf, "Die Gesetzgebung der entstehenden Territorialstaaten," in H. Coing (ed.), *Handbuch der Quellen und Literatur der neueren europäischen Privatrechtsgeschichte,* vol. I, *Mittelalter (1100–1500). Die gelehrten Rechte und die Gesetzgebung,* Veröffentlichungen des Max-Planck-Instituts für europäische Rechtsgeschichte (Munich, 1973), pp. 408–18, 594–605; D. Willoweit, "Die Entstehung und Verwaltung der spätmittelalterlichen Landesherrschaft," in K. G. A. Jeserich, H. Pohl, G.-C. von Unruh (eds.), *Deutsche Verwaltungsgeschichte,* vol. I, *Vom Spätmittelalter bis zum Ende des Reiches* (Stuttgart, 1983), pp. 66–143.

33. Bresslau, *Chronik Heinrichs Taube,* pp. 123–32.

34. For example, the biography of Bishop Marquard of Hageln (d. 1324), *Gesta episc.,* pp. 593f., has at the beginning:

Presul Marquardus, meritis redolens quasi nardus
Et virtutum dos, speculum, rosa, pontificum flos,

and at the end,

Extulit ecclesiam Marquardus honoribus istam
Rebus et innumeris, paucis vixit quibus annis.
Laus, insigne genus, species, sapientia, virtus:
Hic presul meritis alios precellit in istis.

35. Ibid., p. 608.

36. Kraft, *Bischofschronik des Grafen Wilhelm Werner von Zimmern.*

37. See H. Patze, "Die Herrschaftspraxis der deutschen Landesherren während des späten Mittelalters," in W. Paravicini and K. F. Werner (eds.), *Histoire comparée de l'Administration (VIe–XVIIIe siècles),* Beihefte der Francia, vol. IX (Zürich and Munich, 1980), pp. 363–91; H. Schlosser, "Rechtsgewalt und Rechtsbildung im ausgehenden Mittelalter," *ZRGGA* 100 (1983): 9–52 on the Bavarian *Landgebote;* L. Schnurrer, *Urkundenwesen, Kanzlei und Regierungssystem der Herzöge von Niederbayern 1255–1340,* Münchener Historische Studien. Abteilung Geschichtliche Hilfswissenschaften, vol. VIII (Kallmünz/Opf., 1972); H. Lieberich, "Die Anfänge der Polizeigesetzgebung des Herzogtums Baiern," in Albrecht, et al. (eds.), *Festschrift für Max Spindler,* pp. 307–78; Volkert in HBG ii, pp. 475–558.

# Maps and Genealogical Tables

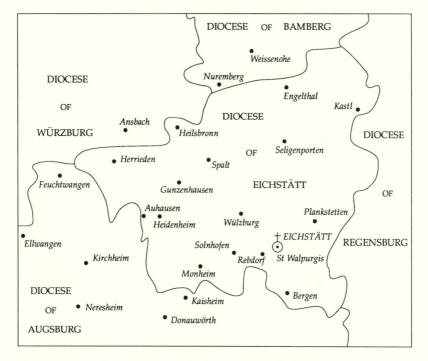

MAP I: Diocesan boundaries and religious houses in the Eichstätt region.

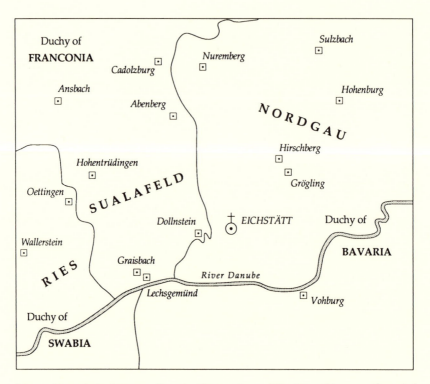

MAP 2: Boundaries between Bavaria, Franconia, and Swabia, with seats of comital and margravial dynasties.

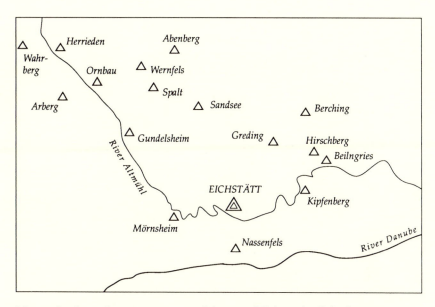

MAP 3: Castles and towns as centers of the see of Eichstätt's *officia* about 1350.

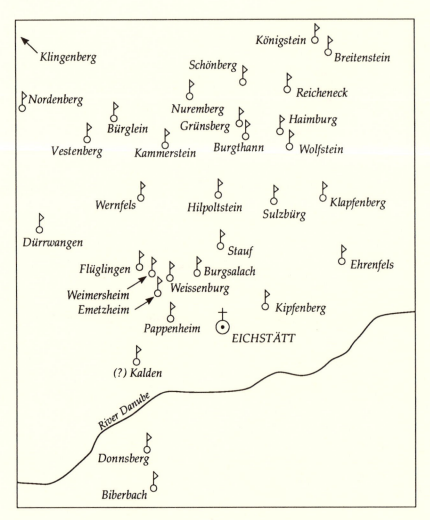

MAP 4: Seats of imperial *ministeriales* connected to the Church of Eichstätt.

## TABLE 4. The Imperial *Ministeriales* of Hilpoltstein

Henry, *senior* of Hilpoltstein, *buticularius* of Nuremberg, d. after 1279  =  Gertrude

- Hermann of Breitenstein
  - lords of Breitenstein and Königstein
- Henry of Haimburg
  - lords of Haimburg
- Hilpolt, d. by 1303  =  Petrissa of Sulzbürg  =  Conrad Kropf of Flüglingen and Kipfenberg
  - Hilpolt, advocate of Hirschberg, 1308–1337  =  Elizabeth of Laaber
    - Bertha  =  Hilpolt, captain of upper Bavaria
      - lords of Hilpoltstein to 1400
  - Henry, provost of Eichstätt Neustift
  - Henry, *Landrichter* of Hirschberg
- Henry  =  Adelheid of Sulzbürg
  - Henry, bishop of Regensburg, 1340–1346

TABLE 3.   The Counts of Hohentrüdingen and Their Connections

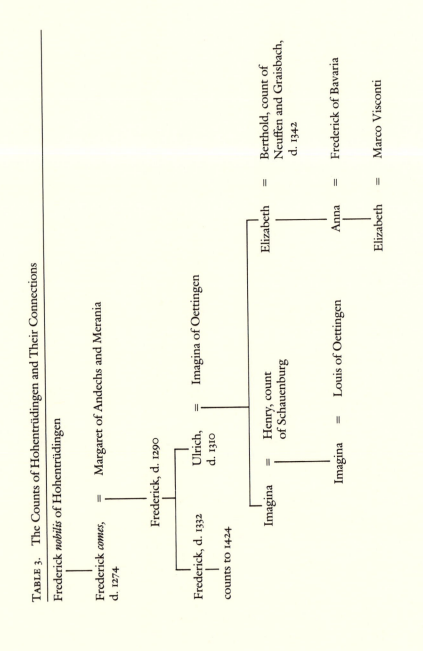

TABLE 2. The Counts of Oettingen and Their Connections

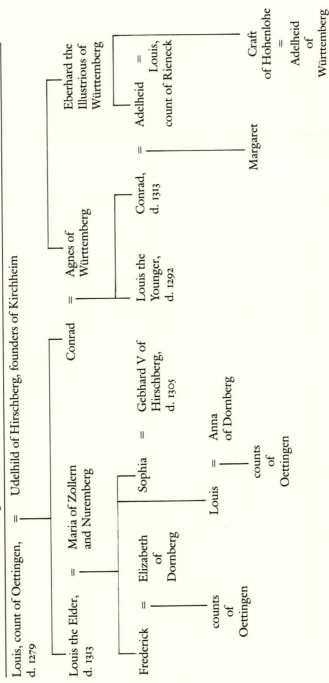

Louis, count of Oettingen, = Udelhild of Hirschberg, founders of Kirchheim
d. 1279

Louis the Elder, = Maria of Zollern          Conrad          = Agnes of          Eberhard the
d. 1313          and Nuremberg                                    Württemberg       Illustrious of Württemberg

Frederick = Elizabeth          Sophia = Gebhard V of          Louis the          Conrad,          Adelheid =
            of Dornberg                  Hirschberg,          Younger,          d. 1313          Louis,
                                         d. 1305          d. 1292                            count of Rieneck

counts          Louis = Anna                                                    Margaret =          Craft
of              of Dornberg                                                                        of Hohenlohe
Oettingen                                                                                          =
            counts                                                                                 Adelheid
            of                                                                                     of
            Oettingen                                                                              Württemberg

TABLE 1.  The Counts of Hirschberg and Their Connections

Ernest of Ottenburg, advocate of Eichstätt, d. 1096

Hartwig of Grögling, advocate of Eichstätt

Gebhard II, bishop of Eichstätt, 1125–1149

Ernest of Grögling

Gerhard of Grögling and Dollnstein, d. before 1188 = Sophia of Sulzbach

Hartwig, bishop of Eichstätt, 1196–1223

Gebhard I of Hirschberg, d. about 1232

Gerhard of Sulzbach

Otto II, duke of Bavaria, 1231–1253

Gebhard II, assassinated in 1245

Gebhard III, d. 1245 or later

Sophia = Gebhard IV = Elizabeth of Tirol, d. 1256

Gerhard, d. by 1280

Gebhard V = Sophia of Oettingen, last count of Hirschberg, d. 1305

Henry XIII

Louis II

Elizabeth = Conrad IV, 1237–1254

Conradin, executed 1268

Louis IV the Bavarian emperor, 1314–1347

Rudolf I of Upper Bavaria, d. 1319

ducal and electoral line to 1777

electoral, palatine, and royal line to 1918

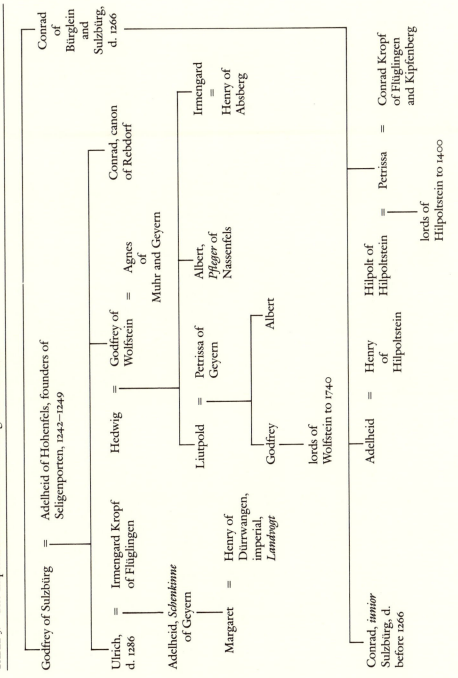

TABLE 5. The Imperial *Ministeriales* of Sulzbürg and Wolfstein

Godfrey of Sulzbürg = Adelheid of Hohenfels, founders of Seligenporten, 1242–1249

Conrad of Bürglein and Sulzbürg, d. 1266

Ulrich, d. 1286 = Irmengard Kropf of Flüglingen

Hedwig = Godfrey of Wolfstein = Agnes of Muhr and Geyern

Conrad, canon of Rebdorf

Adelheid, *Schenkinne* of Geyern

Liutpold = Petrissa of Geyern

Albert, *Pfleger* of Nassenfels

Irmengard = Henry of Absberg

Margaret = Henry of Dürrwangen, imperial, *Landvogt*

Godfrey        Albert

lords of Wolfstein to 1740

Conrad, *iunior* Sulzbürg, d. before 1266

Adelheid = Henry of Hilpoltstein

Hilpolt of Hilpoltstein = Petrissa = Conrad Kropf of Flüglingen and Kipfenberg

lords of Hilpoltstein to 1400

TABLE 6. The Butlers of Hofstetten and Geyern

Benedicta, = Henry of Hofstetten = Agnes of Muhr = Godfrey of Wolfstein
d. after 1282    and Geyern,                              and Sulzbürg
                 d. by 1304

son =                                                      Petrissa = Liutpold of Wolfstein
Adelheid,                                                           lords of Wolfstein to 1740          Hedwig
daughter
of Ulrich
of Sulzbürg

Henry          Gozwin, butler          Agnes =
of Geyern      of Hirschberg           Conrad, seneschal
               = Margaret               of Sulzbach, vicedominus
               of Jettenhofen           of Amberg

Margaret =     Henry of Jettenhofen
Henry of       and Hirschberg
Dürrwangen,
imperial
Landvogt

               Ulrich of Geyern and Weissenburg =
               = Elizabeth of Weiboldshausen                Catherine

               Agnes =                Ulrich      Berthold      Henry
               Henry of
               Reichenau              lords of
                                      Geyern and Syburg to 1803

# Selected Bibliography

The bibliography includes a description of the manuscript sources used in the text, and a selection of the primary sources in print. The list of secondary works is intended to sustain the social and political history of the Eichstätt region into the fourteenth century.

## MANUSCRIPT SOURCES

Munich: Bayerisches Hauptstaatsarchiv München, Abteilung 1. Most of the charters cited were deposited in three categories: (i) Kloster Urkunden, (ii) Brandenburg-Ansbach Urkunden, and (iii) Geistliche Ritterorden 2, Deutschorden Urkunden.

(i)   Kl. Kaisheim 263–631; Kl. Kastl 15–109; Kl. Rebdorf 8–32 and fasc. 4; Kl. St. Walburg 7 and fasc. 6, and those dated Nov. 1344, Mar. 1345; Kl. Seligenporten 8–58 and fasc. 23–26.

(ii)   899–2075, subdivided among Anhausen, Ansbach, Heidenheim, Oberämter, Solnhofen, Weissenburg, and Wülzburg.

(iii)   Kommenden und Ämter 1188–7747. The Plankstetten Klosterliteralien are *Grund- und Salbuch 1461* (no. 1) and *Chronik der Priors Lukas Teyntzer 1514* (no. 24), a later copy.

Nuremberg: Bayerisches Staatsarchiv Nürnberg. The Hochstift Eichstätt Literalien are *Ältestes Salbuch des Hochstifts c. 1300* (no. 165, ES) and *Salbuch des Hochstifts 1407* (no. 9). The *Liber feudorum ad collationem Episcopi Eystetensis spectantium* (EL) is Hochstift Eichstätt Lehenbücher no. 1, a sixteenth-century copy.

## PRIMARY SOURCES IN PRINT

Acht, P. *Die Traditionen des Klosters Tegernsee 1003–1242.* Quellen und Erörterungen zur bayerischen Geschichte, vol. IX. Munich, 1952.
———. *Mainzer Urkundenbuch.* Vol. II, *Die Urkunden seit dem Tode Erzbischof Adalberts I. (1137) bis zum Tode Erzbischof Konrads (1200).* Arbeiten der Hessischen Historischen Kommission, 2 parts. Darmstadt, 1968 and 1971.

Andermann, K. "Das älteste Lehnbuch des Hochstifts Speyer von 1343/47 beziehungsweise 1394/96." *ZGOR* 130 (1982): 1–70.

*Annales Elwangenses, Neresheimenses et Chronicon Elwangense,* ed. O. Abel. MGH Scriptores, vol. X. Hanover, 1852, pp. 15–51.

*Annales Osterhovenses,* ed. W. Wattenbach. MGH Scriptores, vol. XVII. Hanover, 1861, pp. 537–58.

*Annalium Salisburgensium additamentum,* ed. W. Wattenbach. MGH Scriptores, vol. XIII. Hanover, 1881, pp. 236–41.

*Anonymus Haserensis de episcopis Eichstetensibus,* ed. L. C. Bethmann. MGH Scriptores, vol. VII. Hanover, 1846, pp. 253–66.

Bauch, A. *Biographien der Gründungszeit.* Eichstätter Studien. Quellen zur Geschichte der Diözese Eichstätt, vol. I. Eichstätt, 1962 and new ed. in Quellen, new series, vol. XIX. Regensburg, 1984.

———. *Ein bayerisches Mirakelbuch aus der Karolingerzeit. Die Monheimer Walpurgis-Wunder des Priesters Wolfhard.* Eichstätter Studien. Quellen zur Geschichte der Diözese Eichstätt, new series, vol. XII. Regensburg, 1979.

Bitterauf, T. *Die Traditionen des Hochstifts Freising.* Vol. II, *926–1283.* Quellen und Erörterungen zur bayerischen und deutschen Geschichte, new series, vol. V. Munich, 1909.

Boretius, A. *Capitularia Regum Francorum.* MGH Legum, sectio II, vol. I. Hanover, 1883.

Brackmann, A. *Germania Pontificia.* Vol. II, *Provincia Maguntinensis.* Part 1, *Dioceses Eichstetensis, Augustensis, Constantiensis.* Regesta Pontificium Romanorum, new ed. Berlin, 1960.

Bresslau, H. *Die Chronik Heinrichs Taube von Selbach mit den von ihm verfassten Biographien Eichstätter Bischöfe.* MGH Scriptores rerum Germanicarum, new series, vol. I, 2d ed. Berlin, 1964.

Brühl, C., and T. Kölzer. *Das Tafelgüterverzeichnis des römischen Königs (Ms. Bonn S. 1559).* Cologne and Vienna, 1979.

Buchner, F.-X. "Das älteste Salbuch von Herrieden," *Sammelblatt des Historischen Vereins Eichstätt* 29 (1914): 25–46.

*Chounradi Schirensis Chronicon,* ed. P. Jaffé. MGH Scriptores, vol. XVII. Hanover, 1861, pp. 613–33.

Dertsch, R., and G. Wulz. *Die Urkunden der fürstlichen Oettingischen Archive in Wallerstein und Oettingen 1197–1350.* Schwäbische Forschungsgemeinschaft bei der Kommission für bayerische Landesgeschichte, series 2 A, Urkunden und Regesten, vol. VI. Augsburg, 1959.

*Deutsche Reichstagsakten,* vols. VIII and IX, 2d ed. Göttingen, 1956.

Dumrath, K. *Die Traditionsnotizen des Klosters Raitenhaslach.* Quellen und Erörterungen zur bayerischen Geschichte, new series, vol. VII. Munich, 1938.

*Ex Wolfhardi Haserensis Miraculis S. Waldburgis Monheimensibus,* ed. O. Holder-Egger. MGH Scriptores, vol. XV, part 1. Hanover, 1887, pp. 535–55.

Franz, G. *Quellen zur Geschichte des deutschen Bauernstandes im Mittelalter.* AQ, vol. XXXI. Darmstadt, 1967.

Fritz, W. D. *Die Goldene Bulle Kaiser Karls IV. vom Jahre 1356.* MGH Fontes iuris Germanici antiqui in usum scholarum, vol. XI. Weimar, 1972.

Füsslein, W. "Das älteste Kopialbuch des Eichstätter Hochstiftes nebst einem Anhang ungedruckter Königsurkunden," *Neues Archiv* 32 (1906–1907): 605–46.

*Genealogia Ottonis II. ducis Bavariae,* ed. P. Jaffé. MGH Scriptores, vol. XVII. Hanover, 1861, pp. 376–78.

*Gesta Episcoporum Eichstetensium continuata,* ed. L. C. Bethmann and G. Waitz. MGH Scriptores, vol. XXV. Hanover, 1880, pp. 590–609.

Grünenwald, E. *Das älteste Lehenbuch der Grafschaft Oettingen (14. Jahrhundert bis 1477).* Schwäbische Forschungsgemeinschaft bei der Kommission für bayerische Landesgeschichte, series 5, Urbare, vol. II. Augsburg, 1976.

*Gundechari Liber Pontificalis Eichstetensis,* ed. L. C. Bethmann. MGH Scriptores, vol. VII. Hanover, 1846, pp. 239–53.

Heinemeyer, W. *Chronica Fuldensis. Die Darmstädter Fragmente der Fuldaer Chronik.* Archiv für Diplomatik Beihefte, vol. I. Cologne and Vienna, 1976.

Helbig, H., and L. Weinrich. *Urkunden und erzählende Quellen zur deutschen Ostsiedlung im Mittelalter.* AQ, vol. XXVI, 2 parts. Darmstadt, 1968 and 1970.

*Hermanni Altahensis continuatio tertia,* ed. G. Waitz. MGH Scriptores, vol. XXIV. Hanover, 1879, pp. 53–57.

Hillenbrand, E. *Vita Caroli Quarti. Die Autobiographie Karls IV.* Stuttgart, 1979.

Hoffmann, H. *Das älteste Lehenbuch des Hochstifts Würzburg 1303–1345.* Quellen und Forschungen zur Geschichte des Bistums und Hochstifts Würzburg, vol. XXV. Würzburg, 1972.

———. *Die ältesten Urbare des Reichsstiftes Kaisheim 1319–1352.* Schwäbische Forschungsgemeinschaft bei der Kommission für bayerische Landesgeschichte, series 5, Urbare, vol. I. Augsburg, 1959.

———. *Die Urkunden des Reichsstiftes Kaisheim 1135–1287.* Schwäbische Forschungsgemeinschaft bei der Kommission für bayerische Landesgeschichte, series 2A, Urkunden und Regesten, vol. XI. Augsburg, 1972.

Hofmeister, A. *Ottonis de Sancto Blasio Chronica.* MGH Scriptores rerum Germanicarum in usum scholarum, vol. XLVII. Hanover and Leipzig, 1912.

———. *Ottonis Episcopi Frisingensis Chronica sive Historia de duabus Civitatibus.* MGH Scriptores rerum Germanicarum in usum scholarum, vol. XLV, 2d ed. Hanover and Leipzig, 1912.

Holder-Egger, O. *Monumenta Erphesfurtensia saec. XII. XIII. XIV.* MGH Scriptores rerum Germanicarum in usum scholarum, vol. XLII. Hanover and Leipzig, 1899.

Holder-Egger, O., and B. von Simson. *Die Chronik des Propstes Burchard von Ursberg.* MGH Scriptores rerum Germanicarum in usum scholarum, vol. XVI, 2d ed. Hanover and Leipzig, 1916.

Höppl, R. *Die Traditionen des Klosters Wessobrunn.* Quellen und Erörterungen zur bayerischen Geschichte, new series, vol. XXXII, part 1. Munich, 1984.

Jaffé, P. *Monumenta Bambergensia.* Bibliotheca rerum Germanicarum, vol. V. Berlin, 1869.

Kraft, W. *Das Urbar der Reichsmarschälle von Pappenheim.* Schriftenreihe zur bayerischen Landesgeschichte, vol. III, new ed. Aalen, 1974.

———. *Die Eichstätter Bischofschronik des Grafen Wilhelm Werner von Zimmern.*

Veröffentlichungen der Gesellschaft für fränkische Geschichte, series 1, Fränkische Chroniken, vol. III. Würzburg, 1956.

Lohmann, H.-E. *Brunos Buch vom Sachsenkrieg*. MGH Deutsches Mittelalter. Kritische Studientexte des Reichsinstitut für älterer deutsche Geschichtskunde, vol. II. Leipzig, 1937.

Mohr, C. *Die Traditionen des Klosters Oberalteich*, Quellen und Erörterungen zur bayerischen Geschichte, new series, vol. XXX, part 1. Munich, 1979.

Monumenta Boica. Vols. XLIX and L, *Die Urkunden des Hochstifts Eichstätt*. Munich, 1910 and 1932.

Monumenta Germaniae Historica. Constitutiones et acta publica imperatorum et regum (Legum, sectio IV); Diplomata rerum Germaniae ex stirpe Karolinorum; Diplomata regum et imperatorum Germaniae.

Moritz, J. *Stammreihe und Geschichte der Grafen von Sulzbach*. Abhandlungen der historischen Classe der königlich bayerischen Akademie der Wissenschaften, vol. I, part 2. Munich, 1833, pp. 103–58 comprising the Latin and German chronicles of Kastl.

Muffat, K. A. *Schenkungsbuch der ehemaligen gefürsteten Probstei Berchtesgaden*. Quellen und Erörterungen zur bayerischen und deutschen Geschichte, vol. I, part 3. Munich, 1856.

*Nürnberger Urkundenbuch*. Quellen und Forschungen zur Geschichte der Stadt Nürnberg, vol. I. Nuremberg, 1959.

Puchner, K. *Die Urkunden des Klosters Oberschönenfeld*. Schwäbische Forschungsgemeinschaft bei der Kommission für bayerische Landesgeschichte, series 2 A, Urkunden und Regesten, vol. II. Augsburg, 1953.

Schlögl, W. *Die Traditionen und Urkunden des Stiftes Diessen 1114–1362*. Quellen und Erörterungen zur bayerischen Geschichte, new series, vol. XXII, part 1. Munich, 1967.

Schmidt, A. *Enea Silvio Piccolomini, Deutschland. Der Brieftraktat an Martin Mayer*. Die Geschichtschreiber der deutschen Vorzeit, vol. CIV, 3d ed. Cologne and Graz, 1962.

Schuhmann, G., and G. Hirschmann. *Urkundenregesten des Zisterzienserklosters Heilsbronn*. Part 1, *1132–1321*. Veröffentlichungen der Gesellschaft für fränkische Geschichte, series 3, vol. III. Würzburg, 1957.

Stillfried, R. Graf von, and T. Maercker. *Monumenta Zollerana. Urkunden der schwäbischen und fränkischen Linien*. Vols. I and II. Berlin, 1852 and 1856.

Stimming, M. *Mainzer Urkundenbuch*. Vol. I, *Die Urkunden bis zum Tode Erzbischof Adalberts I (1137)*. Arbeiten der Historischen Kommission für den Volksstaat Hessen. Darmstadt, 1932.

Waitz, G. *Chronica regia Coloniensis. Annales maximi Colonienses*. MGH Scriptores rerum Germanicarum in usum scholarum, vol. XVIII. Hanover, 1880.

Waitz, G. and B. von Simson. *Ottonis et Rahewini Gesta Friderici I. Imperatoris*. MGH Scriptores rerum Germanicarum in usum scholarum, vol. XLVI, 3d ed. Hanover and Leipzig, 1912.

Weinfurter, S. *Die Geschichte der Eichstätter Bischöfe des Anonymus Haserensis. Edition—Übersetzung—Kommentar*. Eichstätter Studien, new series, vol. XXIV. Regensburg, 1987.

Weinrich, L. *Quellen zur deutschen Verfassungs-, Wirtschafts- und Sozialgeschichte bis 1250*. AQ, vol. XXXII. Darmstadt, 1977.

Weller, K. *Hohenlohisches Urkundenbuch*. 3 vols. Stuttgart, 1899–1912.

Widemann, J. *Die Traditionen des Hochstifts Regensburg und des Klosters S. Emmeram*. Quellen und Erörterungen zur bayerischen Geschichte, new series, vol. VII. Munich, 1943, and new ed., Aalen, 1969.

*Wirtembergisches Urkundenbuch*. Herausgegeben von dem königlichen Staatsarchiv in Stuttgart, vols. IV and IX. Stuttgart, 1883 and 1907.

Wittmann, F. M. *Monumenta Wittelsbacensia. Urkundenbuch zur Geschichte des Hauses Wittelsbach*. Quellen zur bayerischen und deutschen Geschichte, vols. V and VI. Munich, 1857 and 1861.


SECONDARY WORKS


Adamski, M. *Herrieden. Kloster, Stift und Stadt im Mittelalter*. Schriften des Instituts für fränkische Landesforschung an der Universität Erlangen, Historische Reihe, vol. V. Kallmünz/Opf., 1954.

Appel, B., E. Braun, and S. Hofmann. *Heilige Willibald 787–1987. Künder des Glaubens. Pilger, Mönch, Bischof.* Katalog der Ausstellung der Diözese Eichstätt. Eichstätt, 1987.

Arnold, B. "*Ministeriales* and the Development of Territorial Lordship in the Eichstätt Region, 1100–1350." Ph.D. thesis, Oxford, 1972.

Bayer, A. *Sankt Gumberts Kloster und Stift in Ansbach*. Veröffentlichungen der Gesellschaft für fränkische Geschichte, series 9, vol. VI. Würzburg, 1948.

Beckmann, G. "Die Pappenheim und die Würzburg des 12. und 13. Jahrhunderts," *Historisches Jahrbuch* 47 (1927): 1–62.

Beumann, H. "Reformpäpste als Reichsbischöfe in der Zeit Heinrichs III." In *Festschrift Friedrich Hausmann*, edited by H. Ebner. Graz, 1977, pp. 21–37.

Bigelmair, A. et al. "Herbipolis Jubilans. 1200 Jahre Bistum Würzburg," *Würzburger Diözesangeschichtsblätter* 14–15 (1952–1953): 1–319.

Blendinger, F. "Weissenburg im Mittelalter," *Jahrbuch des Historischen Vereins für Mittelfranken* 80 (1962–1963): 1–35.

Bog, I. "Dorfgemeinde, Freiheit und Unfreiheit in Franken. Studien zur Geschichte der fränkischen Agrarverfassung," *Jahrbücher für Nationalökonomie und Statistik* 168 (1956): 1–80.

Bosl, K. "Das Nordgaukloster Kastl," *Verhandlungen des Historischen Vereins von Oberpfalz und Regensburg* 89 (1939): 3–186.

———. "Die Reichsministerialität als Träger staufischer Staatspolitik in Ostfranken und auf dem bayerischen Nordgau," *Jahresbericht des Historischen Vereins für Mittelfranken* 69 (1941): 1–103.

———. *Franken um 800. Strukturanalyse einer fränkischen Königsprovinz*. 2d ed. Munich, 1969.

———. *Oberpfalz und Oberpfälzer. Geschichte einer Region. Gesammelte Aufsätze*, edited by K. Ackermann and E. Lassleben. Kallmünz/Opf., 1978.

————, (ed.). *Zur Geschichte der Bayern.* Wege der Forschung, vol. LX. Darmstadt, 1965.

Buchner, F.-X. *Das Bistum Eichstätt. Historisch-statistische Beschreibung auf Grund der Literatur, der Registratur des bischöflichen Ordinariats Eichstätt sowie der pfarramtlichen Berichte.* 2 vols. Eichstätt, 1937–1938.

Cahn, E. B. *Die Münzen des Hochstifts Eichstätt.* Bayerische Münzkataloge, vol. III. Grünwald bei München, 1962.

Dannenbauer, H. "Bevölkerung und Besiedlung Alemanniens in der fränkischen Zeit." In *Zur Geschichte der Alemannen,* edited by W. Müller. Wege der Forschung, vol. C. Darmstadt, 1975, pp. 91–125.

————. *Die Entstehung des Territoriums der Reichsstadt Nürnberg.* Arbeiten zur deutschen Rechts- und Verfassungsgeschichte, vol. VII. Stuttgart, 1928.

Diepolder, G. "Ober- und niederbayerische Adelsherrschaften im wittelsbachischen Territorialstaat des 13. bis 15. Jahrhunderts," *ZBLG* 25 (1962): 33–70.

Dollinger, R. "Die Stauffer zu Ernfels," *ZBLG* 35 (1972): 436–522.

Eigler, F. *Die Entwicklung von Plansiedlungen auf der südlichen Frankenalb.* Studien zur bayerischen Verfassungs- und Sozialgeschichte, vol. VI. Munich, 1975.

————. "Weissenburger Reichsforst und Pappenheimer Mark. Ausgangspunkte für die früh- und hochmittelalterliche Besiedlung der südlichen Frankenalb," *ZBLG* 39 (1976): 353–77.

Endres, R. "Die Bedeutung des Reichsgutes und der Reichsrechte in der Territorialpolitik der Grafen von Öttingen," *Jahrbuch des Historischen Vereins für Mittelfranken* 80 (1962–1963): 36–54.

————. "Zur Burgenverfassung in Franken." In *Die Burgen im deutschen Sprachraum. Ihre rechts- und verfassungsgeschichtliche Bedeutung,* edited by H. Patze. VF, vol. XIX, part 2. Sigmaringen, 1976, pp. 293–329.

Englert, S. *Geschichte der Grafen von Truhendingen.* Würzburg, 1885.

Fahlbusch, F. B. "Weissenburg—Werden und Wachsen einer fränkischen Kleinstadt," *JFLF* 48 (1988): 19–38.

Feine, H. E. "Die kaiserlichen Landgerichte in Schwaben im Spätmittelalter," *ZRGGA* 64 (1948): 148–235.

Flachenecker, H. *Ein geistliche Stadt. Eichstätt vom 13. bis zum 16. Jahrhundert.* Eichstätter Beiträge, vol. XIX, Abteilung Geschichte, vol. V. Regensburg, 1988.

Flohrschütz, G. "Machtgrundlagen und Herrschaftspolitik der ersten Pfalzgrafen aus dem Haus Wittelsbach." In *Die Zeit der frühen Herzöge. Von Otto I. zu Ludwig dem Bayern,* edited by H. Glaser. Beiträge zur bayerischen Geschichte und Kunst 1180–1350, vol. I, part 1. Munich and Zurich, 1980, pp. 42–110.

Fried, P. "Hochadelige und landesherrlich-wittelsbachische Burgenpolitik im hoch- und spätmittelalterlichen Bayern." In *Die Burgen im deutschen Sprachraum,* vol. II, edited by H. Patze. Sigmaringen, 1976, pp. 331–52.

————. "Vorstufen der Territorienbildung in den hochmittelalterlichen Adelsherrschaften Bayerns." In *Festschrift für Andreas Kraus zum 60. Geburtstag,* edited by P. Fried and W. Ziegler. Münchener historische Studien. Abteilung bayerische Geschichte, vol. X. Kallmünz/Opf., 1982, pp. 33–44.

————. "Zur Herkunft der Grafen von Hirschberg," *ZBLG* 28 (1965): 82–98.

———. "Zur 'staatsbildenden' Funktion der Landfrieden im frühen bayerischen Territorialstaat." In *Festschrift für Max Spindler zum 75. Geburtstag,* edited by D. Albrecht, A. Kraus, and K. Reindel. Munich, 1969, pp. 283–306.

Gabler, A. *Die alamannische und fränkische Besiedlung der Hesselberglandschaft.* Veröffentlichungen der Schwäbischen Forschungsgemeinschaft bei der Kommission für bayerische Landesgeschichte, series 1, vol. IV. Augsburg, 1961.

Geiger, R. and Voit, G. *Hersbrucker Urbare,* Schriftenreihe der altnürnberger Landschaft, vol. XV. Nuremberg, 1965.

Glässer, A. "1200 Jahre Herrieden, Ursprung und Geschichte im christlichen Abendland," *Jahrbuch des Historischen Vereins für Mittelfranken* 92 (1984–1985): 1–33.

Goez, W. "Über die Rindsmaul von Grünsberg. Studien zur Geschichte einer staufischen Ministerialenfamilie." In *Hochfinanz, Wirtschaftsräume, Innovationen. Festschrift für Wolfgang von Stromer,* vol. III, edited by U. Bestmann, F. Irsigler, and J. Schneider. Trier, 1987, pp. 1227–49.

Grupp, G. *Oettingische Regesten.* Nördlingen, 1896–1908.

Guttenberg, E. von. *Das Bistum Bamberg.* Part 1, *Das Hochstift Bamberg.* Germania Sacra, series 2, Die Bistümer der Kirchenprovinz Mainz, vol. I. Berlin and Leipzig, 1937.

———. "Stammesgrenze und Volkstum im Gebiete der Rednitz und Altmühl," *JFLF* 8–9 (1943): 1–109.

Haering, H. *Der Reichskrieg gegen Graf Eberhard den Erlauchten von Württemberg und seine Stellung in der allgemeinen deutschen Geschichte.* Stuttgart, 1910.

Hannakam, K., L. Veit, and O. Puchner. *Archiv der Freiherrn Schenk von Geyern auf Schloss Syburg.* Bayerische Archivinventare, vol. XI. Munich, 1958.

Heidingsfelder, F. *Die Regesten der Bischöfe von Eichstätt.* Veröffentlichungen der Gesellschaft für fränkische Geschichte, series 6, vol. I. Innsbruck, Würzburg, and Erlangen, 1915–1938.

Herrmann, E. "Zur mittelalterlichen Siedlungsgeschichte Oberfrankens," *JFLF* 39 (1979): 1–21.

Hirschmann, G. *Eichstätt (Beilngries, Eichstätt, Greding).* Historischer Atlas von Bayern, Teil Franken, series 1, vol. VI. Munich, 1959.

Hofmann, H. H. "Bauer und Herrschaft in Franken," *Zeitschrift für Agrargeschichte und Agrarsoziologie* 14 (1966): 1–29.

———. "Fossa Carolina." In *Persönlichkeit und Geschichte,* edited by H. Beumann, in Karl der Grosse. Lebenswerk und Nachleben, vol. I. Düsseldorf, 1965, pp. 437–53.

———. *Gunzenhausen-Weissenburg.* Historischer Atlas von Bayern, Teil Franken, series 1, vol. VIII. Munich, 1960.

———. "Nürnberg. Gründung und Frühgeschichte," *JFLF* 10 (1950): 1–35.

———. "Territorienbildung in Franken im 14. Jahrhundert." In *Der deutsche Territorialstaat im 14. Jahrhundert,* edited by H. Patze. VF, vol. XIII, part 2. Sigmaringen, 1971.

Jahn, J. *Augsburg Land.* Historischer Atlas von Bayern, Teil Schwaben, vol. XI. Munich, 1984.

Jenks, S. "Die Anfänge des Würzburger Territorialstaates in der späteren Staufer-zeit," *JFLF* 43 (1983): 103–16.

Johnson, E. N. *The Secular Activities of the German Episcopate 919–1024.* University of Nebraska Studies, vols. XXX–XXXI. Lincoln, 1932.

Kalisch, H. "Die Grafschaft und das Landgericht Hirschberg," *ZRGGA* 34 (1913): 141–94.

Klebel, E. "Bayern und der fränkischer Adel im 8. und 9. Jahrhundert." In *Grund-fragen der alemannischen Geschichte,* edited by T. Mayer. VF, vol. I. Lindau and Constance, 1955, pp. 193–208.

———. "Die Grafen von Sulzbach, Hauptvögte des Bistums Bamberg," *MIöG* 41 (1926): 108–28.

———. "Eichstätt und Herrieden im Osten," *JFLF* 14 (1954): 87–95.

———. "Eichstätt zwischen Bayern und Franken." In *Probleme der bayerischen Verfassungsgeschichte.* Schriftenreihe zur bayerischen Landesgeschichte, vol. LVII. Munich, 1957, pp. 341–44.

Klohss, K. *Untersuchungen über Heinrich von Kalden, staufischen Marschall, und die ältesten Pappenheimer.* Berlin, 1901.

Kluckhohn, P. *Die Ministerialität in Südostdeutschland vom zehnten bis zum Ende des dreizehnten Jahrhunderts.* Quellen und Studien zur Verfassungsgeschichte des deutschen Reiches in Mittelalter und Neuzeit, vol. IV, part 1. Weimar, 1910.

Kraft, W. "Das Reichsmarschallamt in seiner geschichtlichen Entwicklung," *Jahr-buch des Historischen Vereins für Mittelfranken* 78 (1959): 1–36, and 79 (1960–1961): 38–96.

———. "Über Weissenburg und den Weissenburger Wald in ihren Beziehungen zu den Marschällen von Pappenheim," *Jahrbuch des Historischen Vereins für Mit-telfranken* 66 (1930): 145–74.

Kraft, W. and E. von Guttenberg. "Gau Sualafeld und Grafschaft Graisbach," *JFLF* 8–9 (1943): 110–222, and 13 (1953): 85–127.

Kraus, A. "Marginalien zur ältesten Geschichte des bayerischen Nordgaus," *JFLF* 34–35 (1975): 163–84.

Kudorfer, D. "Das Ries zur Karolingerzeit. Herrschaftsmodell eines reichsfränk-ischen Interessengebiets," *ZBLG* 33 (1970): 470–541.

———. *Die Grafschaft Oettingen. Territorialer Bestand und innerer Aufbau, um 1140 bis 1806.* Historischer Atlas von Bayern, Teil Schwaben, series 2, vol. III. Munich, 1985.

———. *Nördlingen.* Historischer Atlas von Bayern, Teil Schwaben, vol. VIII. Munich, 1974.

Kurz, J. B. *Die Eigenklöster in der Diözese Eichstätt.* Eichstätt, 1923.

Landwehr, G. *Die Verpfändung der deutschen Reichsstädte im Mittelalter.* Forsch-ungen zur deutschen Rechtsgeschichte, vol. V. Cologne and Graz, 1967.

Lieberich, H. *Landherren und Landleute. Zur politischen Führungsschicht Baierns im Spätmittelalter.* Schriftenreihe zur bayerischen Landesgeschichte, vol. LXIII. Munich, 1964.

Löwe, H. "Bonifatius und die bayerisch-fränkische Spannung. Ein Beitrag zur Geschichte der Beziehungen zwischen dem Papsttum und den Karolingern," *JFLF* 15 (1955): 85–127.

Mader, F. *Geschichte des Schlosses und Oberamtes Hirschberg*. Eichstätt, 1940.

Maurer, H. *"Confinium Alamannorum*. Über Wesen und Bedeutung hochmit-telalterliche 'Stammesgrenzen.'" In *Historische Forschungen für Walter Schlesinger*, edited by H. Beumann. Cologne and Vienna, 1974, pp. 150–61.

Merzbacher, F. *Judicium Provinciale Ducatus Franconiae. Das kaiserliche Landgericht des Herzogtums Franken-Würzburg im Spätmittelalter*. Schriftenreihe zur bayerischen Landesgeschichte, vol. LIV. Munich, 1956.

Müller, H. O. *Das kaiserliche Landgericht der ehemaligen Grafschaft Hirschberg. Geschichte, Verfassung, und Verfahren*. Deutschrechtliche Beiträge. Forschungen und Quellen zur Geschichte des deutschen Rechts, vol. VII, part 3. Heidelberg, 1911.

Oefele, Freiherr von. "Vermisste Kaiser- und Königsurkunden des Hochstiftes Eichstätt," in *Sitzungsberichte der historischen Classe der königlich bayerischen Akademie der Wissenschaften zu München*, vol. I. Munich, 1893, pp. 288–301.

Pappenheim, H. Graf zu. *Regesten der frühen Pappenheimer Marschälle vom XII. bis zum XVI. Jahrhundert*. Würzburg, 1927.

Pfeiffer, G. "Comicia burcgravie in Nurenberg," *JFLF* 11–12 (1953): 45–52.

———. "Erfurt oder Eichstätt? Zur Biographie des Bischofs Willibald." In *Festschrift für Walter Schlesinger*, edited by H. Beumann. Mitteldeutsche Forschungen, vol. LXXIV, part 2. Cologne and Vienna, 1974, pp. 137–61.

Pfisterer, K. *Heinrich von Kalden. Reichsmarschall der Stauferzeit*. Quellen und Studien zur Geschichte und Kultur des Altertums und des Mittelalters, vol. VI. Heidelberg, 1937.

Pitz, E. *Die Entstehung der Ratsherrschaft in Nürnberg im 13. und 14. Jahrhundert*. Schriftenreihe zur bayerischen Landesgeschichte, vol. LV. Munich, 1956.

Polenz, P. von. "Vorfränkische und fränkische Namenschichten in der Landschafts- und Bezirksbenemung Ostfrankens," *JFLF* 20 (1960): 157–74.

Prinz, F. "Bayerns Adel im Hochmittelalter," *ZBLG* 30 (1967): 53–117.

———. "Zur Herrschaftsstruktur Bayerns und Alemanniens im 8. Jahrhundert," *BDLG* 102 (1966): 11–27.

Puchner, O., and H. Kunstmann. "Sandskron und Nagelhof," *Jahresbericht des Historischen Vereins für Mittelfranken* 74 (1954): 13–38.

Rassow, P. *Der Prinzgemahl. Ein Pactum Matrimoniale aus dem Jahre 1188*. Quellen und Studien zur Verfassungsgeschichte des deutschen Reiches in Mittelalter und Neuzeit, vol. VIII, part 1. Weimar, 1950.

Riedenauer, E. "Kontinuität und Fluktuation im Mitgliederstand der fränkischen Reichsritterschaft. Eine Grundlegung zum Problem der Adelsstruktur in Franken." In *Gesellschaft und Herrschaft. Eine Festgabe für Karl Bosl zum 60. Geburtstag*. Munich, 1969, pp. 87–152.

Sage, W. "Die Ausgrabungen in den Domen zu Bamberg und Eichstätt," *Jahresberichte der bayerischen Bodendenkmalpflege* 17–18 (1976–1977): 178–234.

Schlunk, A. C. *Königsmacht und Krongut. Die Machtgrundlage des deutschen Königtums im 13. Jahrhundert—und eine neue historische Methode*. Stuttgart, 1988.

Schmid, A. "Die Territorialpolitik der frühen Wittelsbacher im Raume Regensburg," *ZBLG* 50 (1987): 367–410.

Schnelbögl, F. "Nürnberg im Verzeichnis der Tafelgüter des römischen Königs," *JFLF* 10 (1950): 37–46.

Schrader, E. "Vom Werden und Wesen des würzburgischen Herzogtums Franken," *ZRGGA* 80 (1963): 27–81.

Schubert, E. *Die Landstände des Hochstifts Würzburg*. Veröffentlichungen der Gesellschaft für fränkische Geschichte, series 9, vol. XXIII. Würzburg, 1967.

Schuh, R. "Territorienbildung im oberen Altmühlraum. Grundlagen und Entwicklung der eichstättischen Herrschaft im 13. und 14. Jahrhundert," *ZBLG* 50 (1987): 463–91.

Schwammberger, A. *Die Erwerbspolitik der Burggrafen von Nürnberg in Franken bis 1361*. Erlanger Abhandlungen zur mittleren und neueren Geschichte, vol. XVI. Erlangen, 1932.

Schwarz, K. "Der 'Main-Donau Kanal' Karls des Grossen. Eine topographische Studie." In *Aus Bayerns Frühzeit. Friedrich Wagner zum 75. Geburtstag*. Schriftenreihe zur bayerischen Landesgeschichte, vol. LXII. Munich, 1962.

Schwemmer, W. *Die ehemalige Herrschaft Breitenstein-Königstein*. Schriftenreihe der altnürnberger Landschaft, vol. XIII. Nuremberg, 1965.

Schwertl, G. *Die Beziehungen der Herzöge von Bayern und Pfalzgrafen bei Rhein zur Kirche (1180–1294)*. Miscellanea Bavarica Monacensia, vol. IX. Munich, 1968.

Spielberg, W. "Die Herkunft der ältesten Burggrafen von Nürnberg," *MIöG* 43 (1929): 117–23.

Spindler, M. *Die Anfänge des bayerischen Landesfürstentums*. Schriftenreihe zur bayerischen Landesgeschichte, vol. XXVI. Munich, 1937, and new ed., Aalen, 1973.

———, (ed.). *Handbuch der bayerischen Geschichte*. Vols. I–III. Munich, 1967ff.

Spindler, M. and G. Diepolder. *Bayerische Geschichtsatlas*. Munich, 1969.

Steinberger, L. "Ein unbekanntes Schreiben Erzbischof Peters von Mainz an König Heinrich VII," *Neues Archiv* 40 (1915–1916): 427–31.

Stengel, E. E. "Heinrich der Taube. Neue Nachrichten über den Eichstätter Chronisten," *MIöG* 71 (1963): 76–86.

Störmer, W. "Adel und Ministerialität im Spiegel der bayerischen Namengebung bis zum 13. Jahrhundert. Ein Beitrag zum Selbstverständnis der Führungsschichten," *DA* 33 (1977): 84–152.

Sturm, H. *Nordgau—Egerland—Oberpfalz. Studien zu einer historischen Landschaft*. Veröffentlichungen des Collegium Carolinum, vol. XLIII. Munich and Vienna, 1984.

Tillmann, C. *Lexikon der deutschen Burgen und Schlösser*. 4 vols. Stuttgart, 1957–1961.

Voit, G. *Die Wildensteiner*. Sonderheft der Mitteilungen der altnürnberger Landschaft. Nuremberg, 1964.

Wandernitz, H. "Traditionsbücher bayerischer Klöster und Stifte," *AD* 24 (1978): 359–80.

Weigel, H. "Ostfranken im frühen Mittelalter," *BDLG* 95 (1959): 127–211.

———. "Studien zur Eingliederung Ostfrankens in das merowingisch-karolingische Reich," *Historische Vierteljahrschrift* 28 (1934): 449–502.

Weinfurter, S. "Das Bistum Willibalds im Dienste des Königs. Eichstätt im frühen Mittelalter," *ZBLG* 50 (1987): 3–40.

———. "Sancta Aureatensis Ecclesia. Zur Geschichte Eichstätts in ottonisch-salischer Zeit," *ZBLG* 49 (1986): 3–40.

———. "Von der Bistumsreform zur Parteinahme für Kaiser Ludwig den Bayern. Die Grundlegung der geistlichen Landesherrschaft in Eichstätt um 1300." *BLDG* 123 (1987): 137–84.

Wendehorst, A. *Das Bistum Würzburg*. Vol. I, *Die Bischofsreihe bis 1254*, and Vol. II, *Die Bischofsreihe von 1254 bis 1455*. Germania Sacra, new series, vols. I and IV. Berlin, 1962 and 1969.

———. "Die geistliche Grundherrschaften im mittelalterlichen Franken. Beobachtungen und Probleme." In *Die Grundherrschaften im späten Mittelalter*, edited by H. Patze. VF, vol. XXVII, part 2. Sigmaringen, 1983, pp. 9–24.

———. "Eichstätt." In *Lexikon des Mittelalters*, vol. III, edited by R.-H. Bautier et al. Munich and Zurich, 1986, cols. 1671–73.

Wiessner, W. *Hilpoltstein*. Historischer Atlas von Bayern, Teil Franken, series 1, vol. XXIV. Munich, 1978.

Winkelmann, E. "Über die Herkunft Dipolds des Grafen von Acerra und Herzogs von Spoleto," *Forschungen zur deutschen Geschichte* 16 (1876): 159–63.

Wohlhaupter, E. *Hoch- und Niedergericht in der mittelalterlichen Gerichtsverfassung Bayerns*. Deutschrechtliche Beiträge, vol. XII, part 2. Heidelberg, 1929, pp. 141–335.

Zimmermann, G. "Vergebliche Ansätze zu Stammes- und Territorialherzogtum in Franken," *JFLF* 23 (1963): 379–408.

Zinsmaier, P. "Ungedruckter Stauferurkunden des 13. Jahrhunderts," *MIöG* 45 (1931): 200–04.

# Index

University of Pennsylvania Press
MIDDLE AGES SERIES
Edward Peters, General Editor

Books in the series that are out of print are marked with an asterisk.

F. R. P. Akehurst, trans. *The* Coutumes de Beauvaisis *of Philippe de Beaumanoir.* 1991
David Anderson. *Before the Knight's Tale: Imitation of Classical Epic in Boccaccio's Teseida.* 1988
Benjamin Arnold. *Count and Bishop in Medieval Germany: A Study of Regional Power, 1100–1350.* 1991
J. M. W. Bean. *From Lord to Patron: Lordship in Late Medieval England.* 1990
Uta-Renate Blumenthal. *The Investiture Controversy: Church and Monarchy from the Ninth to the Twelfth Century.* 1988
Daniel Bornstein, trans. *Dino Compagni's Chronicle of Florence.* 1986.
Betsy Bowden. *Chaucer Aloud: The Varieties of Textual Interpretation.* 1987
James William Brodman. *Ransoming Captives in Crusader Spain: The Order of Merced on the Christian-Islamic Frontier.* 1986
Otto Brunner (Howard Kaminsky and James Van Horn Melton, eds. and trans.). Land *and Lordship: Structures of Governance in Medieval Austria.* 1991
Robert I. Burns, S.J., ed. *Emperor of Culture: Alfonso X the Learned of Castile and His Thirteenth-Century Renaissance.* 1990
David Burr. *Olivi and Franciscan Poverty: The Origins of the* Usus Pauper *Controversy.* 1989
Thomas Cable. *The English Alliterative Tradition.* 1991
Leonard Cantor, ed. *The English Medieval Landscape.* 1982*
Anthony K. Cassell and Victoria Kirkham, eds. and trans. *Diana's Hunt. Caccia di Diana. Boccaccio's First Fiction.* 1991
Brigitte Cazelles. *The Lady as Saint: A Collection of French Hagiographic Romances of the Thirteenth Century.* 1991
Willene B. Clark and Meradith T. McMunn, eds. *Beasts and Birds of the Middle Ages: The Bestiary and Its Legacy.* 1989
G. G. Coulton. *From St. Francis to Dante: Translations from the Chronicle of the Franciscan Salimbene (1221–1288).* 1972*
Richard C. Dales. *The Scientific Achievement of the Middle Ages.* 1973
Charles T. Davis. *Dante's Italy and Other Essays.* 1984
George T. Dennis, trans. *Maurice's Strategikon: Handbook of Byzantine Military Strategy.* 1984*
Katherine Fischer Drew, trans. *The Burgundian Code: The Book of Constitutions or Law of Gundobad and Additional Enactments.* 1972
Katherine Fischer Drew, trans. *The Laws of the Salian Franks.* 1991

Katherine Fischer Drew, trans. *The Lombard Laws.* 1973

Nancy Edwards. *The Archaeology of Early Medieval Ireland.* 1990

Margaret J. Ehrhart. *The Judgment of the Trojan Prince Paris in Medieval Literature.* 1987

Patrick J. Geary. *Aristocracy in Provence: The Rhône Basin at the Dawn of the Carolingian Age.* 1985

Julius Goebel, Jr. *Felony and Misdemeanor: A Study in the History of Criminal Law.* 1976*

Avril Henry, ed. *The Mirour of Mans Saluacioune: A Middle English Translation of* Speculum Humanae Salvationis. 1987

J. N. Hillgarth, ed. *Christianity and Paganism, 350–750: The Conversion of Western Europe.* 1986

Richard C. Hoffmann. *Land, Liberties, and Lordship in a Late Medieval Countryside: Agrarian Structures and Change in the Duchy of Wrocław.* 1990

Robert Hollander. *Boccaccio's Last Fiction: "Il Corbaccio."* 1988

Edward B. Irving, Jr. *Rereading* Beowulf. 1989

C. Stephen Jaeger. *The Origins of Courtliness: Civilizing Trends and the Formation of Courtly Ideals, 939–1210.* 1985

William Chester Jordan. *The French Monarchy and the Jews: From Philip Augustus to the Last Capetians.* 1989

William Chester Jordan. *From Servitude to Freedom: Manumission in the Sénonais in the Thirteenth Century.* 1986

Ellen E. Kittell. *From* Ad Hoc *to Routine: A Case Study in Medieval Bureaucracy.* 1991

Alan C. Kors and Edward Peters, eds. *Witchcraft in Europe, 1100–1700: A Documentary History.* 1972

Barbara Kreutz. *Before the Normans: Southern Italy in the Ninth and Tenth Centuries.* 1991

Jeanne Krochalis and Edward Peters, ed. and trans. *The World of Piers Plowman.* 1975

E. Ann Matter. *The Voice of My Beloved: The Song of Songs in Western Medieval Christianity.* 1990

María Rosa Menocal. *The Arabic Role in Medieval Literary History.* 1987

A. J. Minnis. *Medieval Theory of Authorship.* 1988

Lawrence Nees. *A Tainted Mantle: Hercules and the Classical Tradition at the Carolingian Court.* 1991

Lynn H. Nelson, trans. *The Chronicle of San Juan de la Peña: A Fourteenth-Century Official History of the Crown of Aragon.* 1991

Charlotte A. Newman. *The Anglo-Norman Nobility in the Reign of Henry I: The Second Generation.* 1988

Thomas F. X. Noble. *The Republic of St. Peter: The Birth of the Papal State, 680–825.* 1984

Joseph F. O'Callaghan. *The Cortes of Castile-León, 1188–1350.* 1989.

William D. Paden, ed. *The Voice of the Trobairitz: Perspectives on the Women Troubadours.* 1989

Kenneth Pennington. *Pope and Bishops: The Papal Monarchy in the Twelfth and Thirteenth Centuries.* 1984*

Edward Peters. *The Magician, the Witch, and the Law.* 1982

Edward Peters, ed. *Christian Society and the Crusades, 1198–1229.* Sources in Translation, including The Capture of Damietta by Oliver of Paderborn. 1971

Edward Peters, ed. *The First Crusade: The Chronicle of Fulcher of Chartres and Other Source Materials.* 1971

Edward Peters, ed. *Heresy and Authority in Medieval Europe.* 1980

Edward Peters, ed. *Monks, Bishops, and Pagans: Christian Culture in Gaul and Italy, 500–700.* 1975*

Clifford Peterson. *Saint Erkenwald.* 1977*

James M. Powell. *Anatomy of a Crusade, 1213–1221.* 1986

Donald E. Queller. *The Fourth Crusade: The Conquest of Constantinople, 1201–1204.* 1977*

Joel T. Rosenthal. *Patriarchy and Families of Privilege in Fifteenth Century England.* 1991

Michael Resler, trans. *EREC by Hartmann von Aue.* 1987

Pierre Riché (Jo Ann McNamara, trans.). *Daily Life in the World of Charlemagne.* 1978

Jonathan Riley-Smith. *The First Crusade and the Idea of Crusading.* 1986

Barbara H. Rosenwein. *Rhinoceros Bound: Cluny in the Tenth Century.* 1982

Steven D. Sargent, ed. and trans. *On the Threshold of Exact Science: Selected Writings of Anneliese Maier on Late Medieval Natural Philosophy.* 1982

Robert Somerville and Kenneth Pennington, eds. *Law, Church, and Society: Essays in Honor of Stephen Kuttner.* 1977*

Sarah Stanbury. *Seeing the* Gawain-Poet: *Description and the Act of Perception.* 1991

Susan Mosher Stuard, ed. *Women in Medieval History and Historiography.* 1987

Susan Mosher Stuard, ed. *Women in Medieval Society.* 1976

Ronald E. Surtz. *The Guitar of God: Gender, Power, and Authority in the Visionary World of Mother Juana de la Cruz (1481–1534).* 1990

Patricia Terry, trans. *Poems of the Elder Edda.* 1990

Frank Tobin. *Meister Eckhart: Thought and Language.* 1986

Ralph V. Turner. *Men Raised from the Dust: Administrative Service and Upward Mobility in Angevin England.* 1988

Harry Turtledove, trans. *The Chronicle of Theophanes: An English Translation of* anni mundi *6095–6305 (A.D. 602–813).* 1982

Mary F. Wack. *Lovesickness in the Middle Ages: The* Viaticum *and Its Commentaries.* 1990

Benedicta Ward. *Miracles and the Medieval Mind: Theory, Record, and Event, 1000–1215.* 1982

Suzanne Fonay Wemple. *Women in Frankish Society: Marriage and the Cloister, 500–900.* 1981

This book has been set in Linotron Galliard. Galliard was designed for Mergenthaler in 1978 by Matthew Carter. Galliard retains many of the features of a sixteenth century typeface cut by Robert Granjon but has some modifications which give it a more contemporary look.

Printed on acid-free paper.